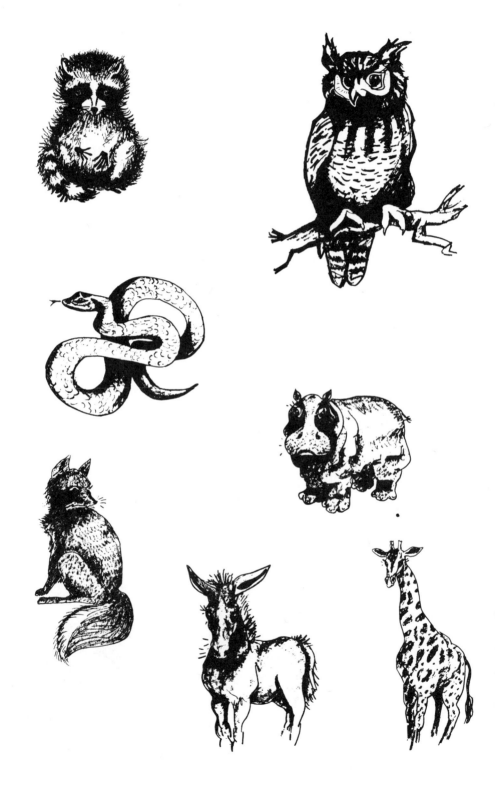

THAD STEM'S
ark

THAD STEM'S
ark

by

THAD STEM, Jr.

Animal Illustrations by Thomas N. Walters

MOORE PUBLISHING COMPANY / DURHAM / NORTH CAROLINA

.

Copyright © 1979 by Moore Publishing Company, Box 3036, Durham, North Carolina 27705.

Library of Congress Catalog Card Number: 79-89864

ISBN: 0-87716-107-0

Printed in the United States of America.

*Amid loving reverence this book
is dedicated to my mentor and
dear friend,*

Jonathan Worth Daniels

OTHER BOOKS

by

THAD STEM, JR.

Picture Poems
The Jackknife Horse
The Perennial Almanac
The Animal Fair
Penny Whistles and Wild Plums
The Flagstone Walk
Spur Line
Impact: 1919-1969
Journey Proud
The Tar Heel Press
Entries From Oxford
Senator Sam Ervin's Best Stories
(co-author Alan Butler)
Thad Stem's First Reader
Ransacking Words and Customs

ACKNOWLEDGEMENTS

I wish to express my profound gratitude to my wife, Marguerite L. Stem and to Faye Apple and Joy Averett for numerous acts of generous assistance and invaluable technical aids.

The day before I commenced work on this book I was told that I had suffered complete renal failure, and the entire book was written while I have been in the regular process of being on dialysis.

A PERSONAL FOREWORD

Most personal confessions are abhorrent to me because most of these are in egregiously poor taste. Yet, the reader may be interested, if morbidly, to learn that I began this book to fill time until I filled a hole in the ground. Any therapy was purely coincidental, and unlike Moxley Sorrel, in his incomparable *Memoirs of a Confederate Staff Officer* I was not running a race with the undertaker. Sorrel was a noble soul, and I am not. (The unsophisticated reader is able to see Sorrel's pen racing to get his marvelous story told before the final, inexorable roll call.)

Writing is my line of work, and if I knew, beyond peradventure, I had but a single day to live, I should spend that day writing, just as the peasant in the field told Tolstoy he would spend his last day plowing.

I am especially anxious, and proud, to go on record to thank Tom and Linda Walters for the drawings and the jacket photographs. Tom Walters, a most talented writer and artist, can't live on hot air and sweet words, but old George Herbert probably envisioned Tom with: "Raise thy head;/Take stars for money." I agree, and I think Tom agrees, with Willa Cather: "Life rushes from within, not from without. There is no work of art so big or so beautiful that it was not all once contained in some youthful body."

I concede there are pages and pages of James Joyce's prose that endure for me as coded communications for which I have no cipher. But, in general, I am with Joyce in his assertion that "The artist, like the God of creation, remains within or behind or beyond or above his handiwork, invisible, refined out of existence, indifferent, paring his fingernails."

As a friend and as a writer, I am delighted that Tom's drawings are linked with my prose, that we have managed to become hyphenated in the most exciting of all ways. My gratitude is boundless, and to see his drawings of sundry animals alongside my prose makes me just as happy as hell, and I say "hell" for the self-same reasons that Sir James Barrie said, "Heaven for climate, and hell for good company."

I thank Linda and Tom Walters for their splendid enhancements of my prose, and I thank them, even more, merely for existing.

CONTENTS

INTRODUCTION

"Animals are nothing but the forms of our virtues and vices, wandering before our eyes, the visible phantoms of our souls."

— Victor Hugo

"I think I could turn and live with animals, they are
        so plac'd and self-contain'd;
I stand and look at them long and long.
They do not sweat and whine about their condition;
They do not lie awake in the dark and weep for their sins;
They do not make me sick discussing their duty to God."

— Walt Whitman

In general I agree with Vachel Lindsay (1879-1931) that we have more interests in demi-gods than in heroes. My America, my small slice of society, is a blend of high idealism and buoyant fantasy, compounded of beauty and ballyhoo, and all of this gives me a ring-side seat at a perpetual county fair, with

Every soul resident
In the earth's one circus tent.

The shadings, the nuances, have altered somewhat since Mark Twain said: "When you go up to heaven, leave your horse and your dog outside. Heaven goes by favor, not by merit. If it went by merit, your horse and dog would get in and you would remain outside." (The connotations of "favor" have changed a little in the past eighty years.)

Did Animals Create the Earth?

Ever so often the ancient Cherokee account of the creation surfaces. The story of the creation, as told by the Cherokee, is said to be much older than the version in Genesis. It is light years beyond Charles Darwin, and it was viable when Franciscan friars came to the Cherokee hills seeking gold and Christian converts. (It was these Franciscan friars, DeSoto's men, who came up with the word "Appalachian" in 1539. The word means "The people on the other side," of the mountain, presumably.)

The Cherokees say creation was made by the tiny waterbeetle and the buzzard, although the beaver and the eagle have been rung in at times. The earth consisted of water and animals, and the animals all lived in Galuniati, the arch of the known world. A lot of Little Thunder Boys were in Galuniati, and their favorite sport was rolling stones. And when two stones crashed head-on, a great burst of flames ensued. Obviously, the animals wanted a quiet, safer place. But no animal had the courage to try to discover a better place.

Finally, the tiny waterbeetle decided death was preferable to life in Galuniati, and it decided to find out what was below the water. (In some accounts, the beetle is the beaver's grandchild.) All the ferocious animals shook their heads in doubt, but the tiny waterbeetle dived under the flood and started throwing up mud. It was this mud that formed the earth.

Almost simultaneously, the buzzard (or eagle), the Great-Granddaddy buzzard, flew in all directions. When he reached the old Cherokee County, he was tired and his wings began to droop, to strike the ground. Wherever the wings struck, a valley appeared and where the wings turned up again, there was a mountain.

When all the earth was dry and habitable, the remainder of the animals departed Galuniati, to find homes in the forests, along the rivers, in the valleys, and on the mountains. The oldtime Cherokees said the earth was an enormous island floating in a sea of water. The earth was held up at each corner by cords hanging from the sky, and when the world grew old and weary, the cords would break and the earth would sink beneath the water again.

Of Darwin's Finches, Dayton's Monkeys,
and Bryan and Jonah and the Whale

When Charles Darwin (1809-1882) was making his famous explorations on the *Beagle*, he discovered a large number of birds on Galapagos Islands of the Pacific. (These islands are about six hundred and fifty miles west of Ecuador, and Darwin visited them periodically from 1831 to 1834.)

The thing that fascinated Charles Darwin was that the birds of Galapagos had characteristics he had never seen before. While tabulating the different beak structures, from long and slender to short, thick and conical, Darwin recorded the diets of the birds; and he learned the diets varied with the structure of the beaks. Some species ate insects, while others ate seeds of varying size and toughness. Many ate cactus, and no two species ate the same food.

Darwin seems not to have evolved a theory at that time, but in October 1838, after his return to England, he read Thomas Malthus' (1766-1834) book, *Principles of Population*, in which Malthus stated that a given people in a specific area are bound to outgrow their supply of food, unless war, disease, or some other pestilence reduces the population to a figure compatible with the area's agricultural production.

Darwin reckoned that the birds on Galapagos had solved the paucity of food in the only possible way: On such isolated islands, the self-producing capacity of the land had been over-run, and the birds that survived would be the ones which could adjust to other foods. Hence, a finch with a heavy bill could crack a hard nut or seed; those with slender beaks could ream out a wood-burrowing insect until the insect became unreachable. So what began as a random variation would be strengthened in succeeding generations. Those which had a capacity for variation would live and the others would die.

Darwin also ascribed the variations in plumage to changes in diet, and this speculation was corroborated by the fact that the feathers of the European bullfinch turned black when the bird fed on nothing but hempseeds. It was a result of his voyage on the *Beagle* that Darwin's ideas about natural selection began slowly to take shape. During the next twenty years, amid meticulous research, he added to his evidence. Then in 1850 he was satisfied with his earth-shaking theory on the evolution of species.

Finches are well known in many portions of the globe, and they fly under such names as chaffinch, bullfinch, and grosbeak. Their plumage ranges from dull grays and browns to sparkling yellows.

Monkeys, as such, were not found in the Biblical countries; but the baboon, of the same family, was sacred to the Egyptian god Troth, and baboons were known to the Hebrews by dint of their lengthy sojourn in Egypt. Several species of primates were found in King Solomon's court, having been brought there from Africa and India. The ape was not indigenous to the Holy Land, but one reads of the navy of Thorsine bringing apes, gold, silver and peacocks to Solomon's court on long, arduous voyages from India and Ethiopia.

Monkey is a general name for animals of the highest intelligence, exclusive of mankind, lemurs, baboons, and anthropoid apes. The monkey's limbs are virtually equal in length, and this gave him the old designation of "four-handed." The Old World monkeys are far superior to their New World counterparts, and the Old World has furnished most of the monkeys used as pets, circus performers, and as servant-solicitors for wandering musicians. Monkeys adjust easily to civilized life, and many breed while in captivity.

In insular America the old Italian organ grinder and his little monkey gave impromptu shows up and down the Atlantic Seaboard states. One minute the organ grinder and monkey were not on the main street of a sleepy town, and the next minute they were giving a concert; it was as if they had materialized from thin air. The monkey always wore a hat, a round hat, brilliantly colored, such as bellhops at swanky hotels used to wear. The monkey passed his hat for loose change while the old Italian ground out erratic strains from *Il Trovatore*, punctuating the music with frequent pleas of "Giva da munk some mun."

The monkey's acrobatics and his manner were so deferential, most of a town's spectators did put some change in his cap. And the monkey brought a new kind of "second-story man" to provincial towns, a second-story man bereft of pistol or safe-cracking equipment. He climbed up to second story windows to solicit from office workers who leaned out the window to see and to hear the musicale. He could hang onto a window ledge with one paw as he extended his cap with his other paw.

When the man and his munk departed to the strains of the "Habanera" from *Carmen*, the monkey did an excellent job of aping a man cutting the pigeon-wing. Then he doffed his little hat, did what passed for an ingratiating curtsey, and waved a hearty "Thank you and goodbye."

The monkey became a household word in the United States in 1925 during the trial of John Thomas Scopes, twenty-four-year-old biology teacher of Dayton, Tennessee. Curiously enough, little was known or said about Charles Darwin in the United States until 1925, off campus and out of intellectual soirees. Darwin may have changed human thought as much, or more, than Isaac Newton changed 18th century thought, but, even so, Americans were parenthetical beneficiaries of Darwin's ideas about the evolution of the species. And Darwin or the monkey might not have attained such garrulous viability had not the legislature of Tennessee enacted an imbecilic law. The Tennessee legislators, dominated by fundamentalists and bully-ragged by hellfire and damnation preachers, passed this law:

"It shall be unlawful for any teacher in any of the universities, normals, and all other public schools of the State to teach theory that denies the story of the Divine creation of man, as taught in the Bible, and to teach instead that man had descended from a lower order of animals."

Darwin may have endured as a textbook reference and the monkey as an isolated performer had the copper mines, the area's chief economic source, not petered out around Dayton. George Rappelyea, a mining engineer, was in Robinson's Drug Store, in Dayton, drinking lemon phosphates with a couple of cronies when Scopes dropped into the drug store. Rappelyea proposed that Scopes allow himself to be caught teaching evolution to an innocent child. Scopes, half of him serious and the other half amused, agreed. Rappelyea told Scopes such an action might "put Dayton on the map," revitalize the town's floundering economy.

Thus, young Scopes was detected teaching the rudiments of

evolution to fourteen-year-old Howard Morgan. At the famous, or infamous, "Monkey Trial," young Morgan testified that "it hadn't hurt me any."

Scopes was indicted for violating the "Monkey Law," and Dayton became a three-ring circus. William Jennings Bryan, the thrice-defeated Democratic nominee for President, volunteered as a private prosecutor. Rappelyea wired the Civil Liberties Union in New York, and he obtained for Scopes the services of Clarence Darrow, Dudley Field Malone, and Arthur Garfield Hays.

Mountain folks came in tin lizzies and in wagons to hear firsthand about that strange process known as "Eval-lution," and the streets of Dayton were quick with improvised hot dog stands and bazaars of an infinite variety. Booksellers appeared to hawk tracts and books on evolution, and innumerable street and corn-field ministers extolled the literal gospel, simultaneously. The Western Union installed twenty-two telegraph operators in a room off a grocery store. The facts of this insanity are pretty well known, from several different theatrical presentations of *Inherit the Wind*; but, in every casting, Bryan, Darrow, and Mencken, although given stage names, are easily identified.

The paramount clash came down to Bryan versus Darrow.* On the scorching afternoon of July 20, Arthur Garfield Hays asked that the defense be allowed to put Bryan on the stand as "an expert on the Bible." The crowds were so dense the trial judge, Judge Raulston, held court outdoors. Bryan sat on the witness stand, with a Bible in his lap. He and Darrow, and everyone else, could read an injunction attached to the gate of the courthouse's lawn:

The Kingdom of God
The sweetheart love of Jesus Christ and Paradise is at
hand. Do you want to be a sweet angel? Forty days of
prayer. Itemize your sins and your iniquities for
eternal life. If you come clean God will talk back to
you in voice.

The inside of the courthouse had admonitions such as: "Read

*Darrow appears to have been in Baltimore when the Dayton ruckus began. He had just saved Loeb and Leopold from the electric chair. It appears that Mencken urged him to go to Dayton to crush Bryan and Fundamentalism. Not just incidentally, H. L. Mencken had some cards printed that identified him as "The Rev. Ebenezer Chubb," and it appears that he did some wild, tongue-in-cheek street corner preaching in Dayton.

Your Bible For One Week," and "Be Sure Your Sins Will Find You Out."

Bryan took a bad beating on the witness stand. Darrow asked Bryan where Cain got his wife, the date of the Flood, the significance of the Tower of Babel, and about Jonah and the whale. On the morning of July 21, Judge Raulston mercifully stopped the testimony of Bryan.

The unseen public's attention was focused on Jonah and the whale. But Bryan got off a superlative crack, even if egregiously irrelevant, when Darrow asked him when the world was created. Bryan said the world was created in 4004 B.C., and he ascertained this by adding the lives of the major and the minor prophets. At this juncture Darrow handed Bryan a chipped-off piece of Stone Mountain, saying, "Do you not know that geologists say this piece of stone is several million years old?"

Bryan's answer was: "I am not interested in the age of rocks but in the Rock of Ages."

(As is generally known, Bryan died a week later. His adherents said he sacrificed his life fighting for the true God. Darrow said Bryan killed himself eating.)

Many Americans reread the story of Jonah and the whale. In the Book of Jonah, the expression is a "great fish." But despite the eloquence of Bryan and the astuteness of Darrow, a whale really isn't a "fish," great or otherwise. It is a warm-blooded animal and it suckles its young. Experts think what we call the whale degenerated from a land animal. Its hind legs disappeared entirely. Its front legs, toes and all, are known as flippers. Like the shark it can use its tail as a weapon as well as its teeth. There are no scales on the whale's body, and it has lungs in lieu of gills. The lungs are connected to the top of the whale's head by a single nostril, through which it blows or spouts. Whales have been known to dive as deeply as a mile in the ocean. It really belongs to an old order called *cataceon*, which includes the dolphin, the porpoise, the grampus, and the mabatec or sea-cat.

Like the walrus the whale was indispensable for blubber, from which oil was extracted, until the advent of kerosene, or coal oil.

It is redundant to say that Herman Melville paused in the writing of *Moby Dick* to answer all the questions about whaling anyone might ever ask. Melville's interminable catalogue of whales and whaling reminds one of the book editor who received three hundred and sixty pages of text and beautiful photographs about penguins. The book editor thought a review by a little girl, a twelve-year-old child, would be diverting. This is her book review, in toto: "This book tells me more about penguins than I want to know." The word *leviathan* is used several times in the Writ. *Leviathan* (Hebrew) is compounded of two words that mean a *great fish* and *fastened*. Hence, *leviathan* probably means a huge fish with scales. The Septuagint* renders it as a *drakon* (a dragon) and *ketos* (a whale). Many scholars think the real allusion here is likely to have been a crocodile, although in several places it has been translated as "whale."

Thomas Hobbes (1588-1679) published his *The Leviathan* in 1651, at the end of England's civil war. The book was a product of turbulent times, which left Oliver Cromwell in power. Hobbes insisted his book was not a defense of the Stuart monarchy, as many contended. Indeed, *The Leviathan* appears to be the first realistic book on politics and ethics since Aristotle.

In the first part of the book, called "On Man," Hobbes established the foundation for modern psychology. He said man is by nature in a state of war, in which wrong and right nullify each other. But such a state is intolerable, and reason directs that mankind must give up his personal liberties for the sake of national peace and security. Hobbes' claim that he was the founder of social science has more of substance than of vanity. (Kipling had a poem in which he said if one takes mankind's totality, mankind's chief interests are "women, horses, cards, and wars." Ultimately, Kipling reduces occupations and pre-occupations, down through history to war and women:

And since we know not how war may prove,
Heart of my heart, let us speak of love.

In his once popular book, *Heavenly Dissertation*, the late C.E.S. Wood, writer, poet, soldier, and minister, has actual personages going to heaven. For instance, Billy Sunday calls God "partner," and he tells him of the saloons and sundry evils he obviated. But a delegation of monkeys, carrying protest signs, demands an audience with God to complain about some

*The Septuagint is the Greek version of the Old Testament, in use generally in the Eastern Church. It is so called because it consists of seventy parts, from the legend that the translation was made by seventy emissaries from Jerusalem.

8

unmitigated slander and libel being circulated about them in a strange place called Dayton, Tennessee. In *Mark Twain In Eruption*, Bernard de Voto quotes Twain's aphorism: "I believe that our heavenly father invented man because he was disappointed in the monkey." It was Kenneth Graham, in *The Golden Age*, who wrote: "Monkeys very wisely refrain from speech, lest they should be set to earn their living."

While "monkey" was out of proper context at the Scopes travesty, Americans are always fascinated by the frequency with which a monkey scratches his head and body. But this ceaseless gesture has no relevance to lice, ticks, or other parasites. Experts say monkeys are free from parasites, unless they are kept in mangy cages; and they scratch their bodies because they exude salt in a prodigious flow. And although monkeys sometimes give each other a hand in pulling up an incline, the so-called monkey bridge is a sure figment of man's imagination.

Actually, many erroneous theories are still attached to Charles Darwin (1808-1882). His *Origin of Species* is habitually confused with his *Descent of Man*, published ten years later. It is the latter, not the former, that treats of man's origin. Despite all the ruckus at Dayton, Darwin never mentioned that humankind is descended from monkeys. Albeit, this is the common charge on which Darwin has always been attacked, especially from the pulpit. Instead, Darwin postulated that human beings and monkeys have a common ancestor.

While it suited the moralistic and political uses of certain 19th century men to assume, and to assert, that "survival of the fittest" means "survival of the strongest," Darwin did not contend that, and one must try to remember that Darwin was a naturalist and not an economist. In Darwinian terms, the organism that lives is that which is best suited to its environment. If this were predicated upon "strongest," dinosaurs would be as commonplace as housecats. And there is no racism to Darwin's "survival of the fittest." His theory is light years from developing a rationale for developing a superior breed or an elite corps in society. (Such blabberings are for fifth-rate minds such as Adolf Hitler's.) Conversely, Darwin stresses the importance of adaptability, never brute strength. He is aeons removed from power just for the arrogance of power. Instead he pleads for an adjustment to circumstances which, in essence, is the exact opposite.

9

An Invasion By Dinosaurs?

From the strange interest many youngsters manifest in dinosaurs one wonders if television will not have the world invaded by an army of dinosaurs, revitalized or born again. TV has already staged such harrowing invasions with armies of ants, spiders, and other insects. Thus we may live to see a dinosaur throw out the first ball at a World Series, on television, that is.

According to scientists dinosaurs flourished during the Mesozoic Era, the time of the dinosaur. Scientists say that in many ways dinosaurs were the dominant life forms during the Mesozoic Age; and, as such, they filled many of the roles of terrestial animals, as do the warm blooded mammals of this hour, the same as their distant cousins, the crocodiles. The dinosaur lacked the mechanism for body heat, but it had interior temperature which varied with the air outside. The discovery in 1925, in Mongolia, of many dinosaur eggs corroborates the ancient scientific contention that it was an egg-laying animal.

In size the dinosaurs ranged from that of today's common house cat to many as big as the modern whale. Many were ninety feet long and weighed as much as forty tons. Their habits were as diverse as their sizes; for some were lightfooted and bipedal, while others were unwieldly quadrupeds. Many were armored, but others were bereft of armor. The ones endowed with armor usually had scaly backs, and they were endowed with horns or talons and with lethal teeth. The others' means of safety were their enormous size and their inaccessible habitats. In all probability the dinosaurs' native habitat was the land, and it was the aridity of climate which developed their enormous girth and made them the largest nomads in the entirety of natural history.

The duration of dinosaurian existence must have been immensely long. For their remains are found first in the rocks of the Middle Triassic period, and the remains show a state of development that indicates a lengthy evolution. Certain lines perished millions of years ago, while others lived until the end of the Reptilian Age. Their remains were found first in Germany, but this does not imply a Germanic origin. On the contrary, scientists have found dinosaur fossils in Europe, North and South America, Africa, Madagasscar, and Australia.

Playing Possum

This piece about possums (opossums to the effete) is essentially negative because more lies have been told about the possum than were told by the ancient mule skinner or by the traveling man who sold corsets. Ironically, most of these fallacies occur and take root where possums are abundant.

Baby possums do not hook their tails around their mothers' tails, to curl up on her back; albeit, dozens of magazine illustrations have depicted this myth. The baby possum actually rides his mother's back. He clings to her long hair with his claws, and her tail is pointed backward for balance. It is a fairy tale that possums hang by their tails from limbs, that they sleep like that.

It is true that the possum is the only North American mammal with a prehensile tail, or a tail that may be used for grasping and one that wraps his tail around a limb for balance. But the wildest, and most cherished myth is that the impregnation and birth both occur in the mother's nose. According to this hoary hoax the male establishes sexual union by placing his penis in the female's nose, and at birth she sneezes her young into her pouch.

This whopping liza-jane probably arose because of the extraordinary nature of the possum's sexual organs. The male has a double-headed penis, and the female has a forked vagina and two uteri. This natural back-up system may account for the proliferation of possums wherever they are introduced, and the truth is that the penis is designed to fit the double vagina, not her nostrils. The legend of the sneezing birth owes something also to the fact that the female inserts her nose and mouth into her pouch, as other marsupials do, and licks it down clean. She also licks her vulva to clean it as each baby emerges. Nonetheless, the babies climb into her pouch by themselves.

But the great granddaddy of all myths is the one that relates to "playing possum," lying down immobile and feigning death

12

to elude captivity and death. Anyone who has ever cornered a possum knows that the habitual response is a hissing hostility. Obviously, a possum may lie down because it is hurt, winded, or exhausted; but if one does lie so quietly it seems dead this is a natural consequence of the possum's physical condition, and it has relevance to an Oscar-winning performance of acting.

The animal's build and habits give rise to "possum belly," meaning an extra car beneath a railroad car. And it is not necessarily true that the smallest possums always climb the highest available gum trees. Poker players, anticipating a change from bad to good luck, are fond of saying, "The big possum walks just before day." Well, some are early risers out to forage for food, and some are inveterate ten o'clock scholars.

Although this is merely a personal opinion, based on my own taste buds, the author thinks the highly touted possum supper is the biggest fraud since wily hucksters sold the Brooklyn Bridge to unwary bumpkins. There is enough grease in one possum to slide an elephant from Bangor to Miami. The animal is filthy and it eats anything. So each possum has to be oriented with a diet of green leaves and other purgatives before it is ever put into a pot. And at every ritual possum supper, the cooked blubber is so permeated with slices of sweet potatoes, warmed peach halves, and other goodies that the man who acquires the reputation of being a possum epicure will eat around and down to the greasy hoax.

Almost as many purple lies are told about the innocuous dragonfly as about the poor possum. Many nannies spent as much time yesterday warning their charges about being stung by dragonflies as they spent blowing noses. The stinging dragonfly really is a mean, or certainly a naughty, myth. According to the tons of hoopla, dragonflies sewed up the eyes of children, of adults hardly ever. As a matter of natural fact the dragonfly has no stinger at all. They are completely harmless, save to mosquitoes and goats. Blessedly, the dragonfly can consume mosquitoes on the wing.

There used to be a popular slander about the dragonfly and the poor man, the man as poor as Job's turkey, or the bird so undernourished it had to lean against a fence to gobble. Some men were so poor, it was said, they had to bend a pin to make a fishing hook, and cash was such a scarce commodity the family had to send for dragonflies to sew up the dead man's eyes. This hoax about having a dragonfly sew up a dead man's eyes has to be a relic of the custom brought over from England in which a penny was put over each eye of the dead man. The practice of closing such eyes is extremely old. In Genesis God tells Jacob, "Joseph shall put his hand upon thine eyes." The custom of using copper pennies was popular in England long before the American penny was ever minted. In her *Reveille In Washington*, Margaret Leach writes that a "doctor laid silver half-dollars on the eyelids of the murdered Abraham Lincoln."

It seems especially cruel that such an innocent little creature as the dragonfly was tied in with death, with sewing together the eyes of dead children. It is difficult to understand how this myth gained so much more currency than Linus' steadfast belief in the Great Pumpkin.

"No Bugger Bears Out Tonight"

Bears are scattered throughout the southern hemisphere, but they are absent from Africa, except for the Atlas Mountains. (Zoologically, this is a part of Europe.) In their structure bears are allied to the dog, badgers, weasels, and the skunk. Though they do not bite so tenaciously as dogs, their unusually large molars are most useful in crushing vegetable fare. The feet are powerful, leaving footprints that resemble those made by a man. If most bears are clumsy, some climb trees, and many have been seen climbing power poles in Siberia when the wind shakes the wires to give off buzzing sounds that the bear thinks come from bees making honey.

The bear is thoroughly omnivorous, and it will eat fish, vegetables or whatever is available. The Kodiak bear subsists on fish almost exclusively. It is able to catch fish from the shore by using a paw as a fast fly, and if this fails he enters the water, in the manner of a trout fisherman.

As collections of animals go, bears are not especially numerous. A family will occupy a district and keep it for their own use. When three or four are seen together, they are likely to be the young and old of the same family. Their home is usually a crevice, cave, or hollow tree, or a dense thicket. The young are usually born in the spring, and they remain with their mother until they are fully grown. The bear, innately shy, will rush anyone or anything that seems to jeopardize her young. When they do attack, they do so with teeth and claws. They fight with tremendous courage; and when a bear is provoked, it is among the most dangerous of all animals.

La Fontaine, in 1688, wrote: "Never sell the bear's skin until you have killed the bear." This saying appears in several European languages, and it supplies the origin of the incessant use of *bear* in Wall Street terminology. And a century before La Fontaine, John Lyly, in his *Euphues and His England*, had said:

"I solde the skin before the Beaste was taken, reckoning with-out mine hoast, and setting down bookes as ready money, which afterward I found to be a heavy and desperate debt." And it was Frederick Marryat (1792-1848) who said, in *The King's Own*, "The captain was as savage as a bear with a sore head."

Big Tom Wilson, of Yancey County, N.C., was credited with killing one hundred and seventeen bears, for meat and rugs and bed covering, and most of this was done with an old-fashioned musket. His grandson, Ewart Wilson, of Pensacola, Yancey County, killed one hundred and sixteen bears. He always said he didn't want to tie or break his grandfather's record. In July 1857, Big Tom was vital in the discovery of the body of Professor Elisha Mitchell and the enormous waterfall that has borne the name Mitchell's Falls ever since.

Professor Mitchell, of the University of North Carolina, spent his summer vacation finding and climbing uncharted mountains. Mitchell had gone to the top of what has been known ever since as Mt. Mitchell. Mitchell's measurement was recorded as 6,711 feet. An argument, apparently bloodless and courtly, developed between Mitchell and General Thomas Clingman, about which man had gone atop the highest peak. Clingman, Civil War general and later a member of Congress, said his peak (now called Clingman's Dome) was higher than Mitchell's peak. Accordingly, Mitchell went back to his mountain to re-measure the vast height. He had told his son to meet him at Half-Way House, a mountain shelter and eating place, in three days. When Mitchell did not show up on time, his son got Big Tom Wilson to organize a searching party. After a futile day and night, Big Tom pointed to the leaves of some bushes. He explained to the searching party: "Those leaves are turned outward by a man's hand. Professor Mitchell must have come through here at night. If these leaves had been turned by a bear, many leaves and bushes would be on the ground."

In a few more minutes, Wilson stopped to examine a tiny hole in a rotten log. "Gentlemen, that hole was made by a tack jutting from a man's boot. It wasn't made by a bear." He placed his right ear to the ground and told his associates he heard a "mighty waterfall." He added, "The poor man came through here at night and his path led him straight to the precipice of a great waterfall, and we will find his body there."

16

It turned out precisely as Big Tom had predicted. Zebulon B. Vance, twice governor of North Carolina and a United States Senator, was among the searching party. As a young lawyer in 1857, Vance augmented his legal fees by being co-publisher of a small Asheville newspaper, for which he wrote up the Mitchell details thoroughly. Mitchell had taught Vance at UNC, and Vance's account of the search is the best extant source.

Mt. Mitchell is just a few feet higher than Clingman's Dome. The amazing feature is that Big Tom Wilson had lived on what became Mt. Mitchell all of his life. He had lived on it for years, and yet the virgin topography had concealed from him Mitchell's Falls, until he led the hunting party to this incredibly high and lovely cascade.

(Mitchell's Peak is still a few feet higher than Clingman's Dome, but Clingman, a Confederate brigadier-general, is entitled to secular immortality for a speech he made in 1875, about unsavory southern kitchens. His clincher was, "More men have died in the past decade from eating greasy biscuits than were killed in the war.")

Despite many contrary reports bears do not seem to hug their enemies to death, even if literature abounds in lines such as Alexander Pope's "'Tis a bear's talent not to kick but to hug." Apparently, this erroneous impression originated in the Old World, where the brown bears climb trees to get honey, and where they have climbed power lines under the delusion that the wires singing in the wind were bees swarming.

The bear stands more erectly than other animals, and, hence, it is fairly simple to teach him to box, to wrestle, and to dance. Because of his anatomical structure the bear strikes with his paws, as if grasping. In reality it is hitting, and it can drive its claws deep into an adversary's body.

Curiously enough, Rudyard Kipling was one of the first to write about the Russians as a menace to world peace and to call Russia "the bear that walks like a man." These comments by Kipling are noteworthy because they were written before the Red Revolution of 1917.

Alexander Pope, in the *Duncaid*, repeats a cherished myth:

So watchful bruin forms, with plastic care,
Each growing lump, and brings it to a bear.

17

Pope is merely repeating in his heroic couplet a myth that has existed since the time of Plutarch and Pliny, and perhaps, before these two ancient historians. The myth was that young bears were born as shapeless lumps, and that the mother licked them into shape. From this fairy tale came the phrase of "licking a youngster into shape," but because the word *licking* used to mean a rod, virtually every time it was written or spoken, the word *licking* came to imply a beating.

Nonetheless, bears are fairly easily trained, and they can adjust to a new climate and they can breed as rapidly in confinement as in their native habitat.

The "ice," or polar, bear wanders over the Arctic, and at times it swims many miles. Many bears winter on ice floes and their young are bred and born there.

The American bears—called black, grizzly, cinnamon, Barren-Grounds, brown, Kadiak—are so confusingly alike that many naturalists lump all of them together as one species. The black bear, however, is the most widely spread of the American species. They are hardly ever a threat to humans unless hurt or provoked, and, obviously, many are trained to perform in circuses. But the grizzly of the Black Hills and the Badlands is among the largest and the most dangerous. Through fear, the American Indian had a deep-seated reverence for the black bear, as well as for the Barren-Grounds. (The Indians burned down many parcels of forest so that the grizzlies and Barren-Grounds could be seen at a safe distance.)

Two of the best known bears in the history of animals are ones that never had any physical existence, the Teddy Bear and Winnie the Pooh. The Teddy Bear, one of the most popular playthings extant, has slept with thousands of children, and it has been the child's alter-ego for a long time. Just as children create imaginary friends with whom they cavort and converse, the ones with Teddy Bears carry on the same intimacy with "old Teddy."

The replica of an innocuous cub derived its name from Teddy Roosevelt when the President was photographed and written up for sparing the life of a young bear. But if America furnished the basis for this eternal companion, the small, brown bear, stuffed with soft material and covered with fur-like plush, seems to have been manufactured first in Germany. For a long time, however, various game protectors and conservationists carried

18

around the famous newspaper cartoon that depicted Roosevelt's sparing the life of the tiny bear.

Winnie the Pooh, also an alter-ego of millions of young shavers, stepped from the fecund mind and pen of the late A. A. Milne to occupy such a viable personality in family groups that many folks actually fixed a place at the eating table for Winnie the Pooh.

Yesterday, overshoes were known as "arctics" from the Greek *arklos*, or bear, and *arklos* was applied to the constellation known as the Great Bear, which revolves around the North Pole. Hence, the region and the North Pole came to be referred to as the Arctic and that around the South Pole as the anarctic. Warm, waterproof overshoes were arctics with all Americans. This word is pronounced "ark-tick," but often it is pronounced as "artic."

President Grover Cleveland invited Mark Twain to a White House dinner. Twain was forgetful, and his wife made a habit of sticking written instructions in his pockets. At the White House Twain saw this handwritten message from his wife: "For the Lord's sake, don't wear your arctics in the White House." Below, in different handwriting and ink, were these words: "He didn't. Frances Folsom (Mrs. Grover) Cleveland."

Virtually everyone is cognizant of the old round, or song, "The bear went over the mountain." In the song the bear saw the other side of the mountain, but that's impossible today with all the billboards, diners, refreshment stands, and amusement parks. The bear saw more various hot dog stands than there were trees before the timber was cut. He saw one of his nephews chained in front of a snack bar, and he saw strangers paying a fee to be photographed standing beside his nephew.

The bear saw live Indians from a reservation getting sick trying to smoke peace pipes manufactured in Japan, and standing around parodying themselves with "Ugh's" as they sported mail-order doeskin, and as they attempted to demonstrate the intricate art of firing arrows shipped in from New Jersey. For a buck the bear could hear a cultural lecture and take a cultural nature walk at numerous places.

Many assume the bear made just one trip. He made two because he assumed the first one was an optical illusion. The second time the bear threw up. He threw up in monumental proportions, and the news along the branch-head is that he still cannot take solid nourishment.

19

The Coon's Sordid Reputation

Sometime back that excellent publication *North Carolina Wildlife* carried a piece that said the coon has a shady reputation because it is so adroit at stealing corn, peanuts, eggs, bullfrogs, and even chickens, now and then. It would appear from that catalogue of edibles that Brer Coon has a better ordered diet than some of the oracles who teach home economics.

From our somewhat cursory observation, the coon will continue to steal edibles because of outrageous inflation at the supermarkets and because the supermarkets do not solicit Brer Coon's active patronage, either for cash or until the fall when the coon sells his lugs. An ethical coon might stand on four-square principle and starve, but tomorrow's hungry coons probably will not take the time and trouble to erect a single monument to vanquished valor. (Coons differ from humans in memorials. Most of our monuments perpetuate men whose only contribution was leading other men to their deaths, in some war.)

Wildlife said also that coons do not wash their food, despite certain sanitary legends that have attached to raccoons. But, then again, most people don't wash what they steal, that is, not until laundering money appealed to certain thugs and politicians, or do I repeat myself? Even worse, according to *Wildlife*, old coons teach little coons the subtle arts of successful larceny. Most of this is taught by the coon's mother; and when a coon has done enough on-the-job training around a farm house, Mamma takes him to the river to show him how to catch frogs, crawfish, insects, muskrats, and mice. And no merit badge is given for any of these activities, although the council in ancient Hamelin promised the Pied Piper a fortune to rid the town of rats. Nay more, the young coon, with Mamma's help, does infinitely better than many boy scouts with traps and gigs. However, few coons die from guilty consciences, heart attacks, and peptic ulcers. From the time they are weaned, they are chased by men and dogs, until they are treed and killed. Few live to enjoy the life of a respectable four-legged patriarch, or any retirement benefits. Of course, as any woodsman knows, a coon can whip a dog three times the coon's size, and send the dog whimpering with his head between his trembling legs.

Obviously, in the eternal feud of man against coon, we have to stay with our own human species, but one wonders how a man would feel if he were marked at birth to be chased the remainder of his life by bloodthirsty coons who had invited the neighbors in for baked man, garnished with sweet potatoes, of course.

"I haven't been there in a coon's age," is heard daily to express a tremendous passage of time. But a "coon's age," meaning a very long time, is a misnomer. Southerners used to believe that raccoons lived to attain great age, but the truth is that coons do not seem to live any longer than foxes, martens, minks, and possums. Coons, in protective captivity, have been known to live as long as ten years. (The British used a "dog's age" for long life, as did many early Americans, and a "coon's age" was probably suggested by the earlier phrase about the dog.)

However, the coon was the first "dunker" of record. It soaks its food before eating it. Usually, a coon lives near a stream and much of its subsistence consists of crawfish, stranded fish, and frogs, all taken in shallow water. Despite *Wildlife's* notes, it is generally assumed that the coon formulated this habit, originally, because what he ate was likely to be muddy. And if water is not close by, a coon is said to carry its food to the nearest water to give it a thorough washing. Expert woodsmen have seen coons that preferred hunger to eating food that couldn't be washed, and they are unwilling for a man to do the dunking for them. The washing impulse is so deeply imbedded many coons go through the charade of washing even when there is no water. Because of this habit the Germans called raccoons *Waschbaer*, or "wash bear," and the second word in the raccoon's technical, scientific name, *Procyon lotor*, means a washer. But in all other respects this finnicky eater is not hailed for his cleanliness.

There were more creeks and small streams in Eastern America that bear the name Coon or Beaver than any other animal. While

21

beavers have many admirable qualities of which Benjamin Franklin, the late Bruce Baton, or Norman Vincent Peale would be proud, they have out PR'd the coon in every basis of comparison. Even so, beavers are not all they are cracked up to be. While they carry mud on their backs, they do not carry cargoes on their tails. And they don't use their tails as trowels. Otherwise, they would have to join a union. A beaver cannot fell a tree precisely where he wants it to fall. Anyone who walks the woods sees many trees that fall the wrong way, and many fall upon and kill the beavers that cut them.

Many scout masters have sworn that beavers build their dams with a curvature that withstands bursts of water. Again, any woodland novice must note the vast inconsistency in beavers' dams. And to those who say, "O, for a beaver's testicles," one replies, "Nuts." Some of the Indian tribes treated cuts with beaver's testicles, and the curative myth has come bouncing down natural history. Finally, there is the belief that most of the beavers were slaughtered in the 19th century for their pelts. (Beaver hats were compulsive items.) But this was true in Chaucer's time, and he wrote about it. Thousands of beavers were killed each year between 1800-1850, but by 1900 the fashions had changed. Today, the beaver, not the hat, is back again, strong in numbers even if he causes no audible rancor to Horatio Alger in the businessman's section of Parnassus.

Skunking or Weasling

The first colonists to smell a skunk must have thought the New World was the largest pile of rancid manure extant, that earth and trees were mere camouflage for an odor that would make lions and tigers turn tail. The skunk is a horrible representative of several genera of small carnivorous mammals of the weasel family (*Mystekidae*).

This four-footed privy is noted for its elongated toes, with blunt, non-tractile claws, and an absence of webs. The true skunk is famous, or infamous, for the tremendous size of its anal glands, and the overpowering odor of its secretions.

The skunk, who evidently carries the woodland equivalent of castor oil, can release his almost poisonous secretions at will, even as he runs. About the size of a housecat, the skunk leaves piles of incredibly odoriferous excrement when he is being chased. In this habitual format the skunk calls up those characters in the novels of James Fenimore Cooper who left a trail of tatters of cloth or broken twigs.

The pursuer, be it man or animal, is not thrown off the track nearly so much as his sense of smelling is offended so egregiously, he says, "To hell with it."

There is only one skunk cabbage, but "skunk words" and "weasel words" are used interchangeably. Whether or not Teddy Roosevelt coined the phrase, he popularized it when he criticized President Wilson: "In connection with the world training (of the military) the words *universal volunteer* have exactly the same effect as acid has on an alkali—a neutralizing effect. One of our defects as a nation is the tendency to use what has been called weasel words. When a weasel sucks eggs, the meat is sucked out of the egg. If you use one weasel word after another, there is nothing left of the others. Now, you can have universal training or you can have voluntary training, but when you use the word *voluntary* to qualify the word *universal* you are using a weasel word. The two words flatly contradict each other."

Historians are positive Teddy Roosevelt got this ambiguity from Stewart Chaplin's more succinct "Stained-Glass Political Platform" (June issue, 1900, of the *Century Magazine*):

"Why weasel words are words that suck the life out of words next to them, just as a weasel sucks an egg and leaves the shell. If you left the egg afterwards it's as light as a feather and not very filling when you are hungry, but a basketful of them would make quite a show, and would bamboozle the unwary. I know them well, and mighty useful they are, too. Although the gentleman couldn't write much of a platform, he's an expert on weasling or skunking. I have seen him take his pen and go through a polished plank or resolution and weasel or skunk out every flatfooted word in it. Then the weasel word pleases one man, and the word that's been weaseled pleases another."

A Man On Horseback

In sagebrush novels and in much pseudo-history, an avenger saves the imperiled schoolmarm, the fort, or the town when he rides in on his horse. In fact, "the man on horseback" has been used almost as often as black slaves referred to Canaan, be Canaan Philadelphia or some place where African slavery did not exist.

Down the years, people have asked, fairly often, "Was there a specific man on a specific horse?" The answer is "yes," and the phrase was coined by Caleb Cushing (1800-1879), attorney-general in Buchanan's cabinet. In January 1860 Cushing wrote a letter in which he predicted that the slavery agitation in the country would result in "a man on horseback, with drawn sword, some Atlantic Caesar or Cromwell or Napoleon."

The phrase was popularized in connection with George E. Boulanger (1837-1891), a French military leader who advocated harsh treatment of Germany as revenge for the French defeat in 1870.

Boulanger acquired the title, "Man on Horseback," because he always appeared in public on a magnificent charge. When he became Minister of War, he was extremely popular with the royalists and all elements disaffected with the Republic.

To a smaller, and perhaps, to less pernicious degree, Boulanger anticipated Hitler. Boulanism was a synonym for Nazism. When he was booted from the French cabinet, as a menace to the safety, every district in France wanted to honor him by making him a representative in the legislature.

The army despaired of him and his fulminations, but he remained a bombastic hero with the people. Even the republicans believed he could become dictator of France any time he pleased. But when his courage proved to be nebulous, a warrant was issued for his arrest, and he fled the country. Two years later, "the peerless" leader killed himself on his sweetheart's grave in Brussels.

25

In America "man on horseback" was applied to Teddy Roosevelt, in an entirely different context. In several rural regions "man on horseback" had the same connotations as "plumed knight," or "knight in shining armor."

It was old John Heywood, in one of his innumerable proverbs written in 1554, who declared: "No man ought to look a gift horse in the mouth." This proverb has been traced back to 400 A.D., to Jerome, and it appears in every European language. The bromide is based upon the opinion that a horse's age may be determined by looking at its teeth.

The form of the proverb just quoted suggests that one ought not to try to appraise the value of a gift, to accept the gift as gratefully as it was given graciously. But there is a subsidiary meaning: Always look a gift horse in the mouth. This means that nothing is given as a fee simple gift. All acceptances acknowledge an obligation. Hence, one must take care to see what one is getting before one entails the obligation attendant to a legatee.

One of the most far-reaching horse disasters occurred in Oxford, North Carolina, some years ago. The story may sound incredulous, but it's every word the truth. A local man, Smith, bought a fast-gaited filly, and he said she had enough papers to join the DAR, and her "Christian name" was Meg McGee. The horse owner said it was superlatively coincidental that his "fast" new horse just happened to have the same name as a local lady, Meg McGee.

Whether or not Meg, the lady, was actually promiscuous, she was highly unconventional for Oxford. She smoked in public, "just like a man smokes," as the locals put it, and many of her sentences were salted with fairly mild expletives. There was never any overt scandal, but local men and women, women especially, tagged her as "fast"—"a fast number, I tell you."

Meg, the woman, sought to have the horse's name changed; but Mr. Smith said his attempts to rename Meg as Mollie produced a split personality in the horse, and, what was infinitely more important, she kicked him. The distraught two-legged Meg sought relief from the court, and soon afterward she left town forever. The horse's owner told everyone who would listen that Abraham Lincoln's mother, Nancy Hanks, had her name picked up by the nation's fastest harness horse, and this was accomplished without all the local hurrahing. History corroborates Smith because Nancy Hanks was the nation's champion trotting filly at the same time that Dan Patch was the fastest trotting horse.

The horse came to town when I was around fourteen, but the whole town was caught by the seat of its pants on fast Meghorse versus the fast Meg McGee onslaught. Before the horse came, Smith led as sedentary a life as a monk. Timorousness seemed to pour from his face in the form of sweat. When he talked with a woman on business, his nervous feet drew enough geometric designs to fill a course on the subject. But after the woman's departure, the word *fast* attached to Smith, and he was so handy with the local ladies he almost had to have a social secretary. In a few years most folks forgot about the lady, Meg, but Smith was given the accolades accorded to Rudolph Valentino and John Barrymore. My father, who knew better, added to Smith's fraudulent laurels by chanting to, and around him:

> Oh, young Lochinvar is come out of the West,
> Through all the wide border his steed was the best;
> So faithful in love, so dauntless in war,
> There never was a knight like the young Lochinvar.

Several theories attempt to account for the horseshoe as a good luck charm. The legend about St. Dunstan may be the best. He was noted for his uncanny ability to shoe horses, and one day the Devil, "himself," called on St. Dunstan "for repairs." The Devil held up a single foot, and St. Dunstan hammered his hoof so hard the Devil begged for mercy. St. Dunstan would not let the Devil go until he got a promise, written in his blood, that he would never enter a house to which a horseshoe was affixed. But witchcraft makes a strong claim, too.

During the Middle Ages men the universe over were afraid of witches and their nefarious tricks. There was a general impression that a person was immune from attack by a witch so long as he was in the open air, and witches were so afraid of horseshoes they fled when a mounted person appeared or whenever they saw a horseshoe nailed to a front door. The shoe had to be nailed open-end up, to hold the good luck in the improvised cup.

27

Of course, the horseshoe has the same shape as the crescent moon, and for primitive man, sight of the crescent moon meant freedom from fear and fertility.

There is the story from Gates County, N.C., in the days when the devil frequently adorned himself in a "gentleman's raiment," for purposes of disguise. He won much money betting on horse races. These were usually stake races, with two animals flying over a dirt road. The Devil could conjure a horse with his eyes and that horse would win. But once the Devil overdid his conjuring and the horse (perhaps Sir Archie?) was so magnetized he ran straight over the Devil. Thus the Devil's horned head and cloven feet were exposed, and the Devil was officially banned from Gates County and has never been back since.

As a schoolboy, I never tired of hanging around Tombo Hick's blacksmith shop. He sweated more than the fireman on the Old 97 as he created wrought iron miracles with fire and anvil. As a child, I was impressed as much by his quiet indifference as I was by his massive strength. I think the grist-miller and the blacksmith were our ultimate independent artisans. I didn't have the envy for Tombo that Henry V expressed for the famous Miller of Dee, but Tombo was everything Longfellow put into his poem, and then some. As I became more acquainted with the magic world of books, I equated Tombo with Longfellow's "village smith," with Joe, the blacksmith and young Pip's friend in *Great Expectations*, and with John P. Kennedy's Horseshoe Robinson, from the novel of the same name. Horseshoe was a smith and a part-time soldier who fought with the American forces in and around the Waxhaws.

Children used to read "The Trial at Tom Belcher's Store" and *Black Beauty* almost as quickly as they learned their ABC's. It is difficult to find a passage in poetry that captures a horse's full gait any better than the late Alfred Noyes's "The Highwayman," with the hooves of the horse going clot-clot along the windy highway. Browning caught much of the same up and down rhythms in "How they brought the Good News From Ghent to Aix."

I have already told how fire horses and ice horses were kept in protective custody by the entire community. And many women, far from the street in their kitchens, could identify various horses by the gaits and ruckus they created on the paved street beyond. Many, many times my mother, entirely shut-off from view of the street, would tell me I'd better go out and get the milk or fix the marker that indicated how much ice a family needed, and she made these accurate identifications from the sounds of hooves alone. Obviously, some wagons were junk piles with the DT's, and some creaked as greaseless boots creak. But that era has written itself out just as an old-fashioned post office pen was written down to a blunt, disfigured end.

To set aside such ephemeral heroes as Tom Mix and his "wonder horse," Tony, or Roy Rogers and Trigger, the nation's best known man on horseback must be Paul Revere. After more than two centuries Revere and his mount still strike fireflies from roadstones as they gallop to proclaim, "The British are coming."

At least Henry W. Longfellow endowed Revere with the phrase. In the poem ("Listen my children and you shall hear of the midnight ride of Paul Revere.") from *Tales of a Wayside Inn*, Longfellow created, with ink, a national hero.

It is important, however, to point out that Revere was America's best known silversmith, a gifted engraver, a political cartoonist, an iron founder and inventor, and he even did a little dentistry. The poem, written long after the alleged facts and long after Revere's death, gave Longfellow (1807-1882) an opportunity to create a swashbuckling episode, and with imagination and compression of the facts, the poet succeeded.

Nonetheless, Paul Revere was a zealous advocate of independence, and it was he who rode a horse from Boston to Philadelphia in 1773 to tell patriotic leaders news of the famous Boston tea party. Revere became the official courier of the Massachusetts Provincial Assembly, and he did make three important rides. He made important trips, on Brown Beauty, a fast horse owned by Dean John Larkin. He made two trips in April, 1775, although Longfellow credits him with but one. He rode to Durham and to Portsmouth in Vermont to warn the citizens that General Gage, British commander, planned to make off with the munitions stored in Durham and Portsmouth by the insurgents. It was on the second ride, in April, 1775, that he arranged for lanterns to be hung in the Old North Church.

But the signal lights were not "one if by land and two if by sea." The lamps were to forewarn the other patriots in Boston and environs. It is the second ride, April 18-19, that turned Longfellow on. However, Revere did not ride through "every Middlesex and farm" to yell warnings. At no time did he holler, "The British are coming." He did ride as far as Lexington to warn John Hancock and Dr. Joseph Warren, president of the Massachusetts Assembly, that danger was imminent. He does not seem to have reached Concord, except in Longfellow's poem. Actually, Revere was apprehended along the road by British soldiers, but after a few hours of questioning he was released. When the famous horse, Brown Beauty, was seized by the British, Revere made his arduous way back to Lexington to devote his activities to retrieving a trunk filled with vital independence objects which John Hancock had left behind in his frenetic desire to escape the enemy.

Thus, he barely missed the slight battle at Lexington, and there is the persistent story that he was paid five shillings by patriots for his night's activities. It should be emphasized again, that at no time did Revere yell, "The British are coming." Hanging the lanterns in the Old North Church is erroneous insofar as Revere is concerned because Revere already knew they were coming by land and by sea.

The most anomalous phase of his evening's work seems to have been his crossing the Charles River, with oars muffled with a woman's petticoat, to attain the Charleston, Massachusetts, side. And while he did arouse the countryside after crossing the river, his chief objective was to warn John Hancock and Samuel Adams. When he reached Lexington and the home in which Hancock, Adams, and Dr. Warren were staying, a patriotic sentinel upbraided Revere for making such a racket with Brown Beauty.

"Noise," all credit Revere with answering, "You'll have noise enough before long because the regulars are coming this way."

It isn't that Longfellow contrived history nearly so much as he took a poetic fragment and gave it immortal wings. Many poets have "taught" history in this same way. Whittier did it twice: He seems badly in error about the true facts in "Skipper Ireson's Ride" and in "Barbara Fritchie." There is every evidence that Stonewall Jackson, being slightly ill, rode through Frederick, Maryland, in a Confederate ambulance. Jackson never saw Barbara Fritchie and she never saw him, and "respect your country's flag" is all Whittier.

30

Longfellow was the best known poet of his time, whatever this implies about critical acumen, and he wanted a Revolutionary hero; he got one, by compressing some facts and enlarging others. Indeed, there is not a single biographical dictionary published in the 19th century that mentions Revere or his swashbuckling ride.

Much nearer to a hero on horseback is Francis Asbury (1745-1816), who started circuit riding among ministers in America. He is credited with having ridden at least two hundred and seventy-five thousand miles on horseback. Despite the influence of John Wesley, Asbury became the first Methodist bishop in America.

Joyful Noises About Animals

Almost from the outset Americans have sung about animals, and whistled about animals. "Pop Goes the Weasel" was immensely popular before the Civil War. And long before the eras of ragtime and jazz, elements of syncopation were found in songs such as "Turkey In the Straw" and "Salty Dog."

By day the Confederate soldier was unbridled mayhem on two legs, but at night around the campfire he cried at the tender, sad saga of the mockingbird's singing over "sweet Hallie's grave" ("Listen to the Mockingbird"). Too, there is the story of the grandee, born to the manner and the manor, who brained an "ill-mannered lout" for cracking jokes at a quartet who sang Stephen Foster's "Old Dog Trey." And we would like the name and address of the man who has never turned loose singing "The Old Gray Mare." ("She ain't what she used to be," although each community seems to have its private set of ribald lyrics.)

On his folk rounds of American colleges Burl Ives revitalized "The Blue-Tailed Fly," just as the late Carl Sandburg revived "The Boll Weevil," to his own accompaniment on the guitar. A tender addendum to "Now I lay me down to sleep," came when the parents sang, "All the Pretty Little Horses":

Go to sleep, little baby,
When you wake, I'll bring you a cake,
And all the pretty little horses.

Another almost axiomatic epilogue to daytime and a prologue to sleep was "Bye, Baby Bunting":

Daddy is going-a hunting,
To find a baby bunting.

One of a child's first rides comes when a parent crosses his legs, and child and parent ride a cocked horse to Banbury Cross,

32

singing and galloping all the way. Several researchers think the "fine lady upon a white horse/with rings on her fingers and bells on her toes" was Queen Elizabeth I. Actually a large cross stood in the center of the English town of Banbury. It was there until it was destroyed in 1601. While many students think the cross was burned, the dissolution of it endures a mystery.

"Cock A Doodle Doo" retains its vigor after more than three hundred and fifty years:

Cock a doodle do!
My dame has lost her shoe,
My master's lost his fiddling stick
And don't know what to do.

Many versions have been sung since the ditty was printed originally in 1608. The rhyme seems to be a childish diversion upon hearing a cock crow, but several historians are sure the rhyme is a spinoff from a child's testimony at a murder trial.

"Down In Jungle Town" began as an irresistible satire on Teddy Roosevelt's big game hunting. When a child receives his first toy animals, he is almost certain to be taught to sing:

I went to the animal fair,
The birds and bees were there,
The elephant got drunk and sat on his trunk,
And what became of the munk, the munk, the munk.

A few years ago Phil Harris revived the old musical saga of "The Preacher and the Bear." ("O, Lord, if you can't help me/Don't help that grizzly bear.")

After the musical joy ride to Banbury Cross, many parents encored "Higgledy Piggledy":

Higgledy-piggledy, my black hen,
She lays eggs for gentlemen.
Gentlemen come every day
To see what my black hen doth lay.

That version is one of the numerous "purifications" of the Victorian era. The version just quoted was printed in 1853, but the lyrics had originated with "Little Blue Betty lived in a den,/She sold good ale to gentlemen'" And good ale is not the only thing Little Betty Blue sold to gentlemen.

Every child used to be taught "Hickory Dickory Dock," which appeared in print as early as 1744.

From the vantage of simple, irrepressible foot-stomping contagion few English offerings, whether in prose or poetry, match the marvelous ebullience of "Abadaba Honeymoon." "Three Little Fish" ("Down in the meadow in an itty bitty boo" never turned this writer on, but the song grasped America in the 1930's, being popularized by my fellow Tar Heel, Saxy Dowell.) The song is simply too cute for me.

I never hear the infectious sparkle of "Be My Little Baby Bumble Bee" without tears in my eyes or with tears in my heart, because my sainted father liked it so much and sang it so well. ("Honey, keep a-buzzing please/I've got a dozen cousin bumble bees/But I want you for my baby bumble-bee.") Arthur Pryor's "The Whistler and His Dog" has put fight into a chicken too sick to cackle, and I must have danced from Oxford, North Carolina, to Oxford, Mississippi, to the strains of "Crazy Over Horses, Horses, Horses," and "Barney Google," whose delapidated nag, Spark Plug, won the big race.

Just before World War I and into the so-called Roaring Twenties, Americans went overboard, with both best feet forward, in a series of animal dances such as the Turkey-trot, the Pussy-foot, the Bunny-hug, and the Camel-walk.

The list of songs is well nigh limitless. A columnist, who needed a personal item badly, wrote that FDR's favorite song was "Home On the Range," and every delegation of school children who came to the White House sang the saga of "where the deer and the antelope play." But throughout the twentieth century, "O, That Strawberry Roan" and "Yippie Ti, Yi, Ye" have been popular western songs, and neither has ever been sullied by being taken over by the squawkers whom we label "country" or "bluegrass" today.

Betimes the contagious "Froggie Went A-Courtin" maintained its popularity:

Froggie went a-courting,
And he did ride,
Sword and pistol by his side;
Rode up to Miss Mousy's house

34

And asked Miss Mousy for to be his wife.
'Not without Uncle Rat's consent,
Would I marry the President!'

Depending upon the vagaries of human emotions, abetted by the tender nostalgia, "Where, O Where" has made thousands of adults relive one of the starkest tragedies of their young and innocent years:

Where, O, where, has my little dog gone,
O, where, O, where can he be,
With his tail cut short
And his ears cropped long,
O, where, O where, can he be?

I related elsewhere some of the volatilities engendered on school playgrounds by children who said and sang the song about the robin. ("I'm very glad you're here.") But the most tempestuous school ground fracas in my memory erupted over "Bye, Baby Bunting, Daddy's Gone A-Hunting." At our small provincial school some of Darwin's rejections—that is a sizable foregathering of the great unwashed—made ribald, and at times, blatantly ribald, allusions to those who had sung "Bye, Baby Bunting" in the schoolhouse. (Thirty minutes of each day was set aside for singing by an entire grade.)

Among other epithets, "Bye Baby Bunting" was derided as prissy-sissy, and boys who sang it had ruffles on their BVD's. I am sure that several of my classmates, as naive as I, construed the harsh castigation of the song as a dark slur on the mother who had sung it to her child at bedtime. I am sure many shared my personal aggrievement. In a left-handed way, slandering the "family" song slandered the whole group, especially the mother.

One day this culminated in what may be described solely as "one hell of a fight," and I still have a scar on my right hand. My hand and the face of one of the great unwashed really collided.

I mention this bizarre donnybrook to show something of marrow ties between mothers and children, and to indicate the obvious fact that today's small students are far too sophisticated to fight about a song that the tone-deaf called "prissy-sissy."

There is this irresistible follow-up: I was suspended from the fifth grade for a few days "for fighting." Re-entry was predicated on hearty promises to behave better, and to carry a note to school from a parent. My father wrote the essential note, but within a few minutes I was back in his law office.

Without looking up from his desk, he said, "Well, what is it now?" I told him how I had handed over his message and how I had told the principal my personal regret. I told him the principal had said, "Until I say so, you can't attend school, use the lunchroom, the toilet, or check a book out of the library."

"What did you say?" my father asked, still engrossed with the papers on his desk.

"I told him, goddamn it, to go to hell."

"Well, did you tell him to take his excuse, his toilet, lunchroom and library with him?"

It would be criminal to omit Stephen Foster's "Camptown Races," which after more than a century retains enough exuberance to restore the fight in a dead gamecock. Foster lived in the new town of Cincinnati in 1850 when he wrote the song, and it was inspired by hearing roustabouts at the river port. (There is always this enigma: Foster was born near Pittsburgh, July 4, 1824, the very same day as the deaths of ex-Presidents Jefferson and Adams, author-co-signers of the Declaration of Independence.)

How Much Ransom For A Gorilla?

Along the Atlantic Seaboard in colonial times and in the early days of the republic, horse-stealing was a common practice, and justice was dispatched summarily when the victim was caught. Horse-stealing was a capital crime in most of the original thirteen states. At best, the culprit got off with a large "T," for thief, being branded in the palm of his hand. Usually, though, the sheriff assembled a jury hastily, and the thief was hanged. When the rope went over the limb of a tree and around his neck, his feet were placed upon a water bucket. To execute the sentence, the sheriff merely kicked the bucket from under the poor man's feet. Thus it was that "kicking the bucket" became a synonym for almost any kind of death. And horse-stealing in the old west was considered such a heinous crime the victim was usually hanged sans the charade of a jury trial.

It was only fairly recently that animals were stolen from zoos and held for ransom. Not so long ago someone with more raw courage than brains stole a rare baby gorilla and a snow leopard from Chicago's Lincoln Park Zoo. Since subsequent news coverage was scant, one is not sure if these animals were kidnapped for ransom, for meanness, or for distorted kicks.

But whatever the sadistic or lunatic motivation was, this has to be one of the strangest heists since Colonel Luke Lea, at one time a United States senator and a long-time publisher of the main newspaper in Nashville, Tennessee. Some of his fellow officers slipped into Dorn, Holland, shortly after the Armistice of 1918, to kidnap the Kaiser, who had abdicated to Dorn. Among Colonel Lea's party were Gordon Browning, who would become governor of Tennessee, and Larry McPhail, voted into baseball's Hall of Fame in Cooperstown in 1978. Apparently, it was Lea's intention to capture the Kaiser, bring him to this country, and exhibit him from place to place, for a fee.

Moreover, this diabolical heist at the Lincoln Park Zoo is

bound to remind some older readers of O. Henry's captivating short story, "The Ransom of Red Chief." In the story the son of a small-town banker is kidnapped for ransom by two men down on their luck. The little boy abuses them so fiercely, especially when he is playing Red Chief and the abductors take turns being his horse, that they write the father that they will return the boy and forego the ransom. The father says, "Nothing doing," and the two incredibly clumsy kidnappers end up selling their few precious possessions to raise money to give to the father to take back his son.

A Few Obsolete Or Legendary Animals

Interest in the so-called werwolf, or werewolf, was dormant a long time, but today's youngsters are turned on by almost all of the most bizarre facets of the supernatural. One of the first printed references is in Herodotus (5th century B.C.). "The father of historians" says he heard about werwolves first when he sojourned in Sythia: "They talked of a people who once a year changed themselves into wolves and then resumed their original shape. But they cannot make me believe such tales, although they (Sythians) not only tell about them but swear to them."

There is also the legend of the lycanthropes of the Middle Ages, sorcerers, called "loups-garous" by the French. The Middle Ages were redolent with horrendous tales of these wolf-men. The idea was implemented in the Middle Ages by the prevalence of the belief that witches could assume various animal shapes, such as cats, dogs, horses, and wolves. Indeed, the superstitution existed in most of the Balkan states until just recently.

Most werwolves were said to have maniacal hatred for religious men and love and a special appetite for the flesh of religious folk. And the superstition was enhanced by the cruel Middle Ages practice of people who suffered extreme melancholia and other forms of derangement being turned loose to run wild in the deep forests. The people who suffered aberrations in the Middle Ages were sent to the woods as routinely as we send people to insane asylums today.

After considerable dormancy there is much renewed interest in the fabled unicorn, described in ancient accounts as a native of India. This strange and highly respected creature was depicted with the body of a huge horse, a goat's beard, and a lion's tail.

Unicorn is from the Latin that means "one-horned," and this horn ranged up to one and one-half cubits (a cubit runs from 17 to 22 inches). The horn on its forehead was perfectly straight, with a white base, a black middle, and a red tip. Biblical scholars think the unicorn alluded to in the Writ was a wild ox.)

The unicorn's pure whiteness symbolized virginity and purity of action and thought, and this legendary animal was a prime subject for the magnificent tapestries of the Middle Ages. The unicorn was adopted as the supporter of the Royal Scottish arms and it was introduced as the left support of the British Royal Arms.

We have extended the name of the fabled animal to the unicorn, or file, fish, the unicorn plant, and the unicorn root.

The dodo, used frequently in phrases such as "dead as the dodo," was a bird that once inhabited Mauritius, a British Island in the Indian Ocean, east of Madagascar. The word *dodo* is a corruption of the Portuguese *duodo*, foolish or silly. This bird, although larger than a wild turkey, was of the pigeon family. Extremely clumsy, its wings were barely rudimentary. When Portuguese sailors first saw dodos in 1507, they killed several with clubs; but the meat was unpalatable.

Van Neck, a Dutchman, described the dodo in great detail in 1598. A specimen, being shipped to Holland, died en route. But it was preserved and it is on exhibit today in the British Museum. In 1638 a living dodo was taken to England by Sir Harmon L'Estrange, who described the bird's back as a "dunn or deare colour. This dodo was exhibited in London, and the curious paid to see it.

The experts say the dodo's extinction was put into motion when hogs were introduced to Mauritius. The dodo couldn't run fast, and it couldn't fly. Thus, it was rudimentary prey to the rampaging hogs, and the female dodo never laid but one egg at a time. There is no record of a live dodo since 1681, but three skeletons are yet preserved in museums. Scientists say the solitaire, closely related to the dodo, and a native of Rodiquez, became extinct around 1761.

Many people who are entirely ignorant of the historical dodo use the phrase "dead as a dodo" regularly, and the phrase must survive as much by alliteration as actual distinction.

The halcyon endures chiefly to conjure the safe innocence of youth. It comes to us from Greek mythology: Ceyx was drowned, en route to consultation with an oracle. His wife, Halcyon, or Alcyone, daughter of the wind god, discovered his body when the sea washed it ashore. Halcyon, distraught with grief, threw herself into the breakers. And when she was dead, compassionate gods turned Ceyx and Halcyon into the birds known as halcyons, usually identified as species of the kingfisher.

The halcyon was said to spend the seven coldest days of a winter building a floating nest upon the icy waves. This nest of fishbones was the place the halcyon laid her eggs. An extra week was required for brooding, and because such a fragile nest could not possibly survive the high winds and cold waves of deep winter, the gods decided to invoke unutterable calm during the period of fourteen days. Hence, the week before and the week after the winter solstice (shortest days of the year) became the "halcyon days."

Then later on in history it was assumed by primitive men that the halcyon, or kingfisher, was endowed with the magic power to subdue the wind and the wild ocean. Indeed, this myth has some enduring viability along the Atlantic Seaboard in the custom of hanging a dried kingfisher up by its head so that its bill can point the direction of the wind, the same as a weather vane.

This belief was old when colonists settled along the Atlantic Seaboard. In *King Lear* Shakespeare has Kent to say: "Such smiling rogues renege affirm, and turn their halcyon beaks with every gale and vary of their masters." The allusion is to Goneril's steward, Oswald.

Perhaps the dragon is the oldest and best known of all of the legendary animals. Often this mythological monster is confused with the equally fabulous griffin. But the dragon is given bat's wings, with ribs and web, while the griffin has the feathered wings of a bird.

The dragon, with its impenetrable, natural armor and its ability to spit fire, was used as a symbol to express power by the ancient Greeks and Romans. The Roman army termed its standard bearers *dragonarius*, because they carried the dragon as a military emblem. The Greek dragon called *hydra*, owned its devastating prowess to its having seven ferocious heads.

The dragon was a Celtic symbol of sovereignty, and it was a part of the British standard from the pagan era to Henry VIII. And in the world famous Bayeux Tapestry the dragon appears upon the shields of some of the knights represented. In the early days of firearms (17th century) a short musket was hooked to a swivel that was attached to the soldier's belt, because a dragon's head formed the muzzle. The soldiers who carried these weapons were called "dragoons."

In medieval mythology the dragon was the epitome of evil, usually the cause of a public famine and pestilence. In medieval alchemy the dragon was the emblem of Mercury, and it was widely known and found on the chemist's drug pots. It even figures in astrology. The northern coast constellation is called *Draco*.

In Byzantine art the dragon personified evil and was responsible for famine and pestilence. In Christian mythology the dragon had an active existence. The great dragon, Gargouile, lived in the Seine, and he ravaged Rouen. This dragon was slain by St. Romulus, in the 7th century. The French word *gargouille* means waterspout. Hence the spouts draining water off the walls of churches and other large buildings were usually in the decorative form of a dragon.

Sundry countries have had their special dragons and dragon slayers. The French dragon of Languedoc, Tarasque-gargouille, was killed by St. Martha, and the city of Taradcon is said to have derived its name from that event. But the big dog in the dragon slaying business has to be St. George. Several paintings depicting St. George killing a dragon are in London's National Gallery. (St. George, special patron of chivalry and a tutelary saint of England, died in Nicomedia on April 23, 303. Although he was venerated by the Eastern as well as the Western church, his actual history is obscure, and the extant accounts are infinitely more mythology than real history.

(The story in *Acta Sanctorum*, "Deeds of the Saints," says he was born of Christian parents in Cappadocia, that he became famous as a soldier, that he was tortured and put to death after affirming his Christian faith. He was adopted by the Genoese as their patron saint, and in 1212 the council at Oxford ordered that his birthday*, April 23, should be observed as a national holiday.

(Edward III, of England, installed a special order in 1344, with St. George as its patron saint, and in 1350 this was made the Order of the Garter. According to the persistent story the Countess of Salisbury dropped a garter at a ball. To still the guffaws and snickers, the thoughtful Edward picked up the lady's garter, tied it around his own arm, and rebuked the

*If 303, as stated was date of St. George's death, it seems unlikely that this should have happened as early as 1212.

merrymakers with "Honi soit qui mal y pense," or "Shame to him who evil thinks." Edward was speaking in Norman French, and he founded the Order of the Garter. He had given his own garter to be used as a signal at the Battle of Crecy, and many think the motto could have been an admonition to King Philip of France.)

Stone slabs at Persepolis, Ninevah, Perseus, and Andromedia in Greek mythology show the ancient origination of dragons.

In Chinese legends the dragon (*lung*) figures prominently. The Celestials say there are three dragons, one *lung*, for the sky; one *li*, in the sea; and a third *kiau* in the marshes. Lung, the most important, is described as having the head of a camel, the horns of a deer, the eyes of a rabbit, the ears of a cow, the neck of a snake, the belly of a frog, the scales of a carp, the claws of a hawk, and the palm of a tiger. Lung has whiskers on each side of its mouth, and a beard in which a bright pearl is often depicted.

The sea dragon appears in waterspouts, and the Chinese fishermen used to worship the sea dragon through fear. Some authorities account for four Chinese dragons: (1) The Celestial Dragon, which guards the mansions of the gods and supports them so they will not fall; (2) the Spiritual Dragon, which causes the winds to blow and makes rain for mankind's benefit; (3) the Dragon of the Earth, which marks out the courses of rivers and lakes; (4) the Dragon of the Hidden Treasures, which watches over the wealth concealed from mortals.

When China had an emperor, the dragon was his official emblem; and it has five claws. Other dragons have four claws, and the five-clawed dragon was forbidden save on imperial goods. This is invaluable to connoisseurs because the presence of five-clawed dragons proves that bronzes, pottery, and tapestries were made for a royal personage. And in the Chinese zodiac, the dragon is the sign for the month of March.

The Japanese dragon (*rio* or *tatsu*) probably derives from the Chinese, but differs from it. It has only three claws, one of which usually clasped a perfect silver ball, or a large pearl. The Japanese dragon was endowed with the power to make itself invisible. It could shrink to the size of a silkworm, or expand until it covered the universe. Pictorially illustrated in multitudes of Japanese decorative art, the *tatsu* is seen floating among the clouds or rising from the ocean's stormiest waves.

(The Persian dragon has eleven cloven feet, and many fun-loving, satirical people really realized the late Heywood Broun's mockery of knighthood via the clumsy oaf who killed dragons, when stronger knights failed, because he could say the magic word, "Rumpelstiltskin.")

The cockatrice is mentioned in early Biblical translations several times. Some English translators put the cockatrice down as a serpent hatched from a chicken's egg. The translators who came later changed the word "cockatrice" to "adder." But the cockatrice depicted in early drawings is always depicted with a ram's head and hair, a snake's tongue, a feathery body and wings, and with the dragon's tail and feet.

According to Homer, the Gorgons were among the most horrifying creatures of Hades. Homer enumerates three: Stheno, Euyale, and Medusa. Homer said the three "lived beyond the ocean," and at that time people believed the various oceans and seas were one continuous body of water encircling Creation.

All were immortal save Medusa. Their hair was entwined with serpents; their hands were made of brass; and their bodies were covered with impenetrable scales. And each had tusks as long as a wild boar's. They could turn into stone all who looked at them. When Perseus went in conquest of the Gorgons, he was given a special scythe by Hermes, a looking glass by Athena, winged shoes by Pluto. His equipment, the looking glass particularly, enabled Perseus to see the Gorgons but he remained invisible to them. He killed the three Gorgons and gave Medusa's head to Athena, who placed it in her aegis and turned into stone all who looked at it.

The riddle of the sphinx, which contributed to the Oedipus legend, is pretty well known, and the Persians and the Assyrians believed in winged bulls. The hippocampus, a sea satyr, seems to have been an offshoot of the mermaid. The hippocampus, was a sea horse that had the head and forequarters of a horse and the tail and hindquarters of a fish. It appears in Greek and Latin mythology.

The belief in the existence of mermaids had considerable vitality for a long time. As recently as the early part of the 17th century two of Henry Hudson's sailors saw a mermaid, and Hudson made meticulous notes in the ship's log book from the descriptions given him by the two lookouts who said they saw the mermaid. (In the 1930's "Minnie the Mermaid," a pop tune,

44

had a few lines that current Puritans branded as salacious, although none would attract even passing attention today.)

The harpies, in Greek mythology, are one of several loathsome, voracious monsters, with a woman's head and torso and with the wings, tail, and talons of a bird. These are some of the most frightening of all the legendary monsters.

The troll, a supernatural creature in Norse mythology, was depicted as a friendly or a mischievous dwarf, and it was also seen as a huge, venal giant. The word is from the Old Norse *tollt*, meaning a monster or demon.

After an almost interminable verbal hiatus, troll came back via the popular kiddie phonograph record, "Three Billy Goats Gruff," in which the third goat bests the troll who guards the bridge. But long before the recording, Henrik Ibsen (1828-1906), the great Norse dramatist, had Peer Gynt being stopped in the deep woods by a troll. The troll admonishes Peer Gynt solemnly and menacingly that he has to go through the forest, that he can't go around or under the forest.

Almost apropos to nothing there have been sporadic reports of various kinds of animated fish, such as the Gunter Grass's *Weltgeist*, (world spirit). Although the great German novelist uses the fish in fiction, such creatures have appeared in writing and in talk that were not supposed to be fiction. Grass's talking fish is a warty, shrewd creature, possessing a crooked mouth and two freakish eyes, all on one side of its doormat-like face. As is true in the earlier tales of talking sea monsters, Grass's fish promises to bring all of the world's knowledge to the narrator, if, in turn, the fish is thrown back into the Baltic, its perpetual home.

In Ambrose Bierce's (1842-1914) chilling short story, "The Damned Thing," an entire western community is paralyzed from the fear induced by an unseen creature or force. Bierce's lethal "damned thing" is never beheld by human eyes, although the objects of its maniacal mayhem are omnipresent. Bierce, a true iconoclast, implies that just as there are sounds beyond the scope of human ears, there are shapes and forms beyond the powers of human eyes.

If Bierce was merely writing a horror story, or what would be deemed science fiction today, his assumption is based upon a common observation. When a tree in full, lavish foliage is filled with birds, when it is impossible for the birds on the lower limbs to see the bird on higher limbs or to see the lookout bird atop the tree, the whole covey flies off in single concert. It stands to reason that the entire covey responds to a call from the leader-lookout. This call is beyond human ears, although the birds hear it plainly enough. In essence, Bierce seems to have applied a similar supernatural force to "The Damned Thing."

"Blind tiger" emanated from the era of blockade whiskey; and when one called upon a distillery in the deep woods, or on a honky tonk, one was said to have visited a "blind tiger." While "blind tiger" was merely a euphemism, any man who fell and cut himself or suffered broken bones while intoxicated was said to have been attacked by a blind tiger. Thousands of innocent children, fully cognizant of the injuries to their elders, came to believe such wounds were inflicted by a real tiger, and a blind one, at that. If a "wet hen" sufficed for anger ("She was as mad as a wet hen"), then a tiger, blinded, was even more dangerous than one with 20/20 vision.

Goblins took many forms and faces with children, and James Whitcomb Riley's (1849-1916) "Little Orphant Annie" was attended by nervous giggles when recited after dark. Many listening children put their hands to the ears, just as they put their hands to their eyes during terrifying scenes at the "pitchershow."

> An' all us other children, when the supper things is done,
> We sit around the kitchen fire and has the mostest fun
> A-list'nin to the witches tales 'at Annie tells about
> An' the gobble-uns 'at gits you
> > Ef you
> > Don't
> > Watch
> > Out.

The sturgeon, the fish that supplies the roe for caviar, certainly isn't obsolete or imaginary. Even so, many moderns have difficulty believing that sturgeon used to swim in inland waters in several of the Atlantic Seabord states. In several of North Carolina's rivers and inland waters sturgeon were so numerous and so large, around the turn of the century, that they became a glut on the market. Many weighed as much as three hundred pounds, and they were sold for a penny a pound, as vegetable garden fertilizer.

In Jonathan Swift's (1667-1745) classic, *Gulliver's Travels*, the fourth portion is about Lemuel Gulliver's sojourn in the Land of Houyhnhnms, wherein the country is ruled by intelligent horses; and mere mortals, tagged Yahoos by Swift, follow the instructions and injunctions of the brilliant horses. And in George Orwell's *Animal Farm*, there are many talking animals. Major, a garrulous pig, is the Karl Marx of the communal or communistic farm. The other animals see Major as a hero because of his Marxian preachments. The animals are provided the bare necessities by Mr. Jones, who owns the farm, but Major preaches subservience. Finally, after accumulated indignities, Major and his talking colleagues run Jones off the farm.

By definition a goblin is a mischievous, dwarfed creature that can take on human appearance. The lines preceding Robert Burn's "Tam O'Shanter" are Gawin Douglas's: "Of bronyis and of bogilies full is this buke." (Bronyis means friendly goblin, and bogilies are unfriendly goblins.) Many readers will recall that the tipsy Tam, riding home late at night on his horse, Meg, dreads the tongue lashing he will get from his wife. But along the haunted rural bypass,

> Aw, wow, Tam say an unco sight,
> Warlocks and witches in a dance
> Nae coillon brent (brought) from France.

By similar token, Hop-O-My-Thumb, the diminutive elf of Charles Perrault's fairy stories is a friendly goblin. He saves himself and his small brothers from an ogre by means of his seven league boots, which enable him to cover seven leagues (in English and American measurements a league is three miles).

Much credence in the 16th and 17th centuries was given to Robin Goodfellow, a mischievous and merry goblin or elf who often took a domesticated form. Betimes Robin was believed to haunt the British countryside. Some of Robin's powers and tricks are given to Puck by Shakespeare in *A Midsummer Night's Dream*:

> Either I mistake your shape and making quite,
> Or else you are that shrewd and knavish sprite

47

Call'd Robin Goodfellow: are you not he
That frights the maidens of the villagery;
Skim milk, and sometime labor in the guise
And bootless make the breathless housewife churn;
    And sometime make the drink to bear no barm,
    Mislead night-wanderers, laughing at their harm?"

Storytelling was immensely popular with the American Indians, just as it has been with all uneducated people, especially nomadic or semi-nomadic ones. The stories told around the campfire took on reality, and what began as entertainment ended as a myth so unshakeable it passed as gospel. Most of the American Indians had a superstitious fear of animals and they believed animals exercised a strong influence over their personal lives. However, the devastations of certain animals could be contravened by incantations, special prayers, charms, and other shamanistic processes and medicines. The brave carried a piece of the animal he feared to ward off attacks. (Ultimately, this produced the American's carrying the left hind foot of a rabbit for good luck.) The Indian hunter carried a rabbit's foot, and he carried small parts of the animal he wished to kill for meat or covering.

As the Indian learned more about wildlife and the habits of animals, and as he found better means of killing animals, his ancient fear of animals was transposed, especially among the Algonquins, and the animals hated and feared him. The Indians slaughtered so many animals that the remaining creatures of the wilderness held a big pow-wow. Fearing extinction, the animals devised new ways to perpetuate their own species. At the big meeting the deer agreed to visit upon man rheumatism and all other muscular ailments; the reptiles agreed to give man nightmares; wasps and black widow spiders agreed to poison him; the birds agreed to give him infested lungs; and the insects agreed to spread malaria throughout his blood system.

Thus, disease was introduced into the world and man has suffered ever since for his mistreatment of animals. It was the ultimate fear of the American Indian of animals that produced amulets of a diverse nature and range. After the alleged meeting of the animals, the Indians would not kill a chipmunk because they said, of all the animals, the chipmunk was the only one that felt sorry for the plague-ridden Red Man.

Virtually all the Plains Indians held sun dances to perpetuate significant occurrences. The average sun dance lasted from eight to ten days. The sun dance is said to have commenced when a Cree took his family to a mountain top to atone for his wickedness. While praying, or meditating, he met a super-duper medicine man who taught him the importance of the sun dance. Although the habitat of the extraordinary medicine man isn't known, he probably came with the wind or stepped from a cloud. In the dance four venerable braves represented the four wind gods of the earth's four corners. All the dancers wore wreaths symbolic of the sun, the moon, the morning star, and the wind.

The Thunder Bird, presented symbolically at these ceremonial dances, was the personification of lightning and thunder. As a rule the Thunder Bird was friendly, and it was he who carried Wakiah, the hero god of the Kwakiut, on his back on the hero's journey down among the Pacific countries.

(Each Indian tribe had a medicine man and the Indian word "shaman" is close to the Hebrew word for caretaker of the synagogue.)

The ancient Scottish prayer always finds ready tongues around Halloween times, if few people can place it in literature: "From ghoulies and ghosties and long leggety beasties and things that go bump in the night, good Lord, deliver us."

There were sporadic allusions to some sort of fish demon in Loch Ness prior to 1930, and for the past half century a continuous tempest like a tug-of-war has gone on between believers, non-believers, and those who don't give a damn either way. Loch Ness is a beautiful lake on Inverness shore, or the line of continuation of the Caledonian Canal. Long and narrow, Loch Ness is around twenty-two miles long, and it is around one mile across; the bottom has been fixed at approximately seven hundred and eighty feet. It occupies the center of the Valley of Glenmore, and an outlet from Loch Ness pours into Merry Firth.

Fossils of the "Irish elk" are supposed to exist from prehistoric times. This animal has been reconstructed, from remains, as attaining six feet, with horns that often measured as much as eleven feet between the tips. (This sounds a good deal like Paul Bunyan's fabled ox, Babe.) The Irish say their big elk became extinct because his antlers were so cumbersome that he

49

continued to have painful falls, and carrying that much weight would get anything down in the back.

But several experts say it was the Irish climate that did in the elk, a fact that the Dublin Chamber of Commerce isn't likely to bruit about. Others say it was more of a deer than an elk, and that in addition to Ireland, the animal lived in England, central Europe, and western Asia.

Quite obviously, a nightmare has no pertinence to horses. In this connection the word "mare" comes from the Anglo-Saxon *mara*, a specter of a type of goblin. It perched itself upon the chest of a sleeper to deny him any movement or speech.

Jonathan and the Gulls

For change of pace, and because I know so little of the bird's history and breeding habits, it gives me superlative joy to quote from Jonathan Daniels' book, *The End of Innocence*, a passage in the introduction, about gulls. Daniels is talking about 1913. His father has just been appointed Secretary of the Navy in Woodrow Wilson's cabinet:

"An inland child, wandering down that part of Rock Creek which was still unlandscaped and unmotorized, to the Potomac's edge, I was particularly fascinated by the gulls. . .the great black-backed and herring gulls which sacrifice some deftness to size and weight, and the little Bonaparte gulls which are grace and quickness itself, but because they lack the momentum of heavier birds must be continually flapping and flicking their wings to sustain themselves. But the best of all are the ringbills with a capacity for a thousand slight, continuous adjustments of wing and tail to the air in which they move. A boy or a statesman may learn from gulls, even gulls may learn from politicians."

Now I exercise the prerogative of an old and vain author to quote a poem I wrote many years ago, one which appears in a book of mine called *Spur Line*:

Sea-Scape
The mother forsaken sand
Closes her eyes and waits the first assault
Of her wild and devastating lover.

A single gull, propelled by consternation alone,
Reduces the sum of infinity's harrowing loneliness
To three stark caws, trimmed with terror.

An intruding mock-moon backs up on rounded heels
To watch the winds ride the sea's white circus horses
Through fiery hoops made of sunset streamers.

51

The Little Foxes and Caroline

The fox was well known by the ancient Hebrews, and Matthew quotes Jesus as saying: "The foxes have holes and the birds of the air have nests, but the Son of man hath no where to lay his head." The Song of Solomon has this to say: "Take us, the little foxes, that spoil the vine." Twenty years ago the old *New York Post* quoted a woman who had said, "A fox is a wolf who sends flowers."

Political whips, such as the Democratic whip in the U.S. Senate, or the Conservatives whip in Parliament, arose from the whipper-in on fox hunts. The whipper-in, close assistant of the Master of Hounds, attained political and fox hunting viability in the 18th century. In England, especially, the Parliamentary whip may wield his authority metaphorically, but the final result is just as effective as the whips used by the whipper-in.

Although coats and shoulder pieces made of silver fox have been expensive status symbols for many years, experts say "silver fox" is the black fox in which so many hairs are white-tipped they appear silver. The black fox, the platinum fox, the grey fox, and the so-called cross fox all are members of the species of the red foxes. Black, silver, and cross foxes abound in North America and in Siberia. Totally black specimens are rarely found save in the far, far north. As a general rule the fur of a cross fox has a yellowish or orange tone with silver points and dark cross markings on the shoulders. Pelts of silver foxes vary in color from black, with a slight dusting of silver on the shoulders to half black and half silver. All these phases are rare in the wild state, and it is believed that they are usually born in litters of normally red cubs. (The red fox is bred for the fox hunting sport.) And the blue fox is a color phase of the Arctic or white fox, which varies in color from dull blue, to bluish brown, to pure white.

Literature is permeated with many memorable stories and

poems about foxes. Most modern animal stories compare to R. P. Harriss's exquisite, cruelly forgotten *The Foxes* as a rubber tub duckie compares to a whale. D. H. Lawrence's *The Fox* is a top flight novella and Lillian Hellman's play *The Little Foxes* is among the most dramatic triumphs of this century. Few long narrative poems have the power and fascination of John Masefield's *Reynard, the Fox*, and I should throw away books by the wheelbarrow load before I would part with my copy of Siegfried Sassoon's compelling book, *Memoirs of a Fox-Hunting Man*.

Thus, it may be egregiously cheeky of me to insert my own story, "Caroline, the Fox." The abiding importance lies not within the story, but in the fact that in insular America many communities had special animals that the whole population kept in the warmest personal custody. For three or four generations of hunters and walkers saw the same special fox, deer, or bear, and while the animal was pursued, extreme caution was taken not to hurt it or to capture it.

I insert "Caroline, the Fox" for that reason, and also to make a personal confession. For years I went fox-hunting regularly. I know now that the chief compulsion was the deep woods, the cleared slivers that had the big head and called themselves roads, and the many creeks that strutted along blowing penny whistles and beating snare drums. But whatever the compulsion, repugnance for the chase and the possible kill overcame me at the contagious apogee of the hallowings of hunters and bell-throated music of Walker hounds. I decided fox hunting is sadistic, morally indefensible. Ever since that radiant day I have pulled hard for the fox, just as I have tried to put a whammy on bounding hounds crying vengeance in pursuit.

Equally reprehensible to me is the ritual wherein the vested clergyman blesses the hounds. Considering the fact that a fox has been a harassed nomad, with a price on its head since history was recorded, having a clergyman pray for hounds strikes those not born to the manner, or to the manor, somewhat as if a referee gave Mohammed Ali brass knuckles to take on Dagwood Bumstead. D. H. Lawrence said he never saw a wild creature that felt sorry for itself. One doubts that Lawrence ever watched a clergyman bless hounds determined to tear the fox into tiny shreds and tatters of unmitigated gore. (Perhaps the wind, when it has a cat in its tail, offers a prayer for the

53

beleaguered fox.) Anyway, if the official blessing of hounds is going to continue among those who wear pinks and ride blooded horses, it seems entirely appropriate that the inverse Purple Heart of smearing a dead fox's blood on the face of novice riders, and of dividing the dead fox's fur among the other riders, is altogether fitting. The only parallel that a commoner can think of is the defendant being tried for murdering his parents who asked the judge for leniency because he was a "poor orphan boy."

Caroline, the Fox

Local historians disagree in trying to figure out wily Caroline's age. There are those who contend that she first showed the year the big oak tree fell in Frank Freeman's yard, while others hotly interpose: "No, no, man, you're 'way, 'way off. It was the year the Fuller boy turned over the hornet's nest in Little Zion Church." And still others tell how their grandpaps hunted Caroline as lads in short pants. An irascible old Squire Pettigrew argued until the day he died that Caroline broke up a rally for W. J. Bryan in the fall of '96.

Now, some of the oldest men will take you by the sleeve and mutter that Caroline really wasn't born of a fox at all. No, siree, her mammy was a gray cloud and her pappy was a whirlwind. And the old people know it to be an unimpeachable fact that Caroline was born during "Old Christmas," that she was whelped and nurtured by Old Christmas spirits that skinned the cat on a locust tree and then took refuge in an abandoned foxhole.

But all the way from Tally Ho Township where Sweetgum Creek lies sunning in the brush like a silver worm, to Sassafras Fork Township, where Coon Creek rattles down the clay banks like a truant boy playing leapfrog, everyone knew that Caroline could vanish right smack before your eyes. If she willed, she could become a rock in Coon Creek, or an elm tree along a ferny lane, or a hollow tree straddling a hole in a sunken field. She could turn herself into mist, or she could run over the hill and become a part of the dust that her flying heels kicked up. Her eyes were dark stars upon a winter night, and her sleek back was a rain cloud.

The legends came and left like a trail of swamp smoke, but

Caroline just went on and on and on. Puppies grew to houndom, got old and feeble and died. Each great one had his turn and each one toppled before the will-o'-the-wisp. To name a few, there were Turkey Trot, winner of the All-Age and sire of Colonel Henry, the National Bench Champion, sire of Whangdoodle, that gave mouth as if the heavens were falling. Each in his day gave fervent chase to the drop of quicksilver, but on and on Caroline ran, exploding over the hill like wind-blown mist, majestic, supreme, eternally aloof and sublimely untouched.

The oldest men spat from the breeze and passionately vowed that Caroline could turn herself into a leaf when the chase was too hot. She'd turn herself into a leaf and hang onto the tree, frolicking in the breeze while hapless hounds passed by as forlornly as children lost in a maze of woodland tracks. I've heard reliable men say that Caroline once changed herself into a fish and lay up under the creek bank, sucking the cool moss, while hounds ran an absurd circle, menacing their own tails. And one of the Warren boys said he'd be damned and double-damned if the sun didn't lower a golden staircase for Caroline when she grew weary of entertaining irksome hounds.

Choleric old Squire Pettigrew died cursing a monstrous fate and Caroline, for it was the morning of the township hunt when the dark angel got him on a sight race and clipped his brush. The expiring squire finally upbraided the astonished clergyman who was reading prayers with: "Stop all that damned nonsense, man. Open the window! Can't they catch that damned strumpet before I die! Listen. Listen. I'll vow they are right on top of her now! Listen! Oh my God, listen! Of all the rotten, stinking luck. . ."

But even the Squire, if he had lived to continue his diatribe, would tell you that Caroline was the best damned nursemaid there ever was. Yes, sir. The Warren boys would start out with their pack of wondrous Walker hounds, as proudly as a troop of cavalry with banners and guidons streaming. At night they'd return as bedraggled as birds too tired to fly. But old Caroline always ended up the hunt through Gregory's Meadow so that spent hounds would be hard by the kennels, and the Warrens would not have to miss a night from the festivities of dancing by searching the countryside for lost hounds.

When a dry spell was as unending as a farmer's hard luck

talk, and a scent harder to raise than cash in planting time, Caroline would wait under the blackgum bushes by the old railroad cut. This was a tacit agreement between Caroline and the Warrens, men and hounds. She would strut up and down in plain view until the pack came tumbling over the hillside with all the fury of unrequited love. First, she'd lead them down by the gristmill. Henry Tyler, the miller, was an old hunter whom time had winded. But this way he could see a chase and never leave his rocking chair, sit in the shade and see Caroline tear across the new ground like a gray chip blown crazily by a tornado.

Or, if the Warrens ran puppies, Caroline always highballed down to the grassy places, obviously in deference to tender young puppy feet. Sometimes, just for the sport of the thing, she led them to the creek to watch cumbersome puppies floundering in the water as skittishly as ploughboys walking in tight, brand-new, store-bought brogans. But if the sun shone too brightly, you could bet your crop that Caroline would shoot like a meteor to Dewberry Springs and the sweet water that tasted like a chilled julep. But always, when the chase became precarious, she'd vanish like a candle flame before the storm. Where she went no man can any more tell than where the candle flame goes when the wind puts it out.

When the one-gallused Tulgins from Lickskillet Hollow ran their two-dollar potlickers by night, Caroline ran an easy circle. She kept hounds close to the fire, within short reach of the whiskey jug.

For the fancy, duded-up, blooded Trotters and their gaily bedecked horsemen, she sought the open fields where pink coats could bob along like red corks on a rolling green sea. Invariably she ended up the Trotter's hunt in front of the Big House, right when the supper bell was ringing. The old men say this gesture was not predicated alone upon Caroline's innate good manners and her impeccable consideration, but also upon a suppressed histrionic desire.

For, when the gigantic raucous of horses, riders, hounds, hark-to-ers and Caroline came catapulting down the ferny lane, all the countryside turned out to witness the imminent kill. But then something always happened to people's eyesight. The dust got too thick, or the sun slanted the wrong way. Whatever it was, Caroline couldn't be seen. She'd disappear, utterly become a fence rail, or a cloud, or a hickory nut. And thwarted and exasperated hounds tucked their goofish tails and sauntered contritely to the pen. Thus it was that great ladies and grand gentlemen turned to brimming decanters to wash away the sting of this prodigious enigma.

And best of all, oh, happy, happy day, she led the vociferous, vituperative, antisocial branch boys right through the swamp, so that the damned scoundrels would have to expend much golden moonlight seeking hounds lost in brambles.

I'd clean forgotten about Whiskey Jones, the old hardshell preacher who always took his hounds to prayer meeting just in case. I can tell you there was more scrambling at Little Zion Church than there possibly can be at Chestnut Grove Cemetery on Judgment Day morning. There was a rail fence in front of the church that was known as the "merry-go-round." The Whiskey Jones' hounds were tied there. And no sooner would Whiskey Jones line out the first hymn than here'd come Caroline tearing around the sycamores like a sinner with brimstone scorching her tail.

Then such barking that one would think the moon had melted! Fence rails flew like flakes of snow. First, they'd be in Ransome's yard, over by the schoolhouse, and next going down the road lickety-split like a carryall drawn by four runaway horses. And then old Whiskey Jones'd come galloping from the meeting house as if Satan were prodding him with a pitchfork.

"Glory, hallelujah, Amen. Use all the doors, folks, Glory, hallelujah, Amen. Hark to her! Glory, hallelujah. Amen. Hark to her, Betsy! Har Yar, Sambo, Glory, hallelujah. Amen. Brother Higgins, turn them other hounds a-loose."

"O, give me that old-time religion,
Hark to her, Betsy, har yar, Sambo!
'Twas good fer Paul and Silas
And hit's good enough fer me.
Glory, hallelujah, Amen. Amen.
Hark to her, I say."

Just when Whiskey Jones conjured exquisite visions of Caroline's tail flying above his dog pen, the ethereal will-o'-the-wisp would vanish like the sounds of a church bell, permeating the countryside with a mocking void. And he who

57

could find the sounds of vanished church bells could unearth the habitat of Caroline.

So it went. Chasing Caroline was comparable to breaking down an oak tree with a jimson weed. It was like the father whose land is mostly rocks. He continues to chase after good times that he doesn't actually expect to apprehend. But the quest must go on. Men who hunted Caroline as beardless boys lay in the graveyards, and the scrub pines that once held in brittle fingers the music of the hunt were majestic woodlands.

But I am as prolix as the old men in their anecdotage who take forever and forever to get to the point. Some say it was the story of Sampson all over again; that a lousy coon dog bit off Caroline's tail and the ignominy of this made her die immediately of bitter shame. Others say, it being the second day of the celebration, that the Old Christmas spirits fetched her home again. Some of the incurable romantics say that Elijah lowered his golden chariot and personally escorted her to fox heaven.

But actually, and I know, Polycarp Warren found her the morning of the Township Hunt. She was lying there all curled up and warm on Squire Pettigrew's grave. And there wasn't a mark on her. No, sirree, not a hair out of place. But there was no Township Hunt that day. We buried her in a pink coat in the High Church cemetery, right at Squire Pettigrew's feet. And there is a marker for all to see, and the tender legend is cast in metal. There's even a poem there; I know because I wrote it. And the Warren boys sent clean to Raleigh for an artist fellow to draw a picture of Caroline as we described her. This picture is in the courthouse for all to see, right under Senator Broadwhaite's portrait, right next to a cannonball that didn't explode at Seven Pines.

That's about all there is to it, except that the one-gallused Tulgins from Lickskillet Hollow went back to coon hunting and making liquor and ended up in the county jail. And the Warren boys sold the wondrous Walker hounds to some rich Yankee and took to bird hunting. Whiskey Jones, until the day he died, never went to Little Zion Church again, and the meeting house is a briarpatch and the clapper's gone from the bell.

But the old people vow they've seen Old Christmas spirits skinning the cat in a locust tree and playing going-to-Jerusalem around a 'simmon tree. They'll all tell you that Caroline will come flying back one frosty morning, sailing like a gray cloud, flashing by like a bar of lightning. Just you wait and see!

Fish Tales

As has been noted "flying fish," which Kipling professed to remember in "On the Road to Mandalay," are a figment of the author's mind, and so is the revered belief that fish are brain food, although there is more substance to the latter. The flying fish came from the fertile pen and fecund mind of a good author.

The theory that fish contains brain power was advanced in America by Louis Agassiz, of Harvard, and one of the nation's premier men of science. During the 19th century Jacob Moleschott, Ludwick Bucker, and some other German scientists sought to explain all energy in terms of material substances; and these scientists popularized the saying, "No phosphorus, no thought." The French chemist, Jean Dumas, had already established the fact that fish are rich in phosphorus.

Agassiz, an authority on marine life, put the two ideas together and suggested that eating fish might be good food for brain development. But today's scientists know phosphorus is no more essential to thinking than any of a dozen elements in the human body. With an equal degree of truth the German scientists could have asserted that there is no thought without calcium, sulphur, iron, or nitrogen. As a matter of fact, the human brain seems to attain its full adult size during the first six years of a child's life, during which time milk is his chief diet. The fish tale was enhanced, most likely, by the additional fact that fish is lighter and more easily digested than most of the flesh we eat.

Mass produced movies, such as *The Word*, refer to a fish as the first Christian symbol. After careful thought this author now believes that the symbolic use of the fish is not an extension of the miracle of the fishes and the loaves. (But this viewer's opinions are not worth much more than those of the merest laymen.) The fish symbol was easy to draw and it was easily recognized by the faithful few who met clandestinely in the catacombs of Rome. Apparently, this began as a Greek rebus or acrostic. The letters in the Greek alphabet that for the word for "fish" form the first letters of the Greek words "Jesus Christ, Son of God, Savior." However, there are those who think the symbol of the fish was used before the acrostic. But no matter how the symbol began, hardly any thorough historian thinks the symbol ties to the fishes and the loaves. This somewhat tedious explanation is inserted because the tie of the fish symbol to the miracle had wide circulation and credulity for a long time.

Any notorious imbiber is said "to drink like a fish." The trouble with that standard statement is that fish don't drink. The water that a fish takes passes through its gills, where oxygen is extracted. While a fish is "breathing," his gullet is so tightly constricted that little, if any, water gets into his stomach. The water a fish does not need is supplied in large by the moisture content of food.

If the whale or leviathan is the biggest animal alive, the smallest species of fish is known as the *Pandaka pygnea*, found in some of the creeks in the Philippines. This fish attains the length of three eighths of an inch and a maximum length of seven sixteenths of an inch. It is about the size of an ant, and it is likely to be the tiniest backboned fish ever called to the attention of science. The fish's body is so slender it is virtually transparent. Many thousands of these dwarf fish are mixed with batter and baked into little fish cakes that are said to be most tasty.

Two San Francisco scientists captured a living specimen of an elusive luminescent fish after several nights of diving off into Grand Cayman Island in the Caribbean. This is the famous flashlight fish, and one had not been seen since 1907 until recently. In January, 1978, John McCosjer, director of San Francisco's Steinhart Aquarium was notified that a flashlight fish, *K. alfredt*, had resurfaced. McCosker assembled an expedition hurriedly to catch this eerie fish. The Atlantic flashlight fish lives in water deeper than five hundred feet, and it never comes close to the surface save to feed at night. Its light organs, or apparatus, are seen as far as fifty feet away by divers. The fish contains certain glowing bacteria, and the fish will be studied to determine how it uses its bright lights. Some specimens are now on display at the Reinhart Aquarium.

61

Dozens of various species of birds swoop down the sky in the manner of Baron von Richthofen to ensnare fish they have sighted with the same high-flying accuracy of the Sperry Rand bombsight. But the European catfish, known more popularly as Wels or Glannis, catches and eats large birds that skim the surface of the catfish's water. (There is a case of documented record in which a Wels ate a small child, although this nuance seems to have eluded Byran at Dayton, Tennessee.) The common angler fish, the sea devil of fishing prey, *Lophuiss Piscatorius*, known in European and American waters, often swallows a bird too big for its mouth. In all of these fish, especially the deepwater fish, the stomach and throat stretch like a rubber balloon, but in greed some have choked to death on fish or birds too big to digest, or as Professor Hugh Holman of the University of North Carolina once said of Henry James, "He chews more than he can bite off."

"That's like water off a duck's back" is spoken endlessly to convey a notion of indifference or adamance. But, save for Donald, ducks don't get wet when they are fishing because their feathers are kept in an oily condition, by oil from the duck's tail. During a heavy rain ducks frequently paddle along a pond, completely impervious to inclemency. In addition to the perpetual oil supply, a duck's feathers are exceedingly close together, and this, too, aids in keeping water out.

Even more anachronistic is the bird called dipper or water ouzel, which exhibits remarkable dexterity under water. The dipper can walk along the bottom of a stream in search for insects and mollusks, for food. While submerged the dipper uses his wings for flippers, and when submerged the wings-turned-flippers help keep the bird under water. Their bodies are only three-fourths as heavy as water and the dipper will rise, cork fashion, when its thick down beneath its feathers is oiled from a gland in its tail. When a water ouzel moves from one place to another, all observers say, "It is flying underwater."

From all appearances the dipper manipulates its wings under water the same way it does when it flies. And although not webfooted, all birds of this species are excellent swimmers and flyers. Cormorants make motions with their wings when diving for fish, but penguins, which cannot fly at all, use their featherless wings like paddles and propel themselves beneath the surface of water.

No Wild State For Goldfish

The bowl of goldfish is almost as irrepressible in the modern home as a few seashells, the stereopticon, and the hall-tree were in the home during the insular era.

Goldfish are highly significant because they do not exist anywhere in a wild state. They are of the long living carp family, and they are plentiful in many of China's streams. Centuries ago Chinese fish culturists interbred light colored specimens to produce many beautiful varieties. Nonetheless, the bright colors of the goldfish are not patently stable.

Often scarlet specimens turn silver; the silver fish turn black; and the black fish turn into gold. When goldfish are restored to their natural environment, the dark color takes over again. If kept in darkness for several years, a goldfish turns white and he becomes completely blind. Those which live in homes in bowls often attain a lifespan of thirty years. Some Oriental specimens have lived out man's allotment of three score and ten years. The size to which goldfish grow is predicated, somewhat, by the size of the bowl.

Goldfish were introduced into England in 1691, and some of the first specimens were sent to Mme. Pompadour, mistress of King Louis V. Thus the tiny goldfish was among the first good will offerings given by one nation to another nation.

Goldfish are produced commercially today, and a hatchery of one hundred fifty acres, near Frederick, Maryland, produces several million annually.

For centuries the elected and appointed officials of Grammort, Belgium, have staged an annual ritual at which each official swallows a live goldfish. American collegians picked up on this during the 1920's and well into the 1930's. Swallowing a live goldfish was one of the first, compulsive "in-things" on the American campus. Indeed, this slug-nutty fad persisted, with diminishing numbers, until the advent of World War II.

It Was To Curry Favel

"To curry favor" endures in American English to denote appeasement or apple-polishing, but *favor* is a corruption of *favel*, the venerable word in France for any roan, sorrel, or chestnut horse. Several authorities derive *favel* from the old French *Faveau*, the color of barren land, and by the 15th century *to curry faveau* meant to rub down a chestnut horse.

Roman de Fauvel, a 14th century book, was almost a companion piece to *Reynard the Fox*. (In *Reynard*, Tibbie, or Tabby, is the name of the cat.) Some scholars think it was the influence of *Reynard the Fox* which changed the application of *faveau* to mean insincere flattery or abject sycophancy. Some experts conclude the phrase attained its current meaning from the habit of groomsmen who curried their master's horse with meticulous diligence, to win the master's favor.

From the 14th century on *to curry favel* meant any type of overt compliance for personal aggrandizement. The theory that *to curry favor* is a corruption of *to curry favel* is borne out by the fact that in German the phrase means, literally, "to rub down a chestnut horse."

For a long time in America, Dobbin was the general word for a horse, especially a draft animal. Dobbin is a diminutive of the proper name Dobmwhich, a variant of Robin and Bob. In *The Merchant of Venice*, written in 1596, Old Gobbo says to Lancelot: "Thou has got more hairs of thy chin than Dobbin my fillhorse, has its tail."

Many cows are still called Bossy, and the Latin word for ox or cow is "bos," and it is likely that the first man to call a cow Bossy was a wag who knew a bit of Latin. Nonetheless, some authorities think the word is related in origin to dialectic English. The bos calf was fed in a stall, and this distinguished him from those that grazed in meadows. (In the Teutonic languages *bos, boose,* and *bus* mean a stall or a barn. In our sagebrush west, prior to the Civil War, a grown buffalo was a boss and the buffalo calf was a bossy.

That loud, often unpleasant guffaw known as the horse laugh dates back to the early part of the 18th century when Richard Steele described it in a 1713 issue of the famous *Spectator*. Steele wrote, "The horse laugh is a distinguishing characteristic of the rural hoyden." (In other words, it was unsophisticated to a Londoner such as Steele.) In his *Life of Frederick the Great*, Thomas Carlyle wrote, "He plays rough pranks, too, and on occasion, he has a big horse laugh in him where there is a fop around to be roasted." (This description is of Prince Leopold, of Anhalt-Dessau).

And as those who attend Sunday school know, Job said, "The horse saith among the trumpets, Ha, Ha."

Some etymologists believe that in this connection horse is a corruption of the word *coarse*. Be that as it may, horse laugh endures to describe anything or person who is loud, uncouth, or coarse. The corruption of "coarse" is intensified as the source when one remembers that many plants, such as horse chestnut, horseradish, horsebeans, horsebane, and horse-faced seem to have emanated from *coarse*.

White Horse of the Berkshires

Although the famous White Horse is a gigantic outline of a galloping horse cut into the slope of a hill in Berkshire, England, about sixty miles from London, it has been there so long that Englishmen talk about it as if it is a true horse. It gives its name not merely to a particular hill, which is around eight hundred and fifty feet high, but also to the whole range, and the "Vale of the White Horse" is the popular name for Valley of Oack, a small river that unites with the Thames from the west at Abingdon. The fabulous White Horse is three hundred and seventy-four feet long, and it was formed by removing the turf to show the white, chalky subsoil. The horse is somewhat rudely sketched because there is little difference in the width of the neck, body, and tail, but the figure is clearly visible from a distance of from ten to twelve miles. If no one knows the precise origin of the White Horse, tradition says it was made by the druids, or the Danes, or the Saxons. Another tradition says Alfred the Great, was born nearby at Wantage, and that Alfred had the White Horse depicted in the chalk cliff to commemorate his victory over the Danes in 871 A.D. However, this battle occurred near Compton Beauchamp, at the end of the Berkshire Downs, in the neighborhood of Reading. But there is reason to suspect the Horse is of great antiquity, that it antedates the Roman occupation.

Periodically, the trench is cleaned of debris, and "scourging the White Horse" used to be a popular local festival. Not just incidentally, the figure of a giant is etched into a chalk cliff just outside the village of Cerne Abbas, in Dorsetshire. Tradition says a giant bearing a huge club was buried in the hill years ago. As late as 1877 John Dodgson, a school master, cut the figure of a horse, three hundred and fourteen feet by two hundred twenty-eight feet, on a hillside near Kilbournm in Yorkshire.

One firmly established myth proclaims that a horse hair turns to a snake or a worm when placed in running water. Even Shakespeare alludes to this in *Anthony and Cleopatra*, when Mark Anthony says of Sixtus Pompeius:

Much is breeding,
Which, like the coarser hair
Hath yet but life.
And not a serpent's poison.

This myth probably began as an uncritical observation, and through mistaken identity, for there are several kinds of worms that resemble the long hairs of a horse's tail. These are called "hairworms," and when one is placed in water it twists and curves from the effect of moisture and microscopic animals playing against it. But for several centuries it was assumed that these "hairs" had assumed life. And for several centuries it was believed that such a snake was bereft of any venom.

There is the lingering belief that a snake will not crawl over a rope made of hair. Because of this belief it became the custom of cowboys, prospectors, and explorers in the west to surround their beds with horse or cowhair ropes. This kept them immune to snakebite as they slept. But repeated tests have proved this is fallacious, too. Many rattlesnakes crawl over a horsehair rope when they could circumvent it by going only a few inches out of the way. If a snake is ever deterred by a rope, it is because the rope has been handled by many human hands; most snakes are disinclined to take on humans, and it is the odor, not the rope, per se, that might drive them away.

Another myth, repeated far more often than the snake and the rope, involves the story of a battle's being lost for want of a horseshoe nail. This appears to be merely the restating of an ancient English bromide of anonymous authorship. The earliest recorded use of the phrase appears in the writings of George Herbert, British poet and clergyman. It was published shortly after Herbert's death in 1633, in his *Jacula Frudebtum*: "For want of a nail the shoe is lost, for want of a shoe the horse is lost, for want of a horse the rider is lost."

The saying seems to have been an established proverb in Herbert's time. Later, in the preface of Benjamin Franklin's *Poor Richard's Almanack*, published in 1758, is this observation: "And, again, he, Richard, adviseth to circumspection and care,

67

even in the smallest matters, because sometimes a little neglect may breed great mischief." Franklin then repeats Herbert almost verbatim. The more elaborate version of the Herbert-Franklin story adds a lost kingdom as the culmination of various losses that attend the absent horseshoe nail.

The horses of St. Mark are four colossal bronze statues in an open gallery over the narthex of the Cathedral of St. Mark in Venice. At one time the orifice was the private chapel of the Doge, and a law of the republic required merchants who traded in foreign lands to bring back some object of art for the adornment of the fane. These horses, five feet tall, were brought to Venice in 1204 A.D., in the time of Doge Enrico Dandago. While the sculptor is unknown, the horses are frequently ascribed to the Greek sculptor Syssiphus. Another theory is that they were made for installation on the arch of triumph of the Emperor Nero, and that Constantine removed them to Byzantium about three hundred years later. In 1797 Napoleon carried the horses of St. Mark to Paris; but after his final fall in 1815, they were restored to Venice. When the Germans threatened Venice during the First World War, the statues were protected by piling bags of sand around them and later by moving them to Rome, temporarily for safety. (Syssiphus is the sculptor who made such a life-like tree many Greeks tried to pull off the leaves and fruit.)

Pigs Is Pigs

Today few people have heard of Samuel Butler (1612-1680) or his long, native, satirical poem *Hudibras*. But Butler interposes, "As pigs are said to see the wind." This is an extremely old English belief that pigs have much more perception at hearing than humans possess. Hence, a pig would register many awarenesses beyond the ken or hearing of their human masters. The Century Dictionary, of 1889, has this quotation: "As independent as hog on ice." The editors of Century listed the phrase as "an ironical simile." Modern scholars think the reference is to the sluggard stones in the game of curling. But readers are referred to the phrase intermittently to show how difficult it is to make a rational guess, even, about the origin of many phrases.

If the custom has terminated today, pigs used to be used by many sea captains as four-legged compasses. During the era of sailing ships many skippers carried hogs on board. If a ship became lost or if some disaster occurred, one of the hogs was thrown into the ocean because it was believed the pig's native instinct would push him towards the nearest land.

But of all the "unclean" animals the pig was singled out by the ancient Hebrews as the lowest, most despicable and loathsome. The infamy carried over to the swineherd and he was never allowed in the temple. The Prodigal Son could not get any lower than tending hogs during his absence from his father's house. Swine were so despised many Jews construed it as a sin even to mention the word. And if they were touched by a hog's bristles, they believed they would become contaminated.

But this seems more a dietary rule of conduct than the obviation of Mosaic Law. As is true with injunctions against the partaking of several kinds of flesh, the Hebrews were deterred by a wise mandate. The ancient swine were notorious scavengers, and their flesh was susceptible to small parasites that produced

69

diseases (not the least of which is trichinosis. Muslims do not eat meat for the same reason.

The nit-picker will wonder why Jesus drove the unclean spirit into the herd of swine (Matthew and Mark and Luke) since the Jews were forbidden to raise hogs. But this episode took place in the land of Gerasenes, a non-Jewish community. The Gerasenes kept and ate swine, the same as the Egyptians and Romans.

Although "as filthy as a pig" is an enduring epithet, the pig is not entirely at fault for this habitual condition. Even when a pig is in fairly close confinement, he selects a specific place to evacuate his bowels and kidneys, and most of our other domestic animals are cavalier about bathroom habits, will answer nature indiscriminately.

The colonial Americans tagged the pig as one that "liked filth." The main reason for this opprobrium was that the New England pig was usually kept in the worst place on the farm, often in a gloomy sty lower than the barn. But in their natural condition pigs are roaming creatures.

On a hot day a pig will wallow in mud, not because he cherishes his reputation for filth but to try to cool off. The pig has no apparatus for sweat, and wallowing in mud is about the only feasible way to keep down the temperature of the skin. Again, pigs are vilified because they eat garbage. But they are fed garbage in captivity. One forgets that of all the animals the diet the pig prefers is closest to the diet of human beings. Finally, it is roundly said that pigs cannot swim because they cut their throats with their sharp hooves and bleed to death. This is yet another of man's myths.

What's A Guinea Pig?

Innumerable scientific experiments have made Americans fully conversant with *guinea pig*, and many folks ask what a guinea pig is, anyway. The name of this native of South America endures as an etymological mystery. Albeit, several plausible theories have been advanced. The most popular theory says that *guinea* is merely a corruption of *Guiana*, and that this arose from the fact that early writers confused Guiana in South America with Guinea in Africa.

But there is positive evidence that as early as 1607 an animal was called "pig cony," and this produced a second theory that *guinea* is a corruption of *cony*. A third theory does not pertain to a region in Africa, although it appears to have existed in several actual cases, as an application to an animal that came from an unknown country. A fourth theory insists that guinea pig arose via the resemblance to the Guinea hog.

Yet another theory insists that Englishmen carried the rodent to South America by Guineamen engaged in the slave trade. But many scientists believe the guinea pig is descended from the restless cavy of Guiana and Brazil. It is a stout, short-tailed, short-eared rodent about seven inches long. It has a life cycle of only four years and it produces offspring five or six times each year, thus its suitability for scientific experimentation.

Because of this fact, guinea pigs have gone a long way toward replacing rats for scientific experiments. Baby guinea pigs possess their second set of teeth at birth, and they are able to nibble grain when they are only forty-eight hours old. Some scientists say a guinea pig will live as long without water as with water. In 1906 Ellis Parker's once famous sketch, *Pigs Is Pigs*, dealt with this animal's amazing, rabbit-like fecundity.

71

Dividing Between Goats and Sheep

The goat seems to be the most widely dispersed animal extant, but precious little is known of his ancestry. There are ten species of wild goats, but the Rocky Mountain goat, alone, is indigenous to the United States. The other wild goats live in Europe and upon the Himalayan Mountains. The famous Angora goat is traced back to Father Abraham, and it is a native of old Asia Minor. The first goat was introduced into the United States in 1849, from Asia Minor, by Dr. James B. Davis, of Columbia, South Carolina. This strain weighed (weighs) between sixty and one hundred pounds. The three principal functions of this strain are mohair, meat for eating, and the destruction of brushwood and decaying wood.

The Nubian milk goat, inexorably tied to Mrs. Carl Sandburg, was not brought to the United States until 1904 when twenty-six Toggenburies and Saanens were brought over from Switzerland.

In insular America many families kept goats as household pets and to keep the lawn cropped, to gather up sundry litter. Many families had two-wheeled wicker carts, generally known as "wicker baskets," to which the goat was hitched with small harness, to take two or three children around town in what was called a "pleasure spin."

In the residential section the goat usually walked along phlegmatically; but as soon as he was uptown, where human traffic studded the sidewalks, he threw his head back as if he were Traveller taking Robert E. Lee on an inspection tour of the Confederate troops. If the goat lacked the gaits of the horse, he trotted along with grandiose bravado.

Despite his reputation for adamance and recalcitrance, most goats succumbed to kindness and they were not difficult to train. (This writer's family had a goat, Miltiades, which came to the back door of our home for a handout with the same

72

subservience that a hobo sought a meal. My father taught Milt to count up to ten, on one front foot. When Milt came down with what our local amateur vet diagnosed as pneumonia, my father and my brother and I took turns sitting up with our sick goat. And I am just as sure he thanked us as F. X. Aubrey was sure that the big mule was telling him he and other mules would find water.)

But throughout history the goat has been erroneously and cruelly identified and equated with fools and blackguards. The devil was represented in the form of a goat, and on Judgment Day human society would be divided as goats and as sheep. The scapegoat is a national patsy, the fellow on whom any mistake or error in judgment can be blamed. But this is the result of simple confusion.

Mosaic Law decreed that on the holiest day of the Jewish year, the Day of Atonement, two male goats had to be brought into the Tabernacle. The two goats placed on the altar had to be unblemished. The High Priest cast lots to pick one of the two goats to be sacrificed on the spot. The other goat was sent into the wilderness, to escape, and to carry with himself all of the sins of the Jews. The Book of Leviticus (Chapter XVI) gives a detailed account: "And Aaron shall lay both hands upon the back of the live goat and confess over him all of the iniquities of the Children of Israel, and all their transgressions, even all their sins. And he shall put them upon the head of the goat and shall send him away by the hand of an appointed man into the desert. And the goat shall bear upon him all iniquities. And he shall let the goat *escape* into the wilderness." Thus, the escape goat became the scapegoat.

The modern theater is an outgrowth of a popular celebration held in Athens around 2500 years ago. It occurred once each year to honor Dionysius, god of wine and nature. Thousands of Greeks flocked to Athens for the celebration, one intended to celebrate and to propitiate procreative prowess. The people joined in singing ribald songs, and in their singing processions they carried the replica of an enormous phallus. When the educated and refined Greeks began to rebel at these orgies, the lyric chorus was introduced. The chorus was composed of fifty men and boys.

The dramatic tragedy, as the first dramatic form to come into existence, emanated from that early choral lyric performed at

73

the feast of Dionysius. The word *tragedy* means, literally, goat-song. The name may have evolved from the fact that the singers were disguised as satyrs and they were dressed in goat skins. Hence, their music was called "goat-song."

Another school thinks the goat-song evolved from the annual sacrifice of a goat at the feast of Dionysius that the chorus sang over the dead goat's body: A goat was the prize, the accolade, offered at ancient Greece's "art festivals." The winner had the option of slaying the goat as an offering to Dionysius.

Despite all the yards of libel and slander written about them, goats do not eat tin cans. Goats are detected eating at tin cans because the paper label on cans contains a small amount of salt, and salt is essential to a goat's diet, to the inner comfort of goats, as well as many other ruminants. It is true that a goat will nibble at almost anything a man throws away, but this is done for any edible that may be in a specific object. Hence, goats do not eat old shoes, clothing, and newspapers that a man throws away, despite the fairy tales.

In the sense of annoying, frustrating, and irritating, "to get one's goat" is irrepressible in American English. Two theories attempt to account for the origin of the phrase. The tuft of hair on the goat's chin is comparable to a man's goatee; and to tweak one's chin whiskers, his goatee, is highly insulting. The etymologists who hold to this school think that "goatee" was shortened to "goat" by process of time.

Perhaps, the more realistic theory dates to the time when a goat was kept in the same stall with a fractious, restive horse to placate it. Many horses and goats became (become) strongly attached to one another through daily proximity. It has been reported that the night of an important race, unscrupulous gamblers have stolen the goat to make the intracable horse run poorly the next day. For whatever it is worth, it is this writer's opinion that "to get his goat" emerged from the goats stolen from a horse's stall. Thus, the phrase means precisely what it says.

As is generally true of cattle, sheep, antelope and other ruminants, the goat arises, invariably, hind part first. Most other four-legged animals get up front legs first.

The goat has embellished American English with a number of enduring words and phrases: The goatsucker, or bull bat, is a popular name for the nighthawk, although it is called a whippoorwill at times. The goatsucker resembles the owl in its noiseless flight, and it travels in migrations from South America to northern North America. It breeds between Florida and Labrador, and it is often seen in the gloaming in quests of insects. It flies at a considerable height, uttering intermittently its harrowing, rasping cry. At times it seems to dive at a vertical angle, its screaming sounds are reminiscent of a dive-bomber's jarring noises. The word *goatsucker* was suggested for this family of birds by the old fable that one of the European representatives of the group loiters in the vicinity of flocks of goats with an eye to molesting the goats.

The goat fish, allied to the surmullet of the genus *Upeneus* is found in the West Indies and in the Gulf of Mexico; Goat Island is in the Niagara River; goat louse is a parasite; goatsbeard is a small woodland plant allied to spirea. And the goat is the patsy in the card game or the ball player who boots the ball and causes his team to lose a dramatic game.

In the open range era in the American West the frequent clashes between the cattlemen and the sheep herders matched the ferocity of the interminable onset between the Hatfields and the McCoys. The paramount objection of the cattlemen was their valid contention that when sheep finished grazing in a particular field, they cropped the grass so closely no subsistence remained for the cattle.

Genesis tells us that "Abel was a keeper of sheep," although the Writ doesn't explain how or where Abel acquired these sheep. Hence, the sheep must have been the first domesticated animal. After the allusion in Genesis, sheep are mentioned some seven hundred and forty times in the Bible. Some Biblical scholars believe that Jesus was thinking of Amos, the prophet, who tended sheep on the hills of Takoha, when Jesus referred to himself as "the Good Shepherd."

Agricultural experts think the sort of sheep Jesus had in mind was of the fat-tail variety. On such sheep the tail might weigh as much as fifteen pounds, and the fat in the incredibly large tail is considered by Biblical scholars to be the same "fat" mentioned in Leviticus and Exodus as sin, or an offering made for guilt or peace.

Young sheep, especially rams, were sacrificed frequently, and John the Baptist, was thoroughly familiar with this sacrificial format when he called Jesus "the lamb of God." It is redundant to say that the lamb is an enduring symbol for Jesus, and hymn writers have written lyrics about the "lamb of God" numerous times.

Sheep (genus *Ovis*) belong to a family of ruminants known as *Bovidae*, of which the ox (*Bos*) is a member. (Goats, musk oxen, chamois, and antelopes are members of the same family.) The male is a ram or a buck, and the female is a ewe. The unsexed sheep is a wether. Until sheep attain the age of twelve months they are called lambs. The ones from twelve to twenty-four months old are called yearlings. The young lamb has twenty-four teeth, and the grown sheep has thirty-two teeth, much sharper and longer.

Sheep like an extensive range and relatively short grass. Because of their mobile lips and incisor teeth, they are adapted to feeding on short grass. But they like to change pastures frequently, and they prefer to graze on high places; they prefer running water to still water. Most of the domesticated sheep produce offspring once a year. Ewes come in heat during autumn only, and they produce offspring in the spring. The most timorous of animals, the flock of sheep can be easy prey for other animals.

The sheep is the subject of innumerable pieces of literature. "Mary Had A Little Lamb" is known by virtually every literate American. While authorship has been disputed, the credit for "Mary" is given to Sarah Josepha Hale, early exponent of women's rights and editor of the magazine and book *Godey's Lady's Book*. Lowell Mason, musician and author of hymns, asked Mrs. Hale to submit a poem for a twenty-four page pamphlet Mason called *Poems For Our Children*. And a lamb, a family pet, seems to have followed Mrs. Hale to Redstone Hill School when she was a child.

"Little Boy Blue" who went to sleep in the haystack while his sheep and cattle wandered, is also known in almost every American household. Much less known is Robert Graves' poem:

May sudden justice overtake
And snap the froward pen,
That old and palsied poets shake
Against the minds of men.

Blasphemers too bold caught
In far-flung webs of ink
The utmost ends of human thought
Till nothing's left to think.

But may the gift of heavenly peace,
And glory for all time,
Keep the boy Tom, who tending sheep,
First made the nursery rhyme.

A Nation of Sheep obviously was suggested as a title because of the irrepressible habit of sheep following the leader. Sheep are amazingly gregarious, and the old adage, "Where one sheep goes all the others will follow," is true enough, even when following entails a long, dangerous leap, or a plunge into icy water.

The sheep bat is a maggot; the sheep dog is a popular name for a species of collie; sheep-eater is an opprobrium that comes down from the Sioux tribes, as an epithet; sheep laurel or lamb killer is a type of mountain laurel that is poisonous to sheep; sheep tick is a mite; sheepshead is an edible fish; sheepswool is a sponge.

It is in Matthew (25:32) that the celebrated sheep-goats passage occurs: "And before him shall be gathered all nations; and he shall separate them one from another as a shepherd divideth his sheep from his goats.

And it was William Blake (1757-1827) who asked the deathless question:

Little lamb, who made thee?
Dost thou know who made you?
Gave thee life and bid thee feed
By the stream or o'er the mead:
Gave thee clothing of delight,
Softest clothing, wooly white.

For several centuries "woolgathering" has been synonymous with aimlessness, vacuity, or simple abstractedness. The phrase arose in the days when English children were assigned the tasks of gathering bits of wool torn from sheep by bushes and brambles amid their far-flung rambles. Woolgathering could not

77

be accomplished systematically; and as the children gathered the wool, they had time and opportunity to improvise countless games. And to complete the metaphor, the small amount of wool that they gathered was actually of little commercial value.

The nursery rhyme, "Baa, baa black sheep/Have you any wool?" was printed originally in 1744. In some of the older versions the little boy "cries in the lane." This nursery rhyme was proverbial long before it was printed in 1744, and the distinction of the bags, "One for the master/And one for the dame/And one for the little boy who lives in the lane," are supposed to have been allusions to the heavy export tax on wool.

The ram, of course, is the male sheep, and it is also a constellation and sign of the Zodiac. A man named Ram is usually accounted one of King David's prime ancestors, although historians are at a loss to find any modern implication in that man's name. Today, of course, a fullback rams the opposing line, and battering-ram has long, viable historical use. And ram is present in the English word "rambunctious."

In a clever play on words, Dr. Samuel Fox Mordecai, deceased, Dean of the Trinity College-Duke University Law School, has this to say:

Mary had a little lamb,
Its fleece was white as snow,
And everywhere that Mary went,
That lamb was sure to go.

Richard had a rakish ram,
As black as black molasses;
He butted Richard in the rear,
And gun him psorias.

An actual ram is the mascot of many military units and college football teams (such as Rameses at University of North Carolina). The Los Angeles professional team is the Rams, and the word is identified with sporting groups of many levels. Perhaps, the ram that was the official mascot of the Royal Welch Fussiliers in World War I was photographed more than any ram in history.

Our ubiquitous "go the whole hog" arose as a phrase among

shepherds, especially those in Scotland. "Hog" encompassed many edible animals, just as "corn" included virtually all grain. Some shepherds would sheer a little wool at a time, but others allowed the wool to attain its approximate length and measure and shear the sheep, from head to tail, all in one cutting. But in American English "to go the whole hog" means complete action, even wild abandonment, and it relates to pigs and not the original "hogs," or sheep, as in Scotland.

Many folks think they are quoting from the Writ when they say, "God tempers the wind to the shorn lamb." Conversely, this appears in Lawrence Sterne's (1713-1768) novel, *A Sentimental Journey*. And Sterne indicates this is not original with him. Actually, the phrase belongs to Henri Eatienne (1531-1598), and, of course, it was said in French: "Dieu mesure le froid a la brebis tondue." (Froid is not quite the same thing as wind, and there seems to be more sheep than lamb (*agneau*) in *brebis*.)

The Snipe Hunt

There is strong probability that more than a reference or textbook is required to prove to thousands of Americans that the snipe is a real animal. The first real hoax on which thousands of boys are duped is the so-called snipe hunt when boy scouts and sundry groups go on an overnight camping trip in the deep woods.

The lad who gets to hold the sack is given the accolade for his numerous, sterling virtues, or so he is told by those who know the ruse involved, and especially by those who have been the shivering goats on these cons.

Habitually, the novice is posted in the deep woods with a large croaker sack. His compadres, like African brushbeaters, will drive the snipe, or snipes, straight to him and he will fill his sack with succulent snipes. Some boys seem to have difficulty realizing they have been hustled. When, after an interminable and fruitless wait in the woods, they return to the campfire to be berated with: "Well, what happened? Where are all those snipes we drove straight to your sack?"

Most of the excuses seem to be: "I heard several, but they ran by me," or "I saw three or four, but they disappeared in the undergrowth."

But the snipe is a bird often compared to the sandpiper, and the two names are used interchangeably. The true snipe has an immense beak, much longer than its head, and its head is grooved all the way. Its mouth is slit almost completely; and its bill, somewhat black, is flattened and expanded at the end and it is richly endowed with a sharp sense of smell.

There are around twenty known varieties of snipe, including the woodchuck. Wilson's snipe is the only one that is universally common in the United States. It, like its brothers and cousins, makes its nest on the ground, and when flushed it emits a screaming cry. It usually flies from twenty to thirty yards, wildly and erratically, before it sets its true course. In the harrowing space of that twenty to thirty yards, it sounds for all the world as if Judgment Day has come to earth in a wild, feathery fury orchestrated by piercing screams.

The Zero Bird

The ostrich is the tallest bird in the world, often attaining a height of eight feet. Job has much to say about the ostrich, and none of this writing is complimentary. It is true that the ostrich is short on brains, but it does not hide its head in the sand at the approach of danger. Actually, the ostrich can run as fast as forty miles an hour, and any predator, man or animal, has a difficult time catching up with it. But if it is forced to fight, if all efforts at mediation fail, the ostrich comes on with the fury of Jack Dempsey, the Manassas Mauler. It cannot fly but it can fight, and it deals deathlike blows, as its battle cry is compared to that of a suffering bull. Micah must have had this scream in mind when he wrote about "mourning like an ostrich." Today's scholar thinks the King James translators meant "ostriches" many times when "owls" is used.

Ancients were completely convinced that the ostrich could eat anything, especially stones and pieces of iron. This myth persisted until two or three hundred years ago. In *Henry VI* Shakespeare has the rebel, Jack Cade, say to another character: "I'll make thee eat iron like an ostrich, and swallow my sword like a great pin, ere thou and I part." In Ben Jonson's *Man In His Humour*, a character is so hungry he says he could eat sword hilts. In *Vulgar Errors*, Sir Thomas Browne sought to correct this assumption. But Browne adds, "The myth is not to be wondered at for the bird is notoriously voracious."

Scientists say the digestive prowess of the ostrich is enormous. As is true of other birds the ostrich has no true teeth and their function is performed partially by grit and sand that grind up their food. Ostriches require much grit, and are eternally watchful for stones and gravel. Hence, ostriches are hunted often in South Africa for the diamonds they have found on the ground and swallowed. An authentic report contained the information that fifty diamonds were found in a single ostrich, and they have been known to swallow wallets, eyeglasses, keys, rings, and other bric-a-brac.

The ostrich is a vegetarian, basically; and on an ostrich farm it subsists on alfalfa in summer and on alfalfa hay, bran, barley and other grain in winter. But the ostriches do not last long in captivity because curious men give them metallic objects. Many ostriches in the London Zoo have died from eating trinkets handed over by spectators who have a macabre sense of humor.

Despite all the contrary evidence, the figure of speech of the ostrich with its head in the sand seems destined to endure. The myth seems to have originated from the theory that if the ostrich couldn't see a foe, he didn't have to fear it. Even Pliny said that an ostrich thought it was safe with its head in the sand.

In the first place the ostrich pokes its long beak into holes in search of water, which it finds frequently under the desert sand. In the second place it rests by sitting down on its folded legs, with its neck and head stretched near the ground. But the simile of the ostrich with his head in the sand was used by Presidents Wilson and FDR. Before America entered World War I, H. G. Wells wrote: "Everytime Europe looks across the Atlantic to see the American eagle, it observes the rear end of an ostrich."

The Belled Buzzard of Granville County

A number of years ago, Irvin S. Cobb wrote and published a short story called "Belled Buzzard." This fact is noted because the Cobb story had considerable publicity among readers of a vanished era, and may yet be found in some of the older college anthologies. Irvin Cobb was a sharp observer and no doubt this story is an admirable fusion of assorted facts, Kentucky folklore, and local anecdotes.

But in this tale before you, there is no fusion of fancy and fact. Certainly not as I have written it down. Any embellishments are the inadvertent dross that accumulates when tales are passed from the facile lips of one generation to the next.

This is a tiny piece of localized history about an infamous buzzard that used to appear, with all the dark music of a black mass, and perch atop the belltower of the courthouse in Oxford, N.C., whenever a death sentence was about to be passed by the presiding judge of the Granville County Superior Court. Away back then, criminals were executed, by hanging, in a big yard between the courthouse and jail (gaol). There was no central prison for such executions. This buzzard would come while court was in session, even before the jury reached its harrowing verdict, it has been told. Not always, of course. But there is little doubt the buzzard did appear a few times while the jury was still deliberating.

The buzzard didn't always return for the hanging. That is, he wasn't always seen but old folks would swear they heard rasping, funeral music, a discord of chains being rattled the night before the execution. That might have been due to overactive imaginations. Yet, no one ever saw the buzzard unless the infamous beast was atop the belltower.

He was a black shadow in that no one knew whence he came or went. Suddenly in the middle of the day the loathsome monster would be atop the courthouse. Yet when people started

84

rehashing the news, no one could ever remember seeing him come or go. It was even suggested he was an optical illusion, but he was real enough. For one day some damned fools shot off some of his evil feathers.

Now today, hardly anyone has ever seen a belled buzzard. In our society, it is almost hideously preposterous to think of anyone having the unmitigated temerity to put his hands on a damned buzzard, much less to affix a bell. But in many Southern rural communities there is one patriarch who remembers vividly hearing about some belled buzzard. Mind you, the patriarch doesn't say he actually saw one, but he knew about the despicable existence of one.

Everyone may not be actually physically afraid of a buzzard, but no one wants to fool with one, with or without a bell. Just about everyone wants a lot of daylight between himself and this insolent poltroon that strikes goose pimples from afar. A lone buzzard in a dead tree (buzzard tree) is as diabolical as a snake charming a bird. The idiot bird could fly away, if it used its wits and wings. But wherever the damnable buzzard flies, death flies also, or, even more starkly, death is waiting in a crumbled heap at the station.

The buzzard is more insolent than a craven atop a wall with a switchblade knife under his shirt. The buzzard gives you a queasy feeling deep down in your guts. He induces a blood-twisting fear, more psychological than physical, perhaps. The filthy buzzard induces the same dread you feel at the mention of some horrible epidemic. Seeing the slimy buzzard wheeling listlessly inside and outside the carcass of a dead cow or mule gnaws your guts so powerfully you really think you can hear the reverberation. He makes you feel as if a leper is clutching at you in the darkness. You are in one of those frightful dreams when motion is lost and horror is jet propelled.

If you are a motorist, you know the terrific compulsion to run down the buzzard on the highway. But when you get close, you are so careful to avoid contact you would tear the car to hell and back before you'd hit one lousy feather. No force on earth could wash away the tainted blood of a buzzard.

Did you ever notice a real dirt farmer when he sees a buzzard? He never mentions the word without appending son-of-a-bitch or bastard. The farmer sees the scavenger. The farmer spits with silent, frigid fury, and rattles with a ferocious mumble: "Sonafabitching buzzard. Bastard buzzard." But despite the small sizzling vituperation, the farmer keeps right on walking, sharply away from the sonofabitching buzzard.

A lot of folks in the country used to say a buzzard is deaf. Admittedly he is almost impervious to stones and shouts. He may move from the dead tree, but he moves with a studied insolence, with a malignant insolence that his effortless motions just keep from being insufferable arrogance. Like a muted devil he seems to whisper: "O.K., sonny boy. Yell out your lungs. Throw your arms off. I got plenty of time. I am all of Poe's conquering worms come together in one set of a slimy black wings."

When I was a boy all kids believed buzzards were immune to death. They were vastly more prevalent back then because few folks buried dead animals, and the highway department folks didn't clean up messes the way they do now. In every small town and rural community there were the witch trees or buzzard trees. Even the grass and shadows that lay about these dead trees seemed contaminated. No one ever climbed a buzzard tree. Good God, no. A buzzard might come back and the smallest thing that happened would be that you'd break your neck trying to get away. Superstitious folks said a buzzard's shadow would kill the grass about the dead tree.

That, of course, is poppycock, but for a petrified fact, grazing cows and chickens always gave buzzard tree shadows a wide berth. Maybe they still do and maybe they don't, but they damned surely used to.

In the innocent era, when boys got their first .22 rifles or .410 gauge shotguns, they potted away at the buzzards, always at a safe distance. But everyone knew you couldn't kill a buzzard. Many times I have known that I hit one. I could hear the bullet strike the harrowing bone or see a ghastly feather fly. I had a young friend named William, and we shot at the scavengers together. Together we must have fired a thousand shells and cartridges at the sonofabitching buzzards. But we knew all the time that we wouldn't kill one. This was right after World War I and we asked my uncle, a soldier, if a .75 shell would kill a bastard buzzard.

He said: "Boy, you are crazy in the head and the feet, also. If a buzzard ever flew across the Argonne Forest, ten minutes later there wouldn't be a doughboy or Hun any closer than Berlin or Paris."

To get back to the main story, the one about the belled buzzard in Oxford. There was a fellow named Wilcox tried one time for murder. He swore and be damned if he wasn't in Virginia at the time of the crime. Trouble was he couldn't produce a witness. This man said he was possum hunting with a man named Ed Byrd on the night of the murder. But no one could ever locate this Ed Byrd.

The prosecutor argued this Ed Byrd didn't exist except in Wilcox's imagination. To condense the story, the jury got the case and went out to confer, and some people along the street started babbling about the belled buzzard being atop the belltower. Perhaps it had been a long time since the buzzard had been in Oxford. Maybe the buzzard came during the night. If so, he wasn't noticed until the jury went to deliberate its verdict. The jury room is just off the courtroom, on the second floor of the building. But the jurors could hear the talk on the streets below. And if they were men of any imagination at all, they could feel the buzzard on the belltower above them. They could feel his horrendous presence. If they couldn't see the buzzard they must have felt that the buzzard could see through the roof down upon them.

The jury convicted this man Wilcox. The judge passed the death sentence. Everyone in the courtroom was babbling nervously about the belled buzzard. They were huddled together, their heads down, as if from a sense of protection. The judge beat for order several times. The nervous chattering went right ahead, and some man said he would ring the bell and the buzzard would leave. The bell beat a dirge but the buzzard didn't move. He was even uglier and more insolent. A crowd came running from all over Oxford. Some thought there was a fire and others thought an alarm was being rung.

The prisoner, Wilcox, broke loose from the sheriff. He leaped from a window and broke his neck on the cobblestones below. Wilcox had a brother, and this brother grabbed a shotgun and emptied both barrels at the belled buzzard. Some loose feathers spiraled down slowly as evil ashes from a burning haunted house.

Several fights started. Some wanted to track down the buzzard and kill it gruesomely. Others screamed imprecations. No, no. It would be against all the customs. Besides, you couldn't kill this buzzard. Don't anger him. Leave it alone and it will get tired of Oxford and drift away.

The buzzard didn't glide away. Many people saw its tantalizing flight and swore to the fact afterwards. But the next day it was back on the porch again. The presence on the belltower the second day was hideous, paganly so. For no one was being tried for a capital crime, if, indeed, court was still in session.

The next day, the second day, this brother of Wilcox's, the same who had fired at the buzzard, was found dead halfway between Oxford and Shoo-fly, his home ten miles from Oxford. The horse he had been riding was gone, gone forever, they told it. It was obvious that Wilcox's brother had been thrown. His back was broken and he was fearfully scarred and cut. There were terrible abrasions, deep and wicked ones that could have come from a horse's iron foot or maybe they came from a blow from a rock. The horse may have thrown and trampled him. Or he may have been thrown and his head struck the rock. Some whispered he had been waylaid and robbed. A few muttered, behind closed doors, that the buzzard waited for Wilcox's brother, swooped down and killed the man or made him kill himself from agonizing terror.

This theory came from something said by the schoolmaster in Oxford. The schoolmaster came to the courthouse square and told the story in Coleridge's poem, "The Rime of the Ancient Mariner." The schoolmaster talked about the eerie albatross in the poem, about the shooting of the bird. He also recounted several stories reflecting albatross lore and superstition.

So, many people in Oxford decided there was a judgment on Wilcox's brother. The buzzard was tied in with the albatross, immediately and irrevocably. Wilcox's brother was killed because he shot at the belled buzzard. If the buzzard didn't do the actual job itself, the heinous judgment killed the man.

It was a judgment and the judgment might lie on the entire community. It was a strange night, the night Wilcox's brother was killed. Somebody remembered seeing an elderberry bush burning that night, burning as brightly as a fire in a parlor grate. Several others saw blood on the moon, a great blotch of it.

Actually, the omens of ill seen are too numerous for recitation. A house burned in which no one had made a fire. Somebody killed a pig, cut its throat, and the shoat didn't squeal once. A chicken with its fool neck wrung off walked three miles scattering blood in the manner of weird and appallingly ominous hieroglyphics. The crows in the forest that ringed Oxford cawed all night, as if seeking some urgent request that wasn't supplied and whose absence intensified the shattering caw-caw-cawing.

Maybe most of these unaccountable events can be charged off to primitive superstition or to alert imaginations. More likely, they are coincidences, but each grisly tidbit came back to the damning words of the schoolmaster and his correlation between the sonofabitching belled buzzard and the albatross in the Coleridge poem.

The second day, the day after the trial, the day the belled buzzard returned, if he ever left, a man came into the barroom in Oxford and said his name was Ed Byrd. He said he knew nothing about Wilcox being tried for murder. He said, why yes, it was true about him and Wilcox and the possum hunt on the night of the murder.

The other bar patrons spoke up angrily. They said this was the damndest yet. Why, this fellow Ed Byrd could have cleared Wilcox. Why in hell hadn't he showed up at the trial? What the hell, they said, Virginia wasn't on the other side of the world but jam against Granville County in North Carolina. This bastard could have saved an innocent life.

You understand how tempers were, how much consternation and chagrin followed the deaths of Wilcox and his brother and all the fantastic events of the night, the night following the trial. Somebody came in from the street and heard Ed Byrd's story. The bar patrons had merely listened up to now, but this man from the street ran out and brought back a crowd, as many as twenty-five or thirty, possibly. They said the only way of evening the score, of putting baleful matters right, was to hang this Ed Byrd. All around the square the cry went up: Hang him. Hang him, high as Haaman.

Somebody got a rope in the hardware store and the mob set out for the big alley behind the courthouse. The official scaffold wasn't up, none had been used recently, and they were going to hang this Ed Byrd to a tree. They put the rope about his neck; and when they gave him the opportunity for some last words, he tried to tell them how wrong they were. He hadn't done anything. He didn't even know Wilcox had been accused of anything.

89

The mob wouldn't have it, not a lame word of it all. The only feasible way to remove the terrible judgment was to eliminate the author of all the misery. The fellow Byrd in some inexplicable manner, some nebulous fashion, was the root of all the madness.

Just as they were getting ready to put him on a horse, the alley was swept with the maddening sounds of a slowly tolled bell.

They had forgotten about the buzzard. This fellow Ed Byrd had diverted the wrath, absorbed some of the tingling fear. They say, they said, it is told that the bell on the buzzard dingled as if a shroud were being stitched with steel.

The belled buzzard swooped down over the mob. From the way it has been told to me, the buzzard buzzed, like a fighter plane, and swept to the right, wheeled back to the left and came back with increased force. The mob ran into one another. Some hid in corners and behind shrubs. Some ran headlong for the street. There was no direction in this panic. The only motivation was escape. The belled buzzard flew just above the heads of the crowd. He flew up and down the alley, turning, wheeling, and coming back again and again.

They say this Ed Byrd spoke some low words to the belled buzzard, that the buzzard sat on a tree limb above this Ed Byrd's head, listening closely. (Since the mob had dispersed, pell-mell, this must have been seen from a distance, but it was sworn and reaffirmed that the buzzard perched on Ed Byrd's shoulder for a second.) This Ed Byrd spoke some final words and the belled buzzard flew off into a white cloud and disappeared.

This time the people saw him when he left, saw him when he entered the white cloud. And that belled buzzard hasn't been seen in Granville County since that awful day.

This Ed Byrd stayed in Oxford a few years after the belled buzzard left. He amassed a small fortune gambling. No one wanted to play cards with this Ed Byrd; but everyone was afraid not to play, afraid to win, afraid the infamous buzzard might return. Behind his back and behind their hands and doors, folks referred to Ed Byrd as Lazarus. Some whispered he was a strange kind of leper. He was the "belled Buzzard man." They say the grass didn't grow where he spat. He had no friends but no material enemies, either. No one walked beside him on the street, but everyone was overly courteous, foppishly so, when they passed this Ed Byrd.

Then one day he vanished. No one saw him leave. He was gone. That was all, just gone. There have been ten thousand tales about where he went and what he did. He was a road agent out west, a millionaire up north, a cardsharp on ocean liners, and he was even in some President's cabinet under an assumed name.

All of this was a long time ago, but even to this hour when the sky is black crepe and the wind moans the way chains rattle, some old man in Granville County will look furtively all around and whisper threateningly: "It's a season of this Ed Byrd weather. If you hear a tiny bell, run for your life. It's him, this Ed Byrd and that sonofabitchingbelledbuzzard, and ain't no atom bomb in creation can do more'n knock a feather or hair outa either one of them."

Egrets and the Audubon Society

Egret is a name given to those species of white herons which have the feathers of the lower portion of the back elongated and their webs disunited because of the absence of barbules at certain seasons of the year. The long feathers form a soft, flowing train that reaches to the tail, or beyond the tail at times.

Their forms are much more graceful than those of the common herons. The name "egret" is applied properly to the American and European varieties. The American egret has white plumage, and when not white, a sort of creamy color. The egret breeds from Florida to New York and along the Gulf of Mexico to Texas.

At the turn of this century it was a sign of high fashion for women to wear big hats lavishly bedecked with egret feathers. Almost overnight the slaughtering of egrets, especially in the Miami region of Florida, was a most lucrative, criminal activity. When Miami was little more than a few crude houses on stilts, because of the swampy terrain, such law enforcement as existed was supplied by members of the Audubon Society.

Hardly any place worthy of the name of "village" existed between Jacksonville and Miami. And as much as one admires the late Frederick Jackson Turner and his speech book about the influence of the western frontier on American life, one can make a strong case for the east coast of Florida as being the nation's last frontier, unless one counts space. In the days in which the Audubon Society tried to husband egrets and protect humans, a barefooted postman carried the mail on foot from Jacksonville to Miami. And he carried "walking" passengers, too. Several men who had business in and around Miami assembled when the mail boat reached Jacksonville. There they paid a nominal fee to the barefooted postman for guiding them through treacherous trails and alligators and desperadoes. Indeed, the walking postman emulated the western stagecoach by having an extra guard "walk shotgun."

John James Audubon was born in Haiti in 1785, and he died in New York City in 1851. At an early age he was obsessed with all living creatures, birds especially. He studied drawing in Paris; and in 1826 he took his sketches of American birds to London, where he elaborated them into a fascinating series. From 1827-1838 he published in London a series of 1,065 colored birds. This work, *The Birds of America*, is still given front rank as one of the world's most beautiful ornithologies. No reading matter attended these 1,065 colored pictures, but from 1831-1839 five volumes were issued under the name *Ornithological Biography*. The technical parts of these five volumes were done by William McGillivray.

The Audubon Societies are organizations of bird lovers whose paramount effort is to educate the general public. The name was coined in 1881 by George Bird Grinnell, and at that time 48,862 Americans joined the society for the protection of local birds. By 1910 the society had obtained, chiefly by gifts, an endowment fund in excess of $366,000. It was in 1914 that the society began its fruitful program of educating and inspiring people on the local level to use artificial means, such as feeders and baths to induce those favorably situated to engage in the propagation of ducks and other game birds. Today, only seven per cent of the organization's income is spent for administrative purposes. This must be an all-time low in the history of America's sundry protective agencies.

An ageless question, somewhat akin to egrets, does the sea come to the beach or does the beach go out to the water, involves the near extinction of herons and egrets. The fashion in women's hats changed, and the supply of egrets became alarmingly short. So, this is a case of blackjack against thunder.* Rice is the egret's favorite food, and that crop has also been in short supply in modern America.

Paddy rice which is derived from the Malay *padi* means "rice in the straw." The Japanese equivalent is *part*, or "rice in the husk." These terms are all believed to have descended from the Sanskrit *bhakta*, or cooked rice. In Anglo-Indian, *paddy rice* is a

*This is a strange old phrase, and it attained its first wide usage on the Mexican Border in 1916 when John J. Pershing commanded an all-black regiment and was called Blackjack. A reporter said of the war, "It's all blackjack on one side and Pancho Villa's pretentious thunder on the other side."

93

commercial term used to denote rough, unhusked, or unmilled rice, whether cut or still growing in the field. By extension the term is applied as a synonym for rice in general. The flooded rice field is a "paddy field," and the various species of herons, egrets, and Oriental sparrows are known to the English-speaking inhabitants of the East as "paddy birds." This erroneous assumption is ascribed, most likely, to an assimilation of paddy rice, to paddock, a small enclosure or piece of ground.

Ironically, a widely invoked ordinance aided in the egret's depopulation. At the apogee of the big costume hat with egrets feathers adorning it, women wore hat pins. Whether or not these pins did any real physical harm is highly questionable, but town after town passed ordinances that forbade hatpins more than one inch long. Whether or not this doleful news was broadcast over the Everglades, when the demand for feathers dwindled to a trickle, breeders of egrets turned to more profitable pursuits.

Not Birds of a Feather

The cuckoo, spelled "cookow" in all but the recent translations of the Bible, is likely the same bird that is so popular in sections of Europe. It feeds not only on worms but also on frogs, lizards, and small snakes, which render it "unclean" among the Jews. The cuckoo is an excellent imitator of other birds in its calls and in its actions. A singular development is that some cuckoos lay eggs that are blue, and other cuckoos lay blue eggs with black spots. Frequently, it will lay its eggs in the nest of another bird that has similar colorations, and the eggs remain in the stranger's nest to be reared by foster feathered parents.

Thomas Hardy wrote of rough winter days, "This is the weather the cuckoo likes/And so do I."

In *Love's Labor's Lost* Shakespeare has it:

The cuckoo then on every tree,
Mocks married men; for thus sings he,
   'Cuckoo!'

Cuckoo, cuckoo. O word of fear
Unpleasing to the married ear.

The Bard of Avon is endowing the cuckoo with the same mocking of married men that is usually ascribed to the mockingbird in American mores.

Wordsworth sees and hears the cuckoo a little differently:

O, blithe new-comer. I have heard,
I hear thee and rejoice.
O cuckoo! shall I call thee bird,
Or but a wandering Voice?

In the same poem Wordsworth picks up his chant with:

> Thrice welcome, darling of the Spring!
> Even yet thou art to me
> No bird but an invisible thing,
>   A voice, a mastery.

In the rural precinct of the United States the cuckoo is called a rain, or a storm, crow because its haunting note, interpreted as "koo, koo, koo," is usually heard when the bird is in a thicket or where the bird is invisible but the song is heard. But unlike their European cousins, the American cuckoos are not parasitic and they never lay their eggs in another bird's nest.

Most birds have four toes on each foot, three in front and one behind, although members of the parrot and woodpecker families are yoke-toed, two of the toes point forward and two backward. The yoke-toed characteristic is found among members of the parrot family known as road runners, cuckoos, and kingfishers.

Falcons, in the broad sense of birds trained to hunt, are universal, and several species were known in the Holy Land many centuries prior to the birth of Jesus. The Peregrine Falcon has been used as an active adjunct of hunting since time immemorial. (But there is no record that the ancient Hebrews used the falcon in any way.) Today falcon is a term given to many birds of the family *Falconidae*, but more specifically the falcon is a member of the family *Falconi*. Falcons are unparalleled for strength, speed, and for graceful flight. The female Peregrine Falcon was especially valuable for the quickness and dexterity with which she worked.

Some true American falcons are the pigeon hawk, the sparrow hawk and some close kindred species. The falcon proper is distinguished by a hooked beak on the point, a notch on the cutting edge of a tooth in the upper mandible. Falconry, or hawking, is among the oldest "sports." Almost timeless in Asia and the Holy Land, falconry had been practiced regularly in China for more than two thousand years before the birth of Jesus. Falconers and their hawks are depicted in several of the oldest Egyptian murals.

The role of the falconer was somewhat kin to that of master of the hounds or, certainly, to the chief whipper in fox hunting.

Hawks were taken for training at an early age, preferably, but they could be taught this lethal art as nestlings or as fully grown birds. In England falconry was regulated by many laws and social customs. Hence, the square frame on which the hawks were carried to the field was called a "cadge," and the servant who bore it was cadger. A "cast" of hawks meant two taken together. To "man a hawk" meant to tame it, and the old hawk, thoroughly familiar with his line of work, was thrown up to teach fledglings the dark art of killing.

The molting hawk was said to be "mew," and "to plume" when its feathers are pulled off. A female of any species, but especially of the Peregrine, is a "falcon," and the male a "tiercel." One apprehended wild was a "passage hawk" or "haggard." One taken from the nest was an "eyas."

All the hawk's or falcon's activities has specific names: A young one is a "red hawk," and a diving hawk "stoops." The quarry is always known as the "prey." She "binds" when she seizes her quarry in midair, and a hawk is said to "clutch" when she seizes her prey between her two feet, and "carries" when she attempts to fly away with the object. She "checks" when she assails a bird that is not her quarry. When she strikes an object, looses it in natural density, and then finds it in a hedgerow, she "foots well" when she locates the wounded animal that is trying to hide from her. "Mantling" means stretching out the wing on one side, or to stretch out one wing and one leg.

The extensive agricultural changes which occurred in England in the 17th century brought about much enclosed land. Vast improvement was made in wastelands, and towns and cities began to develop more widely. The introduction of firearms obviated much of the usefulness of falcons and falconers, and the sport went into a decline in Europe as well as in England. British peasants, armed with flintlocks, began to kill the "vermin" which the British squires had hunted with falcons.

But the "sport" was one in which women partook as avidly as men, and when mounted for the hunt gave every impression of regal caravans. The hawks, always hooded until turned loose to hunt, were carried by servants on frames suspended from their shoulders, but each aristocratic hunter usually carried a favorite hawk on his gauntleted left wrist. (On the left wrist in Europe and on the right wrist in the Orient.) Dogs, especially small pointers and small greyhounds, were taken on the hunts. It was the purpose of these dogs to flush rabbits and gamebirds. Some falconers kept their hawks blindfolded until the quarry was actually seen, and others removed the hoods immediately after the hunting area was attained so that the falcon could flush as well as intimidate and kill.

The Baboon Is Often Homosexual

The baboon is a large, long-haired terrestial mammal that frequents Africa and old Arabia. All baboons are large, with elongated blunt nostrils, and some have shaggy manes to enhance their natural look of ferocity. Although the baboon is a vicious fighter, it rarely ever attacks a man. All known species try to avoid the forests. They travel in groups of troops, and they are always led by elders of the tribe. It is easy to imagine that a troop of baboons is a military company being drilled by a captain and a top sergeant.

The ancient Egyptians appear to have trained some baboons to pick fruit, but the baboon is not mentioned in the Bible when a cargo of exotic animals was brought to King Solomon's court. The omission from the Bible may be ascribable to the reverence of the Egyptians for the baboon; and, in general, the Hebrews were turned off by anything revered by the Egyptians. Mummies of baboons are found often in tombs in the Nile Valley. Historians assume that the highly volatile antics of the baboon at sunrise, as if worshipping the sun god, is the basis for this type of religion among humans. And while this nuance seems to have eluded Anita Bryant's vigilant attention, many baboons are homosexual by choice. However, for whatever it's worth, one rarely ever sees a baboon ordering Florida orange juice for breakfast. And, thus far, there has been no petition for equal animal rights for gay baboons.

Indeed, one feels certain that the late Hilaire Belloc wasn't thinking of the baboon's propensity for homosexuality when he wrote "Four Beasts."

The Big Baboon

The Big Baboon is found upon
The plains of Cariboo;
He goes around with nothing on
(A shocking thing to do).
But if he dressed respectably,
And let his whiskers grow,
How much this Big Baboon would be,
To Mister So and So.

Of the yak, lion, and tiger, Belloc wrote:

As a friend to the children commend me the Yak;
You will find it exactly the thing;
It will carry and fetch, you can ride on its back,
Or lead it about with a string.

The Tartar who dwells on the plains of Tibet
(A desolate region of snow.)
Has for centuries made it a nursery pet,
And surely the Tartar should know.

Then tell your Papa where the Yak can be got,
And if he is awfully rich,
He will buy you the creature—or else he will not
(I can not be positive which.)

The Lion

The lion, the lion, he dwells in the waste;
He has a big head and a very small waist;
But his shoulders are stark, and his jaws are grim,
And a good little child will not play with him.

The Tiger

The tiger, on the other hand, is kittenish and mild,
He makes a pretty playmate for any child;
And mothers of small families (who claim to common sense)
Will find a tiger well repays the trouble and expense.

In view of the fact that two of Belloc's poetry animals, the lion and tiger, have been dealt with cursorily elsewhere in this work, the yak he commends to children (*Bos grunneous*) is the name natives of Tibet gave to the wild ox. Found upon the mountain ranges of Tibet, the Yak lives near the snow line, and he descends to the valleys in winter.

There are at least two races, the wild yak and one that is domesticated. The latter is usually a half-breed, of sundry colors. Although black and white are the colors of most of the domesticated yaks, each race is about the size of the common ox, to which each has a general physical appearance. But the yak is covered with a thick coat of long, silky hair, and this hair hangs down like the fleece of a lamb, and the hair completely invests the yak's tail, to form a lengthy fringe. This exists in both races, and nature developed it, apparently, as protection for the animal, in its alpine haunts. The long hair forms a mat which defends the yak's body from the effects of severe cold when the animal has to live in snow.

The domesticated yak is tremendously important to the denizens of Tibet. Although the yak is employed as a beast of burden, it is never used for tillage or draught. The milk of the domesticated yak is unusually rich and makes much butter. The flesh of the domesticated or the wild yak is a delicacy in Tibet, and several gourmets have pronounced it superior in taste to veal.

The yak's hair is spun into ropes and made into coverings for tents; and the soft, white hair, the soft fur of the yak's hump, is woven into the finest cloth. Tail hairs are dyed red to make into the chowaries, or fly flappers so popular in India. Attempts to breed the yak elsewhere are always futile because it cannot subsist on corn and it is never healthy save when it lives on elevated land.

It may be a proclivity for water, more or less the same kind of teeth, and a moustache, but many people say that the

101

baboon reminds them of the hippopotamus. The word hippopotamus, known also as "river horse," comes from the Latin, through the late Greek *hippos no potamus*. (There is the unusual singularity that although the ancient Greeks and American Indians never heard of each other, the Algonquin word for water is *potomac*, and the Greek word is *potatmus*.)

The hippopotamus (or behemoth) is one of the largest animals known to the Israelites during their Egyptian confinement. The hippo was found in and near the Nile; and when Job (40:15) talks about the behemoth, there is every probability he was thinking of the hippopotamus. The young are born under water and they can swim before they can walk. They weigh up to a ton at birth, and Job construed this mighty animal as a demonstration of the creative power of God. The Egyptians relished the flesh although the Hebrews branded it as "unclean."

There is absolutely no substance to the centuries old myth that the hippopotamus sweats blood when it is excited or angry. It exudes an oily reddish fluid that resembles blood. In fact, it looks very much like blood, but this fluid seems to be a kind of skin conditioning which the animal requires to prevent dried or crackling skin when it is out of the water. The reddish fluid that pours from the hippo's flesh is more copious, and looks much redder when the animal is injured. But skin conditioning is the only reason for the ancient myth of the hippo's sweating blood.

While Hilaire Belloc did exceptionally well in his verse about the Big Baboon, few words rhyme with rhinoceros. Robert Browning used to boast, good-naturedly, that he could put a word into a rhyme quicker than the quizzer could think up the word. Lord Tennyson, who knew some of the problems of rhymes, sat across from Browning at a dinner. The old matter of a rhyme for any word came up, and after much thought, Tennyson said, "rhinoceros." Browning instanteously rhymed:

> O, if you should see a
>   rhinoceros
> And a tree be in sight,
> Climb quick, for his might
> Is a match for the gods—
>   he can toss Eros!"

Despite the jocular setback for British poetry, Browning might have said that any ordinary cartridge will not pierce the hard skin of a rhinoceros (*rhino* is nose in Greek) unless the rhino is hit between the folds. In his book, *The Zoo*, Dr. Reid Blair, notable naturalist, wrote: "From the immense thickness and apparent toughness of its great folds, it was long considered that the hide of the Indian rhinoceros was bulletproof, except at the joints of the armor-like shield plates. As a matter of fact it can be pierced in any place by a bullet or a knife. [sic] (This tip is written for any embryo Teddy Roosevelts or Ernest Hemingways.) When dried, however, it becomes exceedingly hard and it was formerly utilized by Indian princes in the manufacture of shields for their soldiers." Indeed, shields of tanned rhinoceros were used by the Ethiopian army and hunters. One can't say if the rhino shield still prevails in Ethiopia, but one would hope that it does. When Mussolini invaded Ethiopia, the Ethiopian bands played "The St. Louis Blues." Somehow "The St. Louis Blues" conjured a hippo shield more readily than a tank or a bulldozer.

But unlike the baboon, no one has said whether or not the hippo or rhino is a candidate for censure of Anita Bryant. If some rhinos are homosexual, the same as many baboons, one wonders how Miss Bryant would bring her message of sexual salvation to either animal?

Colonel Blimp On Four Short Legs

The walrus is a most gregarious aquatic mammal related to the seal family, and the walrus is found in the Arctic waters. There is a walrus known as the Pacific walrus, and one is known as the Atlantic walrus. There is only miniscule difference insofar as the laymen can tell, but it is a gross slander, or libel, to say that highly gregarious civic organizations such as Rotary and Kiwanis came from close observation of regular, and large, fore-gatherings of walruses to sing old songs off key.

The male often attains a height from ten to twelve feet, and the walrus' wrinkled skin is virtually hairless. His menacing, protruding tusks run from fourteen to twenty inches long, and the walrus resembles a television dental commercial, before one has had the treatment. The walrus dives and digs out clams and other seafood. While most outlanders are repelled by the walrus' flesh, it is a prime favorite with Eskimos.

He seems to have descended from the Swedish "whale horse," but it differs from seals in its huge and sharp incisors. The tusks serve the walrus as weapons and as tools. Its fur is a tawny brown and the hide is so thick it is likened to a coat of mail. The female often produces nine offspring at one birthing, and conception and birth are likely to occur on an ice floe.

The walrus is relatively docile, but it fights ferociously when it has to fight. When its young seem to be imperiled, the walrus will attack anything from a man to a ship. However, needless slaughter has reduced the walrus population vastly.

It really does have a beautiful, handlebar moustache, and although no one knows for sure whether or not Bruce Bairsfeather ever saw a walrus, the famous British cartoonist could have been inspired to draw the deathless, legendary Colonel Blimp after close observation of a walrus. It is easy enough to see a walrus as Colonel Blimp, using an icicle for a swagger stick as he has his troops execute by the right flank, march from ice floe to ice floe. Then, of course, the arctic Colonel Blimp would be off to that special igloo that is staked out as an officers' club replete with a bar.

Although he swims and dives well, on land the walrus is clumsy, but on land he has all of the grace of a giraffe playing basketball. Although the female walrus is much smaller than the male, most females register temper quickly, and Kipling could have thought of the she walrus when he wrote, "The female of the species is more deadly than the male."

The walrus had tremendous commercial value, furnishing a type of crude ivory from his massive teeth, and he and his double first cousin, the whale, were indispensable for oil until electricity came along. O. Henry liked one of Lewis Carroll's walrus phrases to impart it as a book title, and those who don't read poetry know Carroll's famous lines:

"The time has come," the walrus said,
"To talk of many things;
Of ships and shoes and sealing wax,
Of cabbages and kings,
And why the sea is boiling hot,
And whether the pigs have wings."

Merry-Go-Round

There is the hokey story about the manager of a baseball team when no one on the club was hitting more than the size of his hat. Desperately needing surcease, the manager went to a riding academy to take a diverting canter. During the ride, the horse stopped and said: "I can really hit that apple, and you can sign me for a bale of hay. If I don't hit better than your humpty-dumpty ball players, I'll return the hay."

So the horse was signed, and the next day he was inserted in the seventh inning as pinch hitter. He grasped the bat between his front hooves to smash a line drive single to centerfield. He ran down to first base, but he didn't take a lead. Whereupon, the first base coach whispered, "Take a lead and steal second on the next pitch."

With an admixture of pity and consternation, the horse turned to the coach to say: "Don't be silly. Who in hell ever heard of a horse stealing bases?"

A few years ago three horses in Charleston, West Virginia, smashed a Volkswagen, apropos to absolutely nothing. The car was parked, and no hazard to the horses was present. This could have been the result of inexplicable confusion, or perhaps the three horses remembered the tales of their grandfathers told about being menaced by horn blowers in America's insular era.

Mark Twain must have been thinking about city dogs exposed to Salvation Army preaching when he got off the famous crack about the difference between a hungry dog and a man.

Farmers in Coon Valley, Wisconsin, waited interminably for the federal government to act upon their application for a flood control program. Promises were frequent and sonorous, but action was thinner than a cigarette paper. And while the wizards in Washington were wallowing in red tape and legal hogwash, some non-union beavers built four dams and solved the flood control problem. That, as Twain would put it, is the petrified

106

truth, and as James Thurber would say, "You can look it up."

There is the story about the horse trainer in Loudon County, Virginia, who tried to pacify restive Sir Reginald by saying, "After all, men and horses are pretty much alike, Sir Reginald. Both want to win." "I'm damned if that's so," replied Sir Reginald. "I eat my wheat straight and you shred yours and pour cream and sugar on it."

Not long ago some agricultural demons advocated "feeding parlors" for hogs and toys for hogs to play with between meals. This is bound to be a bummer. One can already hear a hog saying, "All I got was a tea set from Rose's, but Oscar got a brand new catcher's mitt and two new balls." Obviously, there will have to be special collections for toys for deprived hogs. Who knows, the hog tree may even menace the public Christmas tree so many towns like to put up around the first of November.

While no affidavits seem to be extant, people used to talk about a nimble-brained, talking crow in Habersham County, Georgia. This crow could do long division and it knew the capitals of all the states. The crow's master ran a country store, and the crow did most of the bookkeeping, and he entertained the loafers when the proprietor was busy. Everything went well until FDR's wage and hour law came in; then when the store keeper ignored the governmental mandate, the crow sat with folded legs, and in utter silence, for almost a week. He finally broke his silence by saying to the merchant: "Now, you stingy bastard, you'll have to buy yourself an adding machine and sneak in a peon by night to entertain the loafers and do the chores I have always done."

We forget the crow's capacity for taking charge of situations because so many of us have forgotten Lord Tennyson's line, "The many winter'd crow that leads the changing rookery home."

Some readers are mystified because the Bible does not reveal the ordinary black "crow." The raucous crow we know was not present, but the Carion Crow of Eurasis and the Hooded Crow were known to the Hebrews. A logical explanation for the omission of the word "crow" from the Bible may be ascribable to the fact that crow belongs to the raven family; and in many places it is highly probable that "crow" could be substituted for "raven" without changing one iota of the meaning of the text.

107

A few years ago some bloodhounds at a prison camp in Ware County, Georgia tunneled under the wire. In the most egregious travesty of this century, the convicts were assembled and they were dispatched to capture the bloodhounds. Sending a poor convict to capture a bloodhound is worse than asking the head man of United Airlines to endorse the canal boat and the stagecoach. And no bounty or trophy was awarded, and no sentence was shortened, not even by parenthesis. The only reward was swamp water, chiggers, snakes, mosquitoes, thirst, and hunger.

But the cons captured the elusive bloodhounds, and a buck will get you ten the next time an inmate burrows under the wire fence, the bloodhounds will forget their benefactors and take out after the convict-boy as if he is a piece of red meat.

A Few National Superstitions

Perhaps, a superstition is something that others believe that one does not believe oneself. The snake was held in reverential awe by many early African tribes. Once each year most of the African tribes killed a *cobra de capello*, and it was hung up in a tree, tail downward. This meant that all the children born within that year would be brilliant and healthy. Each child had to feel the dead snake because parents believed this put the children under the snake's protection.

The Eskimos used to be firm believers in ghosts, and in transmigration of the soul. The spirits returned in form of several different kinds of animals, or it could return as a force in the wind, in snow, or in moving water. Thus, these ghosts were good and bad, just as the various elements were beneficial or destructive. In portions of Greenland when a child died, a live dog was buried with the small corpse. The dog was to act as the dead child's guide to the "other world."

When questioned about this barbaric practice, the Greenlander answered, "A dog can find his way anywhere."

Many Australians used to believe that the moon was a native cat that fell in love with someone's wife. Thus, the cat was driven away to become an eternal wanderer. In certain bush portions of New Zealand the hands of every dead man were tied together tightly, and his fingernails were removed, lest he scratch his way out of the grave and turn into a werewolf or vampire.

The peasants of old Bohemia rid themselves of the depredations of sparrows to their crops by putting a plank from a coffin in the center of the cornfield. Actually, a splinter from the wood of which a coffin was made would drive the sparrows away. (In old Bohemia it was believed that Judas had hanged himself on a willow, and the willow was said to have a magnetic attraction for projected suicides.)

In China, "the old man of the moon" is known as Yue-loa,

109

and Yau-loa holds within his hands the records of marriages among mortals. "The old man of the moon" ties husband and wives together with a silken cord which is broken only at death.

When a cock crowed in Persia, the master of the house ran to feel the cock's feet. If the cock's feet were cold, death in the family was imminent; but if the feet were warm, that was a propitious sign that many good things would occur.

In Peru the peasants used to set a black sheep in a field, to procure rain. They poured chica over the black sheep and did not feed it until rain fell.

In the Philippine Islands the mountain people had innumerable superstitions and gods. When sickness or death came to a village the priest, or the voodoo leader, killed an ox and a pig. The voodoo leader placed the reeking head of the pig over her own head, to work herself into paroxysms of frenzy. In this manner the spirits of the dead received absolution. (One cannot say if this paganism is still prevalent.)

In Poland the goat is the harbinger of good luck, while the wolf, crow, and pigeon bring misfortunes. And if one who has tuberculosis will place the skin of a dead cat on his chest, he will be cured.

In Ancient Romany the gypsies believed witches used egg shells to make plates, pots, and dishes. (These gypsies believed that a coin carried by a specific person became imbued with the carrier's personality. For this reason the Maria Theresa dollar has been sought the world over by collectors of precious objects.)

The Russian general, Skoboleff, never went into battle save astride a gray horse. He had fought his first battle, in 1863, on a gray horse, and he believed to change to another color would be fatal. (The Russians used rolled up certificates of commendation for the deceased person to hand to St. Peter.)

In Cuba the hooting of an owl used to mean certain death if an owl hooted within sound of a sick room. However, the immediate killing of an owl, or any other bird, broke the evil spell. (The Cubans used to believe that rain that fell in May was especially efficacious, that it held powers not accorded to other rains.) For a long time strangers in Cuba were warned not to go out under the moon hatless. It was thought that bright moonlight brought demons and the hat was a type of protection against dragons and werewolves.

The ancient Egyptians worshipped a black bull with a circular

110

white spot in the middle of its head. When such an animal appeared in any herd, there were wild demonstrations, by men and by cattle. As late as the time of Cleopatra such bulls were shod with gold and their tips with the same material. Herodotus tells of a man who died of grief because he sold a cow that soon gave birth to a black bull calf with the circular white spot.

For a long time Egyptian housewives marked their bread loaves with a cross, and housemaids made the sign of the cross over a beginning kitchen fire to insure a continuous blaze. The sacred ibis of Egypt was supposed, from the color of its feathers, to symbolize the light and shade of the moon. The feathers of this ibis would frighten, even kill, a crocodile. The ibis was said to deliver Egypt from the winged serpents that flew in from Arabia. The ibis was so sacred it could enter any temple with complete immunity; and to kill one, even by accident, meant swift execution. After its death the ibis was embalmed, and literally thousands have been found at Thebes, at Memphis, and in other Egyptian cities.

Several superstitions about the cricket have abounded in England. In Hull terrible luck follows the killing of a cricket, and in Lancashire the crickets cut holes in the stockings of an entire family when one of its members kills a cricket. And in many parts of England the death of a member of the human family is "told" to the bees, just as was described in Whittier's poem about New England. There is the additional belief that if a swarm of bees settles on the dead branch of a dead tree, a death in the human family will occur among the land-owning family within a year.

In the north of England when a dairy maid churned a long time without getting butter, she would stir the cream with a twig of mountain ash and beat the cow with another mountain ash twig. This was certain to break a witch's spell.

Throughout Germany and the Low Countries, the sky, as aforesaid, is sacred. Peasants believed that after the stork settled atop the house, in a wagon wheel left by the family as a basis for a nest, the home would never be damaged by fire. And if one has been unkind to cats during one's life, his exodus to the cemetery brings high winds and rough rains.

The Icelanders have a superstition called "Skipamal," or "the speaking ship." Hardly anyone understands the esoteric language spoken, but it is ascribed to various demons.

111

The Irish peasant was (is) subject to all sorts of supernatural agencies, and especially so during the Lenten season. The cry of the Banshee always means death, and it means double-death throughout Lent. In southern Ireland people are terribly fearful that a robin will enter their house. This is an infallible sign of killing frosts and heavy snowfalls.

Many Italian peasants still seem to think a snake is invulnerable save during the full moon. At this juncture, according to the old Italian myth, snakes got drunk eating grapes in the vineyards. It was not difficult to kill an intoxicated snake. But there was great danger involved. If the snake were allowed to live, it might kill one of the family members, or a piece of valuable livestock; but, at times, one had to guess extraordinarily well, for killing a snake brought down from the sky a plague on the entire family. One of the strongest motivations for this myth was the fact that snakes were taught to hover around prodigious treasures. The snake was there as a faithful, unpaid god of the treasure. Thus, it is possible that the man who killed the snake put himself into a dangerously anomalous place with the persons who owned the treasure.

The evil-eye, long associated with the Hebrews, required the wearing of a charm to ward off harm. In Venice, periwinkle is yet called "Death's Flower," from the old custom of raising periwinkle to obtain garlands for the buried infant. In Java when a search was made for a person believed to have drowned, a live sheep was thrown into the water because the Javanese believed the sheep would locate the drowned person by lying in death beside the corpse.

The merman, or sea monster, was vibrant with the sailors of Norway. This animal had the head of a man and a body covered with hair, much like a gorilla's. The merman sat (sits?) upon the waves and blows a harmonica, and the merman, following the customs of all Norwegian sailors, wears a red cap. It is never seen more than once each seven years, but any ship that ventures into its sight is sunk, by natural or by unnatural causes.

When searching for a drowned sailor, or for one who has died at sea, the small oar-boat that is sent to look for his body always contains a cock. This was done regularly for many years on the belief that the cock would crow, in an eerie manner, when the long-boat reached the spot on the water that contained the dead sailor.

In the Samoan Islands a baked pig is used in lieu of funeral flowers. (Some have quibbled that the dead person can't eat the pig, but the answer has been, "He can't smell funeral flowers, either.")

In Scotland if a fisherman passes a barefooted woman, this will scare all the fish away. Men bearing the name Roose, Fyllie, and White must not be in the same boat at the same time. Such a combination will "hoodoo" the fish. And sailors must never speak of any four-footed animal while on the water.

In the 16th century Spaniards believed spiders indicated gold when spiders were found in abundance.

In Sweden terrible fate awaits anyone who kills a stork, a robin, or a swallow. And if one kills a wren, he will break one of his bones before twelve months pass. Three hairs taken from the cross of an ass (the mark running up the back and out at right angles on the shoulders) will cure whooping cough, but the ass will die. And whooping cough can be cured if one asks an intelligent question of a man riding a piebald horse.

If a Swiss hunter meets an old woman or if he sees a fox cross his path, he returns to his home hastily. If he persists in hunting, despite these omens, he will be sure to kill a man obscured by leaves. In the Alps many people still think that if a cuckoo sings in the direction of the north, it will rain the next day; but if the cuckoo sings to the south, fine weather comes the next day.

The Turks believed that if a cat entered a sick room and managed to cross over the sick body, both the dying person and the cat became vampires, to live eternally as bloodsuckers.

The charms, chromos, sayings, buckeyes and similar oddments carried by people in the United States are too numerous for additional recitation. There are fifty states and one can be sure to find not only fifty sets of superstitions, but these are broken down into regional superstitions within the states.

Greenland was known as Nova Zembia when the vastness was virtually unpopulated. It was said that the weather was so cold men's spoken words froze up in the winter and didn't make sounds until after the spring or summer thaw. No one seems to know if the freezing process applied to the various winged and furred animals.

Exit Brer Mule

There used to be a popular song that expressed the anomalous relationship of some men and their persevering mules:

> Johnson had an old gray mule,
> He drove him to a cart;
> John loved the mule, the mule loved John,
> With all his mulish heart;
> The rooster crowed and Johnson knowed
> That day was about to break;
> So he curried mule, with a three-legged stool,
> And brushed him down with a rake.

The mule as a work animal is almost as old as history. All accounts that tell the achievements of civilized men tell also of the mule as an indispensable work animal. From the onset man was impressed by the mule's endurance, intelligence, sure-footedness, and his freedom from excitability. Until the Bronze Age man was a nomad. It was the crude invention of the plow and the simultaneous domestication of mules, and some other animals, that enabled man to live in permanent locations. It was the surplus food produced by the plow and the domestication of work animals that allowed farmers to produce the surplus food essential to feeding the people in the new cities.

The mule was (is) the best of all the work animals, and no draft animal ever bred has had the endurance of the mule, especially under difficult working conditions. In the excessively hot climate of the tropics the mule worked incessantly long after the horse had wilted. And the mule was capable of prodigious labor without injury to himself. This amazing hybrid, descended from the wild ass of the deserts, has inherited an intelligence which protected him from the dangers incident to expanding civilization. He thrived under adverse conditions that were ruinous to the horse.

Curiously enough, the mule, always associated in America with the south and the mid-west, was not hitched to plow and wagon until the 19th century. In Missouri, perhaps, the best known place for the rearing of superior mules, it was determined from the outset that the risks from raising young mules, particularly in reference to acquiring blemishes, is infinitely less than the risk involved in raising young horses.

But to a disheartening degree the song about Johnson and his old gray mule is shockingly typical of Brer Mule's saga. The piano part of the musical ditty is so obvious it may be illusory. Johnson really loved his mule, but he thought he had to express his affection in the hard knocks to which the mule has been accustomed throughout history.

The mule is a pitiful example for enduring tragedy. This shamefully maligned creature enters the world as an Ishmaelite, a bastard who is denied the succor of ancestry and the inspiration of progeny and posterity. There is in his eyes an incomparable sadness; but this sadness is heart-rendingly poignant and it is tinged with gallantry. And yet, the individual mule, whether hitched to a plow or used as a draft animal in the city, required a lot of killing. For, if wanton neglect and continued abuse were lethal, the mule would have been dead long ago.

Ultimately, humans may be replaced by some sort of machine, and man, as we know him, may become totally obsolete. But Old Man Mule has seen his harness bend and break within his own time. On countless farms the ancient harness room is a playground for mice and spider webs, and often it seems that an evil contest is occurring between the two. Which will usurp the old tack room first, the rats or the spider webs? The wind rattles the raw innards and shakes the decrepit bones of the disused place and a detached sort of leukemia works from the roof downwards. On wall pegs molding mule collars form rancid zeroes through which the luscious greenery of buried springtimes and plowing times has passed to oblivion.

It must be acutely disenthralling to see oneself replaced by a younger, more virile, mechanical counterpart of oneself, but to see oneself run from the rich earth by an iron monster must be almost more than even Brer Mule's long and stolid patience and capacity for suffering can endure. Yet, when one thinks of the earth as man's fertile alter-ego, the mule is still the symbol of sustenance, despite the unholy clattering of ten million kinds of tractors and assorted farm machinery.

Even so, it may strain credulity to remember that a few mules are still led out each working day when the earth is as soft and sweet as a bride's kiss, when spring is a big bird laying golden eggs, when spring decorates her woodlands with sticks of striped candy. A few, only a rawboned handful, farmers are impervious to motorized contraptions which one can't cuss or love in a way that the recipient gets the message.

Friendship with a specific mule across long years is a contributing factor, obviously. There are a few southern farmers who were born in the land as well as to the land. These men and their fortunes have been bound-round with a mule so long that any other means of breaking the land and stringing furrows would constitute a minor sacrilege. Thus, the lone mule and plow go ever forward up and down the rows, even as dynasties topple. The mule has no politics, but the relationship between him and a lone and lonely man may constitute a compelling sort of secular religion.

Yet Old Man Mule is the butt of thousands of harsh jokes. (For instance: A man brags about the willing responses of his mule. Then he swats the mule several wallops with a singletree. The other man asks: "I thought you said your mule minds you everytime?" "He does," the owner replies, "But first I have to get his attention.") People who have never touched or smelled a live mule use him as an example of adamance and perversity. Stupid people have compared mules to other stupid people.

Contrariwise, the "noble" horse is almost defied by gullible sycophants. "Horse sense" endures as an accolade, just as mulish indicates perversity. Nonetheless, any competent authority will explain that the horse is the beneficiary of excellent P.R. men. Under pressure a horse is extremely restive and fractious. He might as well be a high-wire walker during a bad electrical storm, when things go badly. If a horse catches his foot in a wire fence, he will cut it frightfully in his violent anguish to extricate it. The mule will stand docilely until his owner removes his foot.

An overheated horse will drink himself sick, if given half a chance. Under the same circumstances a mule will drink just

116

enough to requite his thirst. The same applies to eating. If one overloads a wagon, the tempestuous horse will break into a lather trying with foolish desperation to pull a load far beyond his strength. Conversely, the mule will stand stolidly until some of the excess weight is removed.

Farmers, with and without mules, are fond of an old saw: "Whoever saw a dead mule?" This endures as an eternal testament to his dietary habits and to his vigilance in caring for his own health. And in many parts of the south there is the ancient saying: "A white mule never dies. No siree. Finally, he turns into a Baptist preacher."

There are millions of paintings, photographs, and pieces of sculpture of the noble horse. Only a brand of chewing tobacco known the world over carries the mule's symbolism. (This author can't remember a decent mule drawing since the death of Robert M. Prince, of Chapel Hill, North Carolina, who did the magazine illustrations for the late Ruark Bradford's stories about the Little Bee Plantation. Said Bradford, "Prince is the only man alive who knows how to draw a mule," and this was many years ago.)

Only a few years ago school children had to say by heart all, or portions, of Thomas B. Reed's poem about the noble horse that carried General Phil Sheridan to Winchester, Virginia, to save the day for the imperiled Federal army. Although Reed didn't say so, one gets the impression that the Yankee soldiers, rifles, and cannons were superflous baggage. The horse got top billing in the poem, and Sheridan is the male lead.

But as recently as World War I, before the full advent of motorized armies, the long suffering mule was indispensable as a pack and draft animal. During World War I Old Man Mule pulled guns and limbers and wagons of ammunition just as if he were plowing in the quiet safety of a cornfield back home. Many of the horses tried for these purposes were almost as much a hazard as the Germans. To roll with a punch is second nature with the mule; and along with the cat, he takes excellent care of his own safety.

In a thunderstorm many horses emulate crazy, distraught humans, but the mule looks around as if to say, "What else is news?" No matter, though, we are writing and talking in the past tense, even if a handful of farmers are so wedded to mules that a tractor seems a freak from outer space. The mule is

117

irrevocably tied to the baseball game at the crossroads, the tumultuous camp meeting, the oldtime political rally, the "sociable" at the schoolhouse, the corn-shucking, the wood-cutting, and the raising of a neighbor's barn. And always beyond the symbols and usages of metaphor, the mule meant bread. Just yesterday the mule was big business. Bread and meat and education, weddings and tombstones, rode on his stout back. He was to southern economy what sex is to Hollywood. His honking-yonking and his hee-hawing, those gestures of supreme defiance, were inseparable from the hopes of a people.

The mule market was not merely important business. Its demise buried a way of life. The mule trader, with his derby hat, yellow vest, celluloid cuffs and collar, put on a superb show. His flashing cane was a pointer, and a baton. And through it all he was as elusive as a lone fly in an empty subway tunnel.

As he described the miraculous prowess of a Tennessee mule, his tongue was a wingless jet going around to all of creation's exotic spots. He knew as much about the Pyramids as he knew about Parisian can-can dancers, to hear him tell it; and he was the close friend of big league ball players, and the political leaders ordinary people knew only by reading a newspaper. He had been everywhere and he had seen everything.

The big mule selling and trading occurred during the quarterly sessions of the county court. Everybody but the lame, blind, and halt attended court week and the concomitant mule trading. The courthouse and the adjacent "mule alley" were golden magnets during the provincial era. In a week's time there was everything from a Greek tragedy to the enactment of a tale that couldn't be improved upon by a Bret Harte or an Augustus Baldwin Longstreet. And the man who wouldn't steal a coal of fire from the devil amid a rousing blizzard delighted in sticking the mule trader, even if the pros always got back a little more than they gave away.

Every community had a story about the novice mule trader who was given a mule, in fee simple, by his father with the injunction to trade the mule and his successors as many times as possible his first day in "mule alley." At sundown the novice always ended up with a pocketknife with a broken blade and no mule at all.

Perhaps, the true ending of the mule's saga came in the spring of 1960 when a tenant farmer in Sampson County, N.C., drowned himself because his decrepit mule died. He left this penciled note: "My old mule is dead and I might as well die too."

The two had toiled together for eighteen searing summers. They saw the same sunsets and they both dined on humble fare. The world and all of its exciting mysteries was bounded by the cornfield. Each was the other's alter ego, and their fortunes were so deeply entwined it seems a great shame the two were not buried in the same grave. Now, the tractor has curried Brer Mule with its caterpillar treads, and it has dug his grave with an iron shovel.

There is this addendum. The dark stripe that runs down the ass's back, crossed by another at the shoulders, was communicated to the animal when Jesus rode on the back of an ass in his triumphant entry into Jerusalem.

Balaam's ass, probably the best known in history, reproached her master when he flogged unjustly. After wandering forty years in the wilderness, the Children of Israel were encamped on the plains of Moab. The Israelites had defeated Palestinian kings, and King Balak of Moab feared he would be the third victim. Hence, he ordered the prophet Balaam to go and put a curse upon the Israelites, to insure their defeat.

Balaam demurred because he had been warned in a dream that he was not to fulfill Balak's command. But when he was threatened by Balak's courier, he saddled his ass and set out with Balak's troops, although he knew his speech would be limited to the words God put on his tongue.

En route, an angel, invisible to the group, placed himself in the middle of the road, to be seen only by Balaam's ass. Thus, the ass turned into a side path. When she did Balaam beat her badly with a stick. The ass resumed the journey on the regular road, but once again she turned aside when the angel, visible only to her, appeared in the road a second time. The same beating occurred again. When the angel appeared in the road a third time, the ass lay down and folded her legs to block the road. Balaam whipped her again, but she still refused to move. Suddenly the ass raised its head to say to Balaam, "What have I done to thee that thou has struck me three times?" "Why," Balaam answered, "thou has made sport of me and if my stick had been a sword I would have slain thee." "But have I not served thee faithfully, to this very day? Have I ever failed thee?"

Balaam was forced to answer, "No," and at that precise moment Balaam saw the angel for the first time. The angel stood with sword drawn. Balaam offered to quit his mission, but the angel told him to proceed; and when he had climbed the hill above Moab, he looked down upon Israel's hosts, not with a curse but with a blessing, and a prophecy of a tremendous victory for the sons of Jacob. The Book of Numbers, which contains the story of Balaam, is a part of what is called the Hexateuch, or the Five Books of Moses plus Joshua. These books are a combination of two versions, one written about the 9th or 10th century B.C., and one written at an undefined later date. They are differentiated by the fact that early versions used the word *Jahweh*, to mean God, and is referred to as the "J" version. The other, which uses *Elohim*, and not *Jahweh* for God, is known as the "E" version. Some of the details vary in the two versions, and yet both agree upon the fact that one could be a proper prophet and still not be a Hebrew.

Talking animals are usually a popular subject. While this is true in folklore, and with the writings ascribed to Aesop, and the literature written by La Fontaine and Joel Chandler Harris, aside from Balaam's ass the only other Biblical talking animal seems to be the serpent in the Garden of Eden.

Ass, from the Anglo-Saxon *assa*, was an opprobrium used widely during the Elizabethan era. In *Othello*, Shakespeare uses, "Egregiously an ass," and later, in 1722 Jonathan Swift, in *The Beasts' Confession*, calls a man an "ass," and amplifies it with "The Nightingale of Brutes." Thomas Fuller (1654-1734) in his once-famous *Gnomologia*, writes: "He that makes himself an ASS, must not take it ill if in Men ride him." It is in her novel, *Romola*, that George Eliot (Mary Ann Evans, 1819-1880) says, "An ass may bray a good while before he shakes the stars down." (It may be worth a passing note to see that Mary Ann Evans made the ass a male.) Mark Twain didn't leave many inexplicable conundrums behind, but many Twain fans still ponder a sentence from *Puddn'head Wilson's Calendar*: "Instead of feeling complimented when we are called an ass, we are left in doubt."

In his excellent study, *Lee and Longstreet At Gettysburg*, the late Glenn Tucker tells this story about the mule's astuteness. The story is told by Major General Lafayette McLaws, a self-effacing man, completely honest and a most capable manager of a Confederate division. McLaws told this story thirty-three years after Gettysburg to illustrate how a conference of Confederate officers the first night of the battle may have promoted an alternate plan that would have obviated the disastrous charge on the third day.

McLaw's mule story occurred when he was in the United States Army, some years before the Civil War: F. X. Aubrey, an energetic French-Canadian trader, was taking a wagon train of sundry goods from San Antonio to El Paso. The train's water supply was exhausted, and the hole in which Aubrey expected to find water was powder dry. The entire area was pulverized by an intense drought, and Aubrey said he and his mules may just as well have been in the Sahara.

A big mule followed Aubrey around the overnight camp, nudging Aubrey gently and whining incessantly. Aubrey said to the mule: "Old fellow, I have no water to give you, but I'll give you whiskey if that will help." So saying, Aubrey filled a bucket from one of the whiskey barrels. The mule drank it, walked a few steps and fell dead.

During the night the other mules broke loose from their halters, and when Aubrey and his assistants followed the mules' tracks they found the mules playing friskily in lush grass, close by a large, bubbling spring. Aubrey told McLaws: "I'll almost take an oath that the big mule that died was trying to tell me to turn him and the other mules loose and that they would find water."

121

All Feet In the Air

A comparison between horses and mules has already been made. The horse is mentioned more than one hundred and fifty times in the Bible, but the horse never replaced the humble ass in the lives of the Hebrews. The horse is described pretty generally as a war animal, a puller of chariots, and King Solomon is alleged to have had fourteen hundred chariots in his army. Nonetheless, eventually the horse was used more for cavalry and less to pull chariots.

For a long time Mosaic law forbade the breeding of horses, and the horses used by the Hebrews were imported from Egypt. But when the superiority of the horse in early warfare was demonstrated effectively, the law forbidding the breeding of horses was treated as cavalierly as Americans treated the Prohibition laws. The large Arabian horse was unknown to King Solomon, and he probably used the small, fast Egyptian horse.

The horse genus is descended from the *Eohippus* genus of the *Eocene* epoch, around forty-five million years ago. Many of the Old World horses developed from a genus about the size of a fox. Thus, no one knows for sure if the American Indian ever saw this species. Some researchers believe the tiny horse crossed a land bridge that used to connect the continents. But this breed was extinct prior to the Indians. It is assumed that the strain died from some local disease to which it had not developed a resistance.

In farm work the horse did not replace the ox until the 19th century. The wild horse of the western American plains, known as the Mustang, is believed to have developed from horses that escaped from Spanish explorers and adventurers in the southwest, up through Mexico.

Almost from the time of Solomon to the cavalry horse on the Russian steppes, regular arguments ensued as to whether or not a horse has all four feet off the ground simultaneously.

Leland Stanford, California politician and tycoon, was a fervent believer in the theory that a running horse has all four feet off the ground. While the magnitude of the bet Stanford made fluctuates with the telling of the story, he did prove his point when, as governor of California, he got Eadwear Muybridge, an English-born photographer, to take a series of photographs of a horse running at full speed (from which the motion picture evolved).

"Sowing (or feeling) wild oats" is a cherished bromide and it is often interposed as an extenuation. When a boy reaches a certain age, he is bound to feel his wild oats. This saying seems to have originated in rural England. The wild oat—tall grass that resembles the cultivated oat—was a common weed on the British Isles. So it was only natural that a common, noxious weed should become the basis for moral comparison. At first sowing wild oats meant having a poor crop, but the figurative transition was almost inevitable. Indeed, the phrase may involve three original ideas: A horse is bound to feel any food as stimulating as oats; some even think the phrase is an implied allusion to Jesus's fable of the sower; and there is the implied comparison between a spirited boy and an unbroken colt.

Semper Fidelis?

While no precise statistics are available, more songs, poems, and stories have been written about the faithful dog than about any other animal. These offerings, almost canonizations, run an endless gamut from Odysseus' dog, Argus, to the late McKinley Kantor's once irrepressible *The Voice of Bugle Ann*. These innumerable accolades may have attained their zenith in the speech made in the United States Senate by Senator George Vest in 1884:

> The one absolutely unselfish friend that man can have in this selfish world, the one that never proves ungrateful or treacherous, is his dog. He will kiss the hand that has no food to offer. When all other friends desert, he remains.

Much has been written about the inexorable friendship of the poor man and his inseparable dog. In most cases neither dog nor master will get a vote for anything but being handy, and yet an H-bomb cannot sever them. The man will split his meager rations with his old dog; and when the man stumps his toe, the dog appears to share the pain.

It was such a dog that James Beauchamp (Champ) Clark used as his campaign music when he almost received the Democratic nomination for President in 1912:

> Every time I come to town
> The boys keep kickin' my dawg around;
> Makes no difference if he is a hound,
> They've got to quit kickin' my dawg around.

Stephen Foster's song, "Old Dog Trey," has brought tears to several generations of eyes and lumps in several generations of throats. Homer had to choke his tears when he told how aged Argus, still wagging his superannuated tail, dropped his head when Odysseus returned. And in his novel, *The Voice of Bugle Ann*, McKinley Kantor seems to condone the homicide of a hunter who kills a man who abused his hound. The dog's owner is sent to the pen, but the compassionate reader makes the trip with him.

"Love me, love my dog," a Latin proverb, appears in almost every European language, including John Heywood's famous *Proverbs*, of 1546. This means that if one is loved, everything about one has to be loved, including his dog." And there is the timeless Scottish proverb: "He that strikes my dog, would strike me if he durst." This is a double first cousin to the old southern proverb that if someone mistreated a dog, the malefactor had to whip the owner also.

The American Indian took his hunting dog with him to the Happy Hunting Ground. As Alexander Pope put it:

He asks no angel's wing, nor seraph's fire,
But thinks, admitted to that equal sky,
His faithful dog shall bear him company.

It was Cervantes, in *Don Quixote*, who penned the immortal, "Every dog shall have his day." It was John Heywood, in his aforementioned *Proverbs*, who posed the standard antidote for a hangover: "I pray thee let me and my fellow have/A haire of the dog that bit us last night."

Lord Byron had this inscription chiseled on the tombstone of his dog, Boatswain, a Newfoundlander buried at Newstead in 1808: "Near this spot are deposited the remains of one who possessed Beauty without Vanity, Strength without Insolence, Courage without Ferocity, and all the Virtues of Man without his Vices. This praise, which would be unmeaning flattery if inscribed over human ashes, is but a just tribute to Boatswain, a Dog." Not just incidentally, this monument to Boatswain is many hundreds of times more impressive than Byron's own tablet at Hucknall-Torkard, where he is buried. At one time Byron asked that he be buried with Boatswain. This was not done.

It was Mark Twain who said, "When you go to heaven, leave your dog and horse on the outside. Heaven goes by favor. If it went by merit, the dog and horse would get in and you would stay out." It was Mark Twain, also, who made this immortal comparison: "If you pick up a hungry, stray dog and feed him, the chances are that he will not bite you. This is the principal difference between a dog and a man."

But the dog didn't begin with encomiums strewn around his head. The dog is referred to at least forty times in the Bible, and he was an eastern outcast everywhere but in Egypt. It is in Deuteronomy (23:18) that the dog is branded as "an abomination." There is Jesus's admonition, "Do not give that which is holy unto the dogs." The pariah dogs, owned by no one, ran in packs to ravage, including human corpses. Nonetheless, the Hebrews learned that dogs could be trained to warn the Hebrews of wild animals and thieves. It is in this manner that Job spoke of "the dogs of my flock." Many authorities think Job was alluding to a dog similar to today's shepherd dog. However, the dog was never a household pet with the ancient Jews. And even now the egregious insult in most eastern nations is to tag someone as a dog.

Bob Taylor, who served as a governor of Tennessee and as one of that state's United States Senators, composed "hound dog" music, and Old Limber, the remarkable hound of Bob's brother, Alf Taylor, was known as well across the country as Alf Taylor, if not better.*

The dog's origin is saturated with mystery. Many early authorities believed the dog descended from the fox, the jackal, or the wolf. But the actual record may start with the tomb of the Egyptian king, Amten, who died in the 4th dynasty, or sometime about 3500 B.C. In this tomb are many excellent figures of animals, and the figure of the dog is quite distinct from that of the jackal. The tomb of King Anafee, who died around 3000 B.C., has four dogs at the monarch's feet.

Experts now believe that the dog was derived from one, or, perhaps several, species of the genus *Canis*. And at a fairly early date in history, man began to breed dogs for special purposes.

The hunting dog may have been the first to endear himself to man. Charles Darwin said this of the dog's ancestry: "Looking at

*In the celebrated "War of the Roses," Democrat Bob Taylor and his Republican brother, Alf, ran against each other for governor. Bob wore a white rose and Alf a red rose. The father of the candidates, a Republican, appears to have supported Alf, but his wife, the boys' mother, rode around Tennessee in her buggy yelling, "Hurrah for Taylor."

the domestic dogs of the whole world, I have, after a laborious collection of all known facts, come to the conclusion that several wild species of *Canidae* have been tamed, and that their blood, in some cases, mingled together, flows in the veins of our domestic breeds." Thus, today's authorities give the dog as much credit for originality as any other animal.

It was Edward N. Wescott who wisecracked in *David Harum*: "They say a reasonable number of fleas is good fer a dog—keeps his mind off being a dog." An old English proverb, probably current by the 8th century, declared: "Every dog is entitled to one bite." This has been rendered as "one bite free." Many have declared that the maxim equals anything set forth in the Magna Carta or the American Constitution. What it really means, or used to mean, was that a dog's owner was not liable to a person bitten by the dog unless it could be proven that the dog had bitten someone else previously.

Once when the State of Virginia was ravaged by hydrophobia, Thomas Jefferson proposed that the disease could be eliminated by the simple expedient of killing all the dogs. But John Randolph, of Roanoke, who seems to have lived, eaten, and slept with dogs, announced he would exterminate Jefferson if Jefferson had all the dogs killed. Jefferson let his anodyne die stillborn.*

Almost everyone has seen a dog turn around several times before he lies down. Charles Darwin reported that he saw a dog turn twenty times before settling upon the ground in a comfortable position he liked. Scientists attempt to explain this habit by the process of evolution: Domestic dogs, the scientists say, descended from wild dogs or wolves. The dog's progenitors lived in forests or in regions heavy with brush, and in order to find a comfortable place to rest they had to trample down high grass or other vegetation. This habit is so deeply ingrained that many dogs who sleep on a hearthrug turn around several times before settling for the night's sleep.

Mushing of course is the term used when sledge dogs in the far north travel over snow. The origin of *mushing* is odd. The early French *voyageurs* and *coureurs* yelled *Marchons*, literally "Let us march" to their sledge dogs. English speaking drivers

*This fascinating bit of minutiae was related to this author by Jonathan Daniels, one of the nation's ablest writers and an authority on Thomas Jefferson.

heard this as "mush on." Not just incidentally, such far northern dogs are still trained to respond to "Gee," Haw," and "Mush on."

The ancient Greeks and Romans called the period of intense heat and torpor from around July 10 to August 10 "dog days," because Sirius, the Dog Star, rose with the sun. The Dog Star is the brightest star in the heavens, and it is comparatively close to our solar system. It is the head of the constellation known as *Caius Major*, or the "Greater Dog." The Greeks and Romans tied the excessively debilitating weather to the conjunction of the Dog Star and the sun.

Dog days was a time of much pestilence, and for a long time it was believed that dogs went mad during this period. (Statistics show that more cases of rabies develop in early spring and in late fall than during dog days. But the Romans sacrificed red dogs during dog days to appease the gods.)

Literature abounds with dog poems and stories, and these run an extensive, diverse gamut. Walter D. Edmonds has an intensely moving scene in his *The Boyds of Black River*, in which an untrained dog is entered, perforce, in a fight for money, with another dog, and is killed. There is a fascinating scene near the end of James Fenimore Cooper's *The Prairie*, in which Natty Bumpo dies with his dog at his feet. By this time Natty Bumpo's dog is dead and he has been stuffed by the Indians who are trying to protect the white man from the knowledge of the dog's death.

Many people, comparably, are still enveloped by the pathos in the late James Street's *Goodbye, My Lady*, the saga of a beautiful dog with a voice that is sweetly lyrical.

Hardly anything in literature conveys more of a master's profound sorrow than some doggerel written by the late Samuel Fox Mordecai, Dean of the Trinity Duke Law School, about the death of Pompey Ducklegs, who accompanied Mordecai to every class and chewed Reynolds' Level Best, the same as Mordecai. The doggerel ends:

> He had a loyal heart, acted well his part,
> What more could he be, if a man were he,
> With blood of the bluest blue.

Rudimentary corruptions are responsible for one of the most enduring commands in the entire animal world: "Sic'm," meaning to incite a dog to attack, is merely the English colloquialism for "seek him," and in this sense *sic* is used chiefly with *at* or with *on*. In Shakespeare's time the common word for this was *tarre*. The Bard uses this several times. In *Troilus and Cressida*, Old Nestor explains:

Two curs shall tame each other: pride alone
Most tarre the mastifs on as 'twere their bone.

Raining Cats and Dogs and Other Minutiae

Anytime there is an unusually hard, thrashing rain many folks will say, "It's raining cats and dogs." This saying is an outgrowth of unpublished poetry and mythology, leavened with loose facts. A hard rain, filled with the wind's shrill, ominous whistles does sound as though thousands of cats with sharp claws are scratching the roof, and this same rain seems to be composed of soaking dogs beating their wet tails against the windowpane and asking to come in to sit beside the fire.

Catadupa is the Greek word (and the obsolete French word) for waterfall. Pliny says *Catadupa* was the actual name of a cascade on the Nile, at a point in Ethiopia where the stream rushed downhill emitting a terrifying roar. To compare rain with a waterfall was natural, but people who lacked geographic knowledge and who did not know the Greek language, imagined that they heard *catadupa* as "dogs and cats."

Nonetheless, the ancient Norseman believed rainstorms were caused by the nefarious influence of dogs and cats. Indeed, many of their sailors popularized the saying that an unusually frisky wind had a "gale of wind in its tail." And when witches rode during a storm, they took the form of cats.

Dogs, in Norse mythology, were the pets of Odin, gods of storms, and ancient Germanic pictures depict the wind in the form of a dog with a blast issuing from the dog's head.

Perhaps, more realistic than any of these explanations is an origin which goes back to the unpaved, narrow streets of 17th century England. During this period many London dogs and cats roamed at large, to be drowned in heavy rains. Many of their corpses were found, drowned, floating down the filthy gutters of the city's streets. Many ignorant people actually seemed to believe that it had "rained cats and dogs," in a most literal way.

"To have kittens," i.e., feeling or showing surprise or astonishment or danger, comes from the era when the Scots

130

believed that a pregnant woman would have kittens if she ate any sort of food on which a cat had ejected its semen. In medieval days women who suffered agonies while pregnant were assured by local witches that the pains in the belly did not come from a growing baby, but from kittens inside the womb. As late as 1654 a woman was tried in a Scottish court because she was so certain kittens were in her belly she attempted an abortion.

Flea is Anglo-Saxon in verbal origin, and the ancient cliche, "to put a flea in one's ear," crystalizes the flea's ability to jump. Feeding on the blood of men and animals, a flea has been known to jump thirty times its own height. And it was Socrates who established this fact. Others established a close relationship between the "flea" and "fleeing." Normally a flea's bite is like the flea, or insignificant, but "to put a flea in one's ear" is an act that acquires prodigious proportions. A flea in a man's ear may drive the man crazy. The continuity of the phrase owes much to the common observation of a dog with a flea in its ear. Sometimes the dog is so frantic it flees in terror. But as far back as 700 A.D., Saxon nobles complained bitterly of flea bites. (Scientists have counted in excess of five hundred species of fleas, and no one seems to know which breed Noah took on his celebrated voyage.) Fleas attained their most aggravating tenure in the time of the medieval knights. The knight, covered with heavy mail, his hands in stiff gauntlets, began worrying more about the flea under their heavy armor than the enemy with the broadsword. For a while fleas had their pick of the human meat at Camelot and elsewhere. Tiring of a repetitive diet, fleas tried to get out, to leave the dark prison of medieval armor, and in its frenetic search for a way out, it got into the knight's ear. It settled there, intermittently biting and jumping for several hours. The knight might slay an infidel on a Crusade and he might even kill a dragon, but that tiny flea in his ear made him the almost witless captive of the tiny insect.

The enduring pertinence of animals is indicated by the fact that we reckon the force of an automobile in horsepower. Businessmen and lawyers play intellectual games called "cat and mouse," and the lucky person is likely "to have the cat's whiskers." Conversely, the cat burglar is a dread, and no one wants to be thoroughly conned or victimized, i.e., become "the cat's paw." Catgut usually comes from horses or sheep.

The Bible says the earth was created in seven days, but God

131

waited until the sixth day to create man. An ancient, anonymous saga explained it this way: "To be able to tell man, whenever he becomes overbearing or when his head is swollen with pride for his own accomplishment, 'Even the flea preceded you in creation'."

The man who throws an enormous fit or tizzy of anger is yet "as mad as raising a red flag to a bull." The phrase comes from Spanish bullfighters, matadors, who attract the bull's attention and provoke it into a maniacal charge by waving a red cloth at the bull. Actually, the bull, in common with many animals, is color blind. It is the movements of the cloth, not the color of the cloth, that incurs his anger. From the outset the torero used a red cloak. In the beginning days of this sadistic and masochistic sport, the matador stood perfectly still on a pedestal in the middle of the arena. He had to hold his breath when the bull charged him. Then for a vacuous interlude the bull merely stood and stared. Because there was no motion the bull walked away. But when the frozen figure on the pedestal made movements, the bull snorted and charged him. The colorful explanation generally accepted about red has no basis in fact.

The duck is not merely a swimming bird, but he is also an able and strong flyer. His short legs are set far back under this torso, and his feet are fully webbed. Ducks are of the family *Anartide*, which includes the manganses, or small duck, geese, and swans. As Matthew Arnold wrote:

> Let the long contention cease,
> Geese are swans and swans are geese.
> Let them have it as they will!
> Thou are tired, best be still."

The name "duck" was given for the precise fact that this water bird dives and ducks under the waves. A few build nests on the ground, but many ducks sleep on water, with one foot dropped down and moving gently so as to keep the bird slowly turning and remaining in very nearly the same spot through the night.

Freshwater ducks embrace the woodchuck, whose meat the epicure really fancies. The canvasback duck may be the most

132

popular with those people who study the merits of various meats with meticulous zeal.

Via ignorance of diction "de ducks" came to mean money withheld from a pay envelope. Many mill workers did all of their trading at the company store, and each Saturday what they owed the merchant was deducted from their pay envelope. If a man was supposed to get thirty dollars a week but found only twenty in his pay envelope, he told his wife, "De ducks et up ten dollars of our money."

In time the phrase was taken over by educated and more affluent people, in the southern states especially. Almost any loss, be it money or a missing love letter, was said to have been "eaten up by the ducks." Indeed, this author has heard the phrase used as an explanation by outlanders who seem to have no idea that the ancient bromide began as "de ducks," and "de ducks" was as close as some poor devil could come to "deductions."

The old duck stool, which usually stood in the center of the town, was used by the courts for punishment. Ibsen left us his fine play *The Wild Duck* and Hans Christian Andersen's story "The Ugly Duckling" still has a host of youthful readers.

Throughout this century, "duck" has been a relatively simple man, pleasant, but not profound. "Dead duck" applies to political candidates who are detected in unsavory or unpopular actions. Goose pimples are duck bumps, and a short man is called a duck-butt. A duck fit is a monumental tizzy, and to get a duck egg at school is to fail a course. Duckie started out to indicate an attractive woman, but is often used facetiously today. White ducks are trousers and duck soup is an uncomplicated action or chore. Duck tail is a type of haircut, and in baseball "ducks on the pond" means men on bases.

The deer, the oldest ruminant, is fleet poetry and grace and motion. The male is called a "buck," and this gave us "buck" in the sense of money. This came about in the days when the colonial barter system was in effect, and the hide of the male was deemed more valuable than the doe's skin. Since most of the male's skins brought at least a dollar, big money in times of barter, the word fastened to the one dollar bill. In Europe the male deer is called a stag, as Sir Walter Scott put it:

The stag at eve had drunk his fill
While danced the moon on Monion's hill.

The female is called a doe or a hind; and the young deer stay
with their mothers until they are one year old, and this is
almost revolutionary among animals.

The grassland deers are highly gregarious and they form herds
when winter starts coming on.

There seem to be few neutrals relative to venison. One likes it
tremendously or one can't abide it. But the hoofs and horns of
the male are ground (or were ground) into many medications.
Burns left this fine picture:

My heart's in the Highlands,
It is not here,
My heart's in the Highlands
A-chasing the deer.

William Cowper's "The Task," a take-off on *Hamlet*, is understood much better if one knows Cowper had a nervous break-
down and spent his life in seclusion:

Why, let the striken deer go weep,
The harp ungalled play;
For some must watch (and stay awake) while
some must sleep:
So runs the world.

Once when he felt one of his attacks coming on, Cowper
wrote: "God moves in a mysterious way/His wonders to
perform." Lord David Cecil called his biography of Cowper *The
Striken Deer*, and it was Shelley, in *Adonais*, who wrote, "A
herd-abandoned deer struck by the hunter's dart."

Peacock Pie

Blackbird is the name given to two distinct species. (1) The grackles, which include a dozen varieties of varying shapes and sizes, and (2) the British song-thrush, or "merle." The best known American blackbird is the crow blackbird, often styled the purple grackle because of its iridescent gloss on its plumage.

The famous nursery rhyme was published in 1744, although portions of the song were proverbial at that time:

> Sing a song of sixpence,
> Pocket full of rye.
> Four and twenty blackbirds
> Baked into a pie.
>
> When the pie was opened,
> The birds began to sing;
> My, isn't that a lovely dish
> To set before a king."

The ditty means what it says. People in medieval England, and for a long time afterward, though the releasing of many blackbirds, from a pie, was a proper act of deference to visiting nobility. Indeed, the format is pretty much the same one used by the Chicago gangsters of the 1920's who had a naked, or scantily attired, girl step from a cake as a high mark of distinction to some notable hood.

And one of the first science fiction stories must be Solomon's flying carpet. King Solomon placed his choice possession and his prettiest wives and concubines on the magic carpet and away they flew. The only trouble was that there was no means of warding off rain or intense rays of the sun. But King Solomon solved this dilemma by the simple expedient of ordering a canopy of singing blackbirds. The birds kept the rain and sun away, even as they twittered and moved at the carpet's terrific pace. Ultimately Solomon solidified the blackbirds into a permanent covering for his flying carpet.

(*Black* endures in words and phrases such as blackbirder, captain of a slave ship; the blackberry plant; Black Rock desert, in Nevada; Black Rood of Scotland, a cross in the form of a casket, believed to have been brought to Scotland by Margaret, Queen of Malcolm III; and Black Saturday, a violent story in Scotland which fell on August 4, 1621. There are the Black Sea; black wad, an ore of manganese; Black Walnut, the tree; Black River, a river in Alabama; and the Black Watch, famous Scottish regiment in the first World War. We still have blacksnake; black-water fever; blackmail; the blackberry lily; the blackbuck, a small deer; the Blackfeet Indians; the blackfish; many black-guards; blackhorse, also a fish; blackleg, a cattle disease; blacklisting, which came so tragically during the late Senator McCarthy's sadistic tenure; Blackpool, the English town; and the word *Black* is the first portion of several American towns, such as Blackstone, Blacksburg, and Black Mountain.)

If blackbirds were for entertainment, peacock pie was an extreme delicacy. Most moderns rightfully construe the peacock as a filthy bird; but during the Middle Ages, peacock pie with the bird's head and tail protruding from the crust, was a prime gourmet dish among England's nobles. In popular parlance any peafowl is called a peacock; but, strictly speaking, the male only is the peacock. The young are known as peachicks. (In this connection, *pea* is derived through Anglo-Saxon from the Latin *payo*, the scientific name of the genus to which the peacock belongs. The peacock started as a native of India and Ceylon and it is found there yet. It is believed that the Macedonians took the first peacocks to Europe at the time Alexander the Great invaded and conquered India. The throne of Iran (Persia) is known as the Peacock Throne. The original peacock throne was constructed at Delphi for Shah Jahan in 1628-1635. It consisted of twelve pillars, each bearing gem-encrusted peacocks, and in 1719 the throne was removed to Persia by Nadir.

Despite the lingering myth, the true tail of the peacock is comparatively short, and it seldom ever attains twenty inches in length. The magnificent train for which the peafowl is heralded does not represent the tail. Actually, it is composed of unduly elongated feathers which grow on the lower part of the back,

136

above the tail, but extending far beyond the tail. Ornithologists call the long train feathers "tail-coverts." When the train feathers are erect and spread into a characteristic fan-shaped disk, the short tail is used as a support. The gorgeously-colored national bird of Guatemala has a comparatively short tail under its long train feathers.

The peafowl can make its train vibrate gracefully by jerking its real tail. The notion that train and trail are one is an old myth. In *Henry VI* Shakespeare gives this speech to Joan of Arc:

Let frantic Talbot triumph for a while,
And, like a peacock, sweep along his tail;
We'll pull his plumes and take away his train,
If Dauphin and the rest will be but rul'd."

The great Montaigne (1533-1592) wrote: "It is the foulness of thy peacock's feet which abates his ride and stoops his gloating-eyed tail." During Montaigne's time the myth was prevalent that the peacock was given hideous feet to check his pride, the buoyant pride which his marvelous plumage would inspire. It was believed that its feet were so ugly if he happened to see them he would let his train fall from unmitigated mortification and chagrin. The unromantic fact is that a peacock must keep his head erect to advance his train so that when his head is lowered, the train, of necessity, falls. But this is all sheer folk mythology. And while "proud as a peacock" is deeply-rooted, perhaps we shouldn't ascribe such elegant high-mindedness to the peacock if we knew that for purpose of copulation he is placated by the juxtaposition of two or three common barnyard hens, the same hens that lay our breakfast eggs.

What's Up, Doc?

Bugs Bunny, in the animated cartoon, made "What's up, Doc" an integral portion of this nation's jargon, and the Carthaginians found so many rabbits in what is now Spain, they gave the country the Punic name, *span* or rabbit. Obviously, *Spain* evolved from *span*.

The word *rabbit*, when used properly, is restricted to a single species, *lepus cunniculus*, of the rodent family. The native American hare belongs to this general family, and the habits of rabbits afford the best distinction between rabbits and hares. The wild species of hare exhibits some structural differences —smaller size, shorter ears, and a uniform brown color. The rabbit, as Americans know it, is of European extraction, and it was brought here from Europe in a domesticated or semi-domesticated state. While hares build nests of the most flimsy material, rabbits live underground permanently, in burrows; large colonies are often found in dry, sandy banks that are overgrown by brush.

As early as Confucius's time (551-477 B.C. and originally called Kung Chin) the Chinese were raising rabbits for sacrificial purposes, and domesticated rabbits are mentioned in the early writings of Greek and Roman scholars.

Some years ago rabbits and hares almost produced financial ruination in Australia and New Zealand. Within a period of ten years, rabbits and hares multiplied so rapidly they became the chief worry of each nation's agricultural department.

These agricultural experts estimated that seven rabbits eat as much as one sheep, and the stock of food of the continent was reduced by a fifth. Various forms of extermination were attempted, and weasels, ferrets, and mongooses were introduced down-under for the specific purpose of exterminating rabbits

138

and hares. Men trapped, shot, poisoned, and gassed rabbits for governmental bounties. Fences were ineffective at first because the rabbits learned quickly to burrow under them or to climb over, and it was determined that the weasels and the other animals imported to kill rabbits failed to distinguish between rabbits and poultry.

Higher, rabbit-proof fences were built, three feet high and sunk deeply into the ground. Such new fences were built around individual farms and around entire districts. One such fence extended for one thousand miles. But, ultimately, the Australians learned to convert a profound pest into big cash money. Rabbits were caught, and the meat was frozen until it could be exported, and the skins were sold for felt hats and items of clothing. This became an annual asset running into several million dollars.

Rabbits got such a foothold in New Zealand in 1875 that farmers considered seriously abandoning their land and moving elsewhere. When a few rabbits were caught and placed on a remote South Pacific island, they multiplied so rapidly they ate up all the vegetation, and this brought about their very own starvation.

Carrying a rabbit's foot for good luck presents an obscure origin, but ancients admired the rabbit for its enormous capacity for reproduction. The most sacred portion of the ancient's body was the part that came in contact with the earth. Footprints were mystical, and from this association of the feet with nature's most prolific animal "produced smiles among the gods." Among southern blacks of the 18th and 19th centuries "Brer Rabbit" was regarded as a supernatural animal, the wisest animal of the fields and forests, and the stories of his outwitting pursuers became legendary. The very best luck is supposed to be insured by carrying in a hip pocket one of the hind legs of a rabbit that has run through a graveyard.

"Harebrained," and not "hairbrained," is an accepted word for recklessness, skittishness, and flightiness. "Hairbrained" was used by several writers prior to 1600. However, in *Henry IV*, Shakespeare has young Henry Percy referred to as "A hare-brained Hotspur, govern'd by a spleen." Shakespeare uses "hare-brained" again in *Troilus and Cressida* to mean cowardice and timidity.

"Jack rabbit" came into popular usage because its unusually

large ears were said to resemble the ears of the jackass. And since a jackass is usually called a plain jack, in time the jackass rabbit was shortened to jack rabbit. The average jack rabbit can attain the speed of thirty-five to forty miles an hour for a considerable distance. It makes bounds from ten to fifteen feet in length when running at top speed.

There is acute danger to a rabbit or hare when a man lifts it by the ears, although lifting by the ears is a common practice. The best way to lift a rabbit and not injure it is to grasp the loose skin above the shoulders with one hand as the other hand supports the rabbit under its body.

Whether the dish is "Welsh rabbit" or "Welsh rarebit" has preempted many bull sessions and seminars. But melted cheese on toast is Welch rabbit. The *Oxford Dictionary* refers to "rarebit" as "an etymologizing alteration of "Welch rabbit." H.W. Fowler, an acknowledged authority on English grammar and diction, wrote in *Modern English Usage*: "*Welch rabbit* is amusing and right and *Welch rarebit* is stupid and wrong."

One may determine the direction a rabbit takes in snow because his tracks form a triangle in the opposite direction from which he was running. When a rabbit runs, it touches the ground with both small front feet together, and he strikes the ground with his two large hind feet apart and ahead of the front feet, thereby forming a triangle. In other words, the hind feet strike the ground or the snow, far ahead of the front feet; consequently, the two foremost tracks are not made by the front feet, as many people assume.

As is true of many animals, rabbits and hares can swim when forced into water; but their fur and skin are not impervious to water, and they will drown gradually with excess weight. The swamp rabbit of the southern marshes is a good swimmer, and many have been seen swimming back and forth across a creek or bayou to confuse and to elude the hunting dogs.

In addition to "hare-brained," American English has been expanded with idioms such as rabbit-salad (any combination of green vegetables), to rabbit foot it (to move quickly), rabbit punch (a chop delivered behind a human's neck), quick like a rabbit (intercourse completed quickly), and turning rabbit (backing off from a fight). The common phrase, "Hold with the hare and run with the hounds," seems to have appeared in print originally in 1572, in Humphrey Robert's book, *Complaint For*

Reformation. And throughout most of this century a boy who is most zealous to express his physical enthusiams would not want to date a girl who is said to have "rabbit blood in her veins."

The wise and highly vocal rabbit, or hare, appears in some of the fables ascribed to Aesop, in the writings of La Fontaine, and in the "Brer Rabbit" stories created by Joel Chandler Harris.

Many Americans, including this scrivener, think that parboiled rabbit is a prime delicacy. Apparently rabbits and hares have been eaten for many centuries, but few Americans would like rabbit as the ancient Greeks prepared it. The following poem was written as a "superior recipe" by Archestratus:

> Many are the ways and the many the recipes
> For dressing a hare—but this is the best of all—
> To place before a set of hungry guests
> A slice of roasted meat fresh from the spit,
> Hot, seasoned only with plain, simple salt,
> Not too much done. And do not you be vexed
> At seeing fresh blood trickling from the meat,
> But eat it eagerly. All other ways
> Are quite superfluous, such as cooks pour
> A lot of sticky, clamsy sauce upon it."

One thinks the Greeks had to be ravenously hungry to get down such a hideous "delicacy."

Although "mad as a hatter" encompasses several legends, reference may have been to the adder, originally. Even so, many experts lean to the established fact that the phrase means what it says. In the days when mercury was used in processing animal skins for hats, the dangerous properties of mercury were not known. Many hatters succumbed to the "shakes" from repeated handlings of mercury. It is more than likely that the phrase entered the English language from this source, and Lewis Carroll (1832-1898) and William Thackeray (1811-1863), who popularized the phrase in literature, seem to have had the mercury mad hatter in mind.

"As wild (or as mad) as a March hare" is closely allied, even if "March" and "marsh" seem closely allied in this connection. Nonetheless, the greater weight of the evidence supports "March" as the original word. Scientists of the Middle Ages supposed that rabbits underwent periods of excessive depression,

141

from eating various plants; and they believed that humans who ate the rabbit's meat succumbed to profound melancholia, also. March is the hare's favorite breeding season, and the spell of sexual need accelerates the rabbit's, or the hare's, innate aberrations. But, then again, such breeding is done in marshes where the hare finds itself bereft of protective trees and bushes. Hence, unable to hide from hunters and to copulate in peace, it goes mad.

But the late Ralph Hodgson has the last word with his poem, "The Bells of Heaven":

'Twould ring the bells of Heaven
The wildest peal for years,
If Parson lost his senses,
And people came to theirs.
And he and they together
Knelt down with angry prayers,
For tamed and shabby tigers
And dancing dogs and bears,
And wretched, blind pit ponies,
And little haunted hares.

Finally, we beg to differ from those who contend that the modern world is bereft of absolutes. One may be absolutely sure that carrots are good for the eyesight because one hardly ever sees a rabbit wearing glasses.

The Heart of the Beasts

The lion, ensign of the House of Judah, and a portion of the official name of the ruler of Ethiopia, is mentioned in the Bible more often than any other wild animal. Albeit, some of the pharoahs are said to have tamed ferocious lions into household pets. And later on, the same sort of lion was popular at King Solomon's Court. The untamed lions were kept in pits ("den" is the Biblical translation), and it was in such a pit that Darius, King of Persia, had Daniel cast. The Bible uses the lion to symbolize God's spiritual strength, but the roaring lion is likened to the devil in virtually all early literature. The devil adored the lion because it was said, "The lion seeketh whom he may destroy."

The lion, unlike many other jungle killers, is an innate killer, and he does not kill merely for food. In his native habitat the lion is the most predatory of all the killers. He will kill for food, but his preference for killing, merely for the sake of savage destruction, is equally as puissant.

According to T. H. White's translation of *The Beastiary* the lion copulates backwards. If this is true the subtle nuances seem to have eluded all the experts from Kraft-Ebbing, to Kinsey, down to Masters and Johnson.

The lion mentioned so often in the Writ appears to be the small Persian lion. But at any size, the lion is properly tagged as a killer because, along with the leopard and the tiger, it ravages with its teeth and its claws.

Lion (*leo*) was turned into Latin from a Greek root. (The beast is called *leon* in Greek.) The less ferocious lions are likely to be those with short, curly manes. The lions with longer, plain hair are the insensate killers. Experts say their courage comes from their hearts. (The British derided King Richard by calling him "Richard, yeah or nay." He was a classic example of ineptitude and vacillation until his courage on the Crusades gave

143

him a new name, Richard, the Lion-Hearted.)

Experts say Leo has four main characteristics: He adores to stand atop a mountain, and today's in-phrase, "King of the Mountain," began with a lone lion standing upon a great hill as if he were surveying his vast possessions. If he is pursued by hunters, he can smell them; but the hunters can't smell him because he garbles the spoors behind with his tail. He appears to sleep with his eyes open; and when his lioness has babies, he returns on the third day to breathe life into them. The babies, usually born in threes, are utterly still and, for all practical purposes, are dead until the father restores life.

(Some notable writers, including T. H. White, see parallels between the various threes of the lion and the threes associated with Jesus, and the lion's seeking the top of the mountain is tied to Jesus's sojourn in the wilderness. This not only makes a travesty of coincidence, but, in this writer's mind, is prodigious bosh.)

The lion observes the rules of health as zealously as the mule. A finicky eater, he prefers abject hunger to eating yesterday's leftovers. When he is sick, he sees a monkey because he thinks eating a monkey will make him well again. He is highly susceptible to bites from poisonous snakes, and he fears the bite of the white snake, with particular awe.

The tiger, of the cat family, is next to the lion in size. The longest specimens are from three or four feet high, and from fifteen to eighteen feet in length, counting its tail. In relationship to its eyes, ears, head, whiskers, and tail the tiger is simply a jungle cat. Obviously, the tiger is slenderer and more agile and active than the lion. Its fur is a bright glowing yellow, and it is banded beautifully with immense black stripes.

The tiger is restricted to the jungles of Asia, but he roams as far west as the Caspian Sea, and as far north as the southern borders of Siberia.

It attains its greatest height and ferocity in the province of Bengal, and the Bengal tiger has the grace of a ballet dancer. It hides in thickets by day and it comes out after dark to forage. Unlike the panther and leopard, the tiger does not climb trees. But neither does it hesitate to attack a herd of cattle, and it is so strong and agile it can throw a buffalo or a small ox across its back and run with this heavy burden.

Like the old-time door-to-door huckster, the tiger hangs

144

around the fringes of villages, especially to carry away small children. Because of this and other depredations, India pays a large bounty for tigers, and the city of Singapore pays a special award to those who bring in a tiger's ears. Nonetheless, tiger hunting was a compelling "sport" with the British when that nation had charge of India. On these hunts, white men rode elephants and the hunters carried high-powered rifles into regions infested with tigers. Natives, in the manner of skirmishers, went ahead of the hunters to beat the brush with spears and to roust out the tigers.

Another tiger catching ruse was the pitfall, a deep, bottle-shaped hole covered with flimsy bamboo onto which a young goat was tied. The bleating of the kid excited the tiger, and he fell into the hole. A strong net was placed against the walls of the hole, and on ground level were what passed for drawstrings.

The Tigris, named for the tiger, is a fairly famous river of West Africa, rising near the Euphrates; and, figuratively, the tiger has enduring expression to mean a strong man or a sugar daddy. In many games of poker a tiger is the lowest hand a player can hold, and this came originally from faro because the player must bluff to win, and perforce "has a tiger by the tail."

As William Blake exhorted:

Tiger, tiger! burning bright
In the forests of the night.
What immortal hand or eye
Could frame thy fearful symmetry.
When the stars threw down their spears,
And water'd heaven with their tears
Did he smile his work to see?
Did he who made the Lamb make thee?

The tiger's name developed from his lethal and amazing agility. Among the Greeks and Persians an arrow was called "tigris," and he is a feline, the same as Leo. He is notable for his courage and rapidity of motion.

If, during the tiger's absence, someone steals one of its babies, it gives immediate pursuit, with the cunning and accuracy of a bloodhound. And if the kidnapper is on a horse, the grown tiger will overtake the man and destroy him. However, experts say that if the man being pursued will hold

145

down a glass ball, the tiger is enthralled at seeing its own reflection, and will stop the chase. It seems that the tiger believes its own reflection in the glass is the missing baby. When the tiger understands it has been victimized by a ruse, it takes up the chase with prodigious speed and venom. If the rider drops a second glass ball, the tiger doesn't seem to remember being taken in by the same subterfuge. She wraps herself around the glass ball, curls herself around the reflection, and lies precisely as if she is about to suckle her baby. Deceived by her malicious zeal, she loses her revenge and her baby.

The pard, or leopard, is multicolored, extremely fast and extremely fond of bloodshed. "Leo pards," according to the ancients, were born via the illicit sex of a lioness and a pard. Pliny says that the lion lies with the female pard, or the male pard with the lioness and in either case their offspring are inferior. Early explorers thought the pard was a cross between a lion and a panther. The leopard was a familiar predator in the Old Testament days, especially in the thick forests of Lebanon, where it was an active menace to grazing flocks. It is one of the animals Isaiah mentions in his word picture of peace. It was Jeremiah who asked the question: "Can the leopard change its spots?" (The late Thomas Dixon appropriated and twisted this image to fit as a title to *The Leopard's Spots*, one of his incredibly racist novels.) Even though matrimony, as such, is unknown in the jungle, the leopard may be said to be a bona fide bastard.

Another beast, the panther, is also of variegated color. It is a most beautiful animal, and compared to the lion and the tiger it is permeated with kindness. The ancients said the panther's only fear was of dragons, even if no one seems able to explain how this was discerned. When a panther has filled his belly with food, he hides in his own den to go into a profound sleep. At the end of three days it awakens and emits a thunderous belch, and following this mighty belch his mouth exudes an exceedingly sweet smell, an odor that has been compared to spice many times. Other animals follow him, almost as the children of Hamelin followed the Pied Piper, because of the enchantment of this smell.

Experts say female panthers have babies in threes, but only once. When the cubs have struck root in their mother's womb, they become impatient. Thus, they tear the mother's womb as if

146

it is an obstruction. The mother's womb is torn so badly she cannot bear again. (Pliny, in his immortal *Natural History*, says many animals with long, strong claws are limited to one litter because these strong claws tear up the mother's womb.)

Lincus, the lynx, obtained his name because of his wolfian qualities. It has the pard's spots on its back, and its urine is said to harden into the precious stone called Ligutius. (Ligarius is simply lync-uruis, as common as lynx piss.) and When they have urinated, they cover the urine as rapidly as possible with sand, and this solidifies into the valuable stone. Ancients believed this was done to try to hide from a man a precious stone. Be that as it may, Pliny says lynxes have only one litter of their young.

These beasts have supplied us with words such as lion-hearted; mean as a hurt lion; tiger, or virile man, and in certain games of poker, the lowest hand one may have; tiger's eye, cheap whiskey, and, perhaps, reinforced by the term from the faro wheel; tiger meat, beefsteak; tigersweat, also cheap alcohol; panther or panther urine, potent, cheap whiskey; and pard, now a friend but used for so-called illicit sex in the 19th century.

The wolf has been a vicious predator since history was first recorded. It was among the meanest known animals of prey in the Holy Land and elsewhere. The shepherd's prime job was to protect his flock from wolves. The savagery and lust of the word are contained in Old Testament analogies thirty times. Jesus warned against "false prophets which come to thee in sheep's clothing, but inwardly are ravening wolves." (Matthew 7:15) To emphasize the dangers his disciples would encounter, Jesus admonished: "I send you forth as lambs among wolves." This appears in Luke and the meaning was palpably clear to the disciples. For Jesus and his close companions were well acquainted with wolves.

In whatever guise the parable now appears "to cry wolf," ("Wolf, wolf") goes back to Aesop's story of the shepherd boy. And it was Terrence who came up with "I have got a wolf by the tail." (The same expression is used today in allusion to a "bear by the tail," chiefly, because modern society is infinitely more aware of bears than of wolves. John Lyly (1554-1606) gave parlous economic the deathless metaphor that it is a hard winter when one wolf eats another wolf.

Thomas Jefferson got into the wolf act with: "It is better to keep the wolf out of the fold than to trust to drawing his teeth and talons after he shall have entered." (From *Notes on Virginia*.) But it was Ann Rowell, composer of "Who's Afraid of the Big Bad Wolf," for the Walt Disney movie, *Three Little Pigs* (1938) who brought infamous recognition of the wolf the world over.

Wolf endures in daily conversations, such as: an aggressive male and a male homosexual seducer; a man whose main efforts are expended chasing after women (along about 1940 *wolf*, as a seducer of women lost its opprobrious connotations, certainly on campuses, and for several years it was almost an encomium).

A "wolf" was a young man who manifested the same aggressive tendencies, and although "wolfless" was heard now and then, "wolf" meant either sex. A "wolf whistle" was established originally by boys who stood in front of a drug store to stare at and to whistle at pretty girls. This whistle had all of the implications of astonishment and lust and incredulity.

No Bag Limit

The Bible contains references to around forty-six birds, but there is no mention of the wren, even if the tiny bird (then spelled brid) used to be viable in England's Christmas celebration. When a wren was caught it was paraded around town in a special "wrenhouse," a miniature painted with doors and windows to resemble a real home. In many parts of the British Isles the wren was "king of all the birds" for the ensuing twelve months. He was greater than the eagle because a wren had been seen riding a soaring eagle's back. Hence, the tiny warbler had gone higher into the hemisphere than any other bird.

The Druids are said to have made their prophecies by listening carefully to the wren's notes, but in some portions of Europe it was caught and killed because its singing is said to have revealed the hiding place of St. Stephen. There is this ancient couplet:

The wren, the king of all the birds,
Was caught on St. Stephen's Day in the furze.*

The wren was a hero in England, a blackguard in Ireland, simultaneously. During one of the rebellions in the north, the Irish had the sleeping British forces completely surrounded, but the English soldiers were awakened and alerted by the pecking of the wrens on British military drums.

On the Isle of Man is the old legend that the siren whose singing lured sailors to their death changed into a wren, immediately afterward, and flew away to elude captivity.

Usually when a wren was killed, for any reason, the feathers

*A small evergreen.

were retained as a talisman or charm. Sometimes the feathers were nailed, horseshoe-like, to the front door.

The kite, a migratory bird which does appear in the Bible, resembles the hawk. Although it is (or was) a magnificent bird and a magnificent flyer, it fed on carion and the Hebrews denounced it as "unclean." This bird is responsible for today's paper kite.

And the lammergeier seems to be the "ossifrage" mentioned in Deuteronomy. It is the largest of the vultures, with a wing spread up to nine feet. These and other vultures became symbols in much heraldry in medieval times.

Ancient legends gave the mythical phoenix to Christianity as a symbol for the resurrection. This made-up bird was described as being incredibly beautiful and it had a life span of five hundred years. At the end of five hundred years it set fire to its nest and it was consumed in the flames, only to emerge from the ashes to commence another five hundred year cycle. (Some scholars think Job was referring to the phoenix with the word translated as "sand" (Job 29:18).

In choosing a bird to represent the lowliest of creatures, Jesus seized upon the sparrow. "Are not two sparrows sold for a farthing? And one of them shall not fall to the ground without your Father (knowing)." Apparently the Biblical sparrow was as gregarious as his 1979 descendants.

The hoopee, with beautiful reddish feathers which expanded when it was alarmed, was ten inches long and was known to the Hebrews prior to the Exodus.

The Bible also mentions the ibis, sacred to Thoth, the Egyptian god of learning. It, too, was familiar to the Jews before the Exodus, and it was a common sight in the papyrus in which the baby Moses was hidden. There were allusions to the stork, but the stork as a bringer of babies probably appeared originally in Germanic countries. The Hebrew word for stork means "kindly one," or "loyal one." Many times storks are seen actually carrying the old and feeble. Before the migratory habits of birds were understood, ancients, including Aristotle, believed the autumnal disappearance of the stork was ascribable to the bird's hibernating in mud or in a cave. Too, storks frequented marshlands, and it was believed that the souls of unborn children waited in such watery places. When a German mother had a baby, it was told she had to remain in bed a few days

150

after the delivery of the infant because the stork had bitten her leg. And today it is exhilarating to see a stork, tall and graceful, its white plumage set off by its black wing quills, with its red beak and legs, as it stands upon one leg atop a chimney.

The chicken seems to be one of the oldest of the domesticated animals, and the bulbul, a sweet singer, was kept in cages by the Hebrews to sing. These bulbul cages were inside the home, much as canary cages are today.

The dove is likely the most familiar bird in the writ. All four gospels speak of the Spirit of God "descending like a dove."

The Biblical bee eater actually subsisted chiefly on a diet of bees. A close relative of the kingfisher, but smaller, it had a most unusual digestive system, one that made swallowing bees fairly rudimentary.

The osprey, spelled "ospray" in Leviticus, is a large fish hawk. An incredibly adroit diver, and possessed of brilliant eyesight, the osprey dives for a fish from a great height, and often after the dive it disappears beneath the surface of the water, only to bob up with a fish in its mouth.

The mockingbird, known for its powers of mimicry, is a native of the southern states in America. In summer months many southern people have felt that they had their very own mockingbird-in-residence, and many construe their mockingbird as the feudal lord construed his private minstrel for troubadour. Honest men swear that their live-in mockingbird reserves his most derisive sarcasm for the early mornings on which they have terrible hangovers or when they have lost money playing poker.

From a distance, and hidden from the human sufferer, the mockingbird seems to sing, "O, my head. O, my aching back." And after one has spent an unsuccessful night at the card table, he jeers the loser with the maddeningly repetitive sounds of "Sixes and sevens, sixes and sevens."

And the same in-residence status is enjoyed today by many woodpeckers. Unlike most of the other birds, which have four toes, the woodpecker is two-toed. Perhaps, it is being two-footed that enables the woodpecker to maintain such amazing balance as he uses a tree or power pole for his own rapid Morse code. Actually, his pecking is extremely diverse. Sometimes he sounds as if he is drilling a tooth for a hippopotamus, and again he is playing a drum for rapid march. And when he attacks metal it is as if all the glockenspiels extant are going simultaneously.

151

The woodpecker is among the most adroit of the feathered logicians. Quite often, downy and hairy woodpeckers excavate special holes in dead stumps and limbs in the fall to use as bedrooms and storm shelters during the harsh winter months.

The cock, or rooster, has fallen upon such parlous times he almost seems up for grabs by bounty hunters. One usually thinks of feckless St. Peter denying his Savior "before the cock crows thrice." In the Bible and in other literature the cock is mentioned most often as crowing an hour or two before dawn. And in ancient times the cockcrow was the third watch. (In his final thoughts Socrates remembered that he owed a cock to Aesculapius.)

Undoubtedly the early farmers, those who used the first plows in the Bronze age, considered the rooster an alarm clock. And for a long time he had similar, if unofficial, status as an alarm clock in insular and small-town America. Anyone who has ever seen a rooster at dawn, strutting with the confident aplomb of a drum major, his red comb and crest flying as the flag flew at Concord Bridge in Emerson's old poem, knows that the rooster really thought his raucous bugle calls scourged the laggard sun into putting on his yellow overalls and commencing the day's skyland occupations.

Many men, honest if irascible, ascribe the rooster's downfall to the chicken salad served up at endless missionary society meetings. In the rural and small-town south, roosters were always sacrificed for chicken salad on the theory that it was hazardous to kill a fat hen that might prove to be an excellent layer of eggs. Irascible men said "sainted" women killed roosters because the audacious and rapacious rooster would express his physical enthusiasm with a hen right out in open, on the front lawn, even on the church lawn, or wherever righteous women were collected. And when chicken salad, made from the meat of a rooster, was served at the various literary and civic clubs manned by women, the rancorous men put a pox on all the women's organizations.

(Bob House, former chancellor of the University of North Carolina, said he ate so much chicken salad at various church meetings when he was a boy in Halifax County, N.C., that he never sees the stuff today without having, simultaneously, a conviction of original sin.)

Shakespeare mentions the cock at least twice, in *Richard III* and in *Hamlet*, respectively:

The early village cock
Hath twice done salutation the morn."

and

The cock, that is the trumpet to the morn,
Doth with his lofty and shrill-sounding throat
Awake the god of the day.

In her novel *Adam Bede*, George Eliot (nee Mary Ann Evans) wrote: "He was like a cock who thought the sun had risen to hear him crow."

Delaware is called the Blue Hen State because Captain Jonathan Caldwell, a soldier in the Continental army, was enamored of gamecocks, and his military company always carried a few as mascots. These cocks were celebrated particularly in Kent County, and they were said to be the offspring of a renowned hen. When the fame, or infamy, of Caldwell's cocks spread throughout the Continental Army, the Delaware troops became known as the Blue Hen's Chickens; and in time Delaware was tagged the "Blue Hen State." Caldwell always insisted no cock could be truly game unless his mother was a blue hen.

Perhaps the ultimate apostasy came during the summer of 1978 when the tobacco town of Wilson, N.C., removed from the top of a public building a rooster that had crowed in breakfast for thousands of Wilsonians across the years. So, wave to the rooster tenderly all who have known the exhilaration of skinny-dipping or the ache of a stone bruise. For a long time, roosters owned the town, which they leased to mortals. Each morning a rooster seemed to crow out in graveled tenor that he had assembled a spanking new day from fragments of nocturnal clouds and mists. His swashbuckling halloo turned on every light in town. But his guttural exhortations seemed to contain admonitions and injunctions. He had made the day and he had set it in motion, and mere mortals must handle it delicately, suck it down to its last drop of sweetness.

It is just possible that the pitifully few remaining roosters are awaiting Dr. Kinsey's reports on them. For if he is antiquated in the solar age, here and there he still cries out the glory and grandeur of a May morning as if he were blowing a trumpet to

153

herald the President. And, although the sounds become weaker and infinitely more sporadic, they do part the last folds of semi-darkness as they usher in the day. And for those of us who were raised in backyards, in concert with real animals and not toy animals, it's really heartwarming that a few alarm clocks in royal scarlet sing in sunlight as if they had put their coat of arms to eternal music.

Comparing a chicken to a rooster is comparable to pitting Blondie against Dempsey, in his prime. And intellectually the comparison is akin to Simple Simon and Albert Einstein. Albeit, in the south's provincial era, chickens almost induced a parallel to the range wars in the old sagebrush country. Long before deep freezers in refrigerators, long before frozen foods, practically all small-town southern people kept chickens in a chicken lot in their backyards. However, the wire enclosure impeded a chicken about as much as the Maginot Line impeded the Nazis in World War II.

Every vegetable gardener said his neighbor's chickens obtained free board in his garden. These depredations turned some antisocial men against chickens so rancorously they wouldn't permit fried chicken on their dinner tables, not even when the preacher dined there. A few militant defenders of gardens shot chickens with fatback and hard beans. And a few, after posting their precious tomatoes and butterbeans, shot to kill. Such men tossed the chicken's carcass onto the owner's lawn, the same way a hit man in Chicago's palmy days delivered the stiff to his former employer.

Some men baited fishing hooks with corn, and there was a note attached to the fishing line. The idiotic chicken would swallow the grain of corn and then blunder around the neighborhood so every literate person could read the tag on the line: "I Am A Bad Chicken And I Am A Thief. I Belong To Mr. George Entwhistle, 110 Magnolia Street, But I Rummage In Mr. Smith's Garden."

In days before frozen foods and deep freezers, housewives ordered frying size chickens from a grocery store. Every grocery store had a delivery wagon, or truck, and the driver put the frying size chickens in a coop in the backyard of the lady who ordered them. Most housewives bought three or four at a time; and, of course, they had to kill the chickens, usually by wringing the necks, and then they had to pick off the feathers in scalding water.

154

Killing chickens was a bit cannibalistic for many young women who had been married only a short time. So, most of these women would give a boy in the neighborhood a nickel to kill a chicken. My older brother and his best friend developed a small-time racket, by preying upon the sensibilities of young married women.

When they needed a nickel, they would steal to the coop and let a fryer out. If they apprehended the fryer on the ground, they got five cents, but if the fool chicken took refuge in a tree, they charged the gullible young woman a dime to ensnare the bird.

One day when a circus, or something of the sort, was coming to Oxford, my brother and his co-conspirator let out five neighborhood fryers before school.

When my brother walked into his seventh grade homeroom, the teacher remarked that his hands were dirty. "I know it," he replied, "but I have been catching chickens all the morning." She answered, "I don't see how catching chickens could make your hands so dirty."

"But, Miss Allen," he said amid a put-upon look, "they were all black chickens."

The cackle of a hen after she lays an egg is an inherited hangover from the wild fowls of India and the Malay Peninsula. Scientists say these wild fowls were the progenitors of today's domestic hen. These birds cross easily with common barnyard chickens, and, indeed, the rooster's crow resembles that of a young leghorn rooster. Many of the eggs sold in India are laid by domesticated jungle fowls, and in their wild state they usually run in small flocks of from six to eight. One cock always accompanies the six or eight hens. When a hen is ready to lay, she steals away from the flock, lays her egg in a concealed nest; and then she cackles to attract the attention of her flock that has wandered away. In response, all the cocks in the neighborhood begin to crow, and thus the lost hen recognizes her mate. The characteristic of cackling has never been bred out of domestic chickens. Even in their current domestic condition, it is not unusual for the roosters in a barnyard to begin a clamor of crowing when the hen cackles. This is just about the only satisfactory reason to explain why a chicken violates the fundamental law of safety by cackling when she lays an egg.

For a long time a minor argument ensued over whether the

mother of the chick is the hen that lays the egg or the hen that hatches it. But the fact that a hen incubates an egg she did not lay gives her no blood relationship to the chick. A hen that incubates an egg laid by another is merely a temporary foster parent. The term "mother" usually indicates actual parentage with animals, but most people who eat eggs regard the hen that incubates as the mother, irrespective of the source of the egg.

But there is considerable validity to one old wives' tale: Washing eggs does cause them to spoil much earlier, according to rural people. The shells of eggs are covered with a natural mucilaginous coating that usually delays the entrance of germs into the interior. Washing eggs softens or removes this viscid coating, thus diminishing the quality of eggs and hastening their deterioration. Clean unwashed eggs fetch the highest price and the Department of Agriculture advises poultrymen against washing eggs before taking them to market.

Why a chicken is called a *biddy* is an etymological mystery. One authority suggests that it may be derived from *chickabiddy*, the instinctive sound adapted to calling chickens. Other writers have attempted to connect *biddy* with the Gaelic *bideah*, meaning "very small." Yet another source believes the word is related to *Biddy*, which in the United States used to be applied to a female domestic, especially an Irish girl. In this connection the name must be a corruption of Bridget. *Biddy* was used by Shakespeare in *Twelfth Night*. Sir Toby says to Molvolio, "Why how now, my bawcock! how dost thou chuck. . .Ay, Biddy come with me."

Bawcock is a corruption of the French *beau coq*, meaning a fine cock, and *chuck*, like *cluck*, is probably of onomatopoeic origin, having been suggested by the noise made by a hen when calling her chicks; although, of course, it may be a modification of *chick*. In Shakespeare's era it was a term of endearment. And the association of *bawcock, chuck*, and *Biddy* in *Twelfth Night* shows clearly that the last alluded to a fowl.

"Mother Carey's chickens," a corruption of *Mater Cara*, used to be a commonplace nickname among sailors for stormy petrels. The phrase seems to have originated with sailors from the Levant (Turkey, Syria, Lebanon, and Israel). Ancient sailors danced with glee when stormy petrels wheeled and dipped near their ships. For dear Mother Mary had sent the "chickens" as a sign that a safe harbor was close at hand. This nickname was applied by sailors to any snow at sea. The webfooted stormy petrel is a close cousin to the albatross, and "stormy" was appended because this bird was seen much more often when the elements at sea were rough or stormy.

"The birds and the bees" are coupled usually when a parent tells a child about sex and procreation. The swarm of bees is provided by a queen that remains totally ignorant of Abraham Lincoln's Emancipation Proclamation. The workers, who live around six weeks during the busy, or creative, season, gather and store honey and wax, clean up and protect the surroundings, and wait upon the queen; and no minimum wage and hour law has been explained to any queen bee.

The average bee is intelligent but not brilliant. Intellectually he stands between a smart sheep and a second rate man. There used to be a belief that bees hate doleful people, people whose faces are so long on a rare day a barber would charge them ten bucks to shave it. In the horse and buggy era they did their best to disperse mourners at funerals because they cannot stand tears, real or crocodile, when the sun is a yellow haired girl playing hopscotch.

Many rural people said everyone should wear a black veil to a funeral; and although bees lay-in-waiting for a funeral, they could not do much damage to a face heavily veiled. A few rural people said a smart bee could tell when a mourner was putting on an act. They said that the person stung was an aspiring legatee whose probate chances were not particularly viable. Thus, a wise and sham-hating bee gave the rural Sarah Bernhart something to cry about.

The bee, the smallest of the "domestic animals," was common in Egypt as far back as 4000 B.C. Honey was used for embalming since it was the least expensive ingredient. The bee's food value was heralded long ago, and the Hebrews seem to have taken their knowledge of beekeeping with them when they left Egypt. Ezekiel may not have seen a flying saucer, as the TV show UFO implies, but he listed honey as one of Judah's prime exports. Evidence that the terror of an assault by angry bees was well established, and the fact is stated in Deuteronomy and again in Psalms. In both references attacks by armed enemies are likened to an attack by a swarm of bees.

Perhaps, because the Egyptians used honey for embalming, bees love to attend funerals, and they like nothing so well as

157

getting under the widow's black veil. This, of course, accounts for the fact that many widows at the graveside carry on as if their late husbands had allowed all of their life insurance to expire.

After the discontinuation of the use of the veil and following the advent of closed automobiles, bees concentrated more on front porch columns that had a little dry rot inside. They bit hell out of people with wanton prodigality. And even if the AMA Journal has not taken official cognizance of the fact, the only cure for a bee sting is a dab of wet chewing tobacco. There used to be a scandalous whisper that the healing prowess of chewing tobacco was advanced by J. B. Duke and R. J. Reynolds. Actually, wet tobacco was the lone anodyne long before Duke and Reynolds were born. But the worse contribution of the bees is what it has done to our mother tongue. And the madder a wife is at her husband, the more likely she is to embroider him with "honey this, and honey that." This whole preposterous charade is ascribed to the bee because *honey* was the initial form of fradulent endearment. After the lips are rolling in honey, it is a simple step to proceed to even more grandiose endearments.

The honeybee is not indigenous in America, and the first handful was brought over from England to Massachusetts by some nut between 1738-1740. The Indians hated bees and called them "the white man's fly." But by 1800 honeybees had crossed the Mississippi, and Stephen Austin, writing in his journal in Texas in 1821, says he obtained a gallon and a half of delicious honey from a single tree.

However fanciful the bee at the funeral may sound, there is no question that throughout most of the 19th century there was the profound rural belief that if a member of the human family died, the bees had to be told immediately or they would swarm and leave. The swarms had to be draped with black crepe and a young girl went about the swarms singing, usually improvising, the news of a death in the human family.

In 1858 in "Telling the Bees," John Greenleaf Whittier turned this bucolic legend into first class poetry. While the whole poem is too long to quote, it begins and ends with these stanzas:

Here is the place; right over the hill
Runs the path I took;

158

You can see the gap in the old wall still,
And the stepping-stones in the shallow brook.

Whittier tells of a death in the human family. Her dog is silent and the "old man" (the husband, perhaps) sits with his cane to his chin, as the chore girl sings the sad tidings:

And the song she was singing ever since
In my ear sounds on,—
'Stay at home pretty bees, fly not hence!
Mistress Mary is dead and gone.'

Samuel Johnson, meaning wax and honey, said the bee supplies mankind his two most essential elements, light and sweetness.

And in a celebrated passage in *Henry V*, Shakespeare uses the bee to tell how men read their own customs into nature, rather than the other way around. Then men find confirmation for them in "the natural order." For centuries people simply assumed that the principal figure in a beehive was a king, a ruler, and the hive was used to substantiate the "natural" order of a monarchy:

For so work the honey bees,
Creatures that by a rule in nature teach
The act of order to a peopled kingdom.
They have a king and officers of sorts;
Where some, like magistrates, correct at home,
Others, like merchants, venture trade abroad,
Others, like soldiers, armed in their stings,
Make boot upon the summer's velvet buds;
Which pillage they with merry march bring home
To the tent royal of their emperor;
Who, busied in his majesty, surveys
The singing masons building roofs of gold.
The civil citizens kneading up the honey.
The poor mechanic porters crowding in
Their heavy burdens at his narrow gate,
The sad-eyes justice with his surly hum,
Delivering o'er to executors pale
The lazy, fawning drone.

Isaac Watts, the hymn writer, in "Divine Songs For Children," wrote:

> How doth the busy little bee
> Improving each shining hour;
> And gather honey all the day
> From every opening flower.

Historians agree it was Watts's little ditty that prompted Lewis Carroll to write:

> How doth the little crocodile
> Improve his shining tail,
> And pour the waters of the Nile
> On every golden scale.

It was the relatively obscure David Moir, in his work of 1824, *The Life of Mansie Waugh*, who furnished the language with the irrepressible phrase, "A bee in his bonnet." Actually Herrick, the parson-poet, and Sir Walter Scott had said the same thing before Moir, although the phrase has become Moir's identical twin.

Robert Bridges (1844-1930), the British poet laureate, seems to have given Shakespeare's passage in *Henry V* a mild jolt with:

> For among Bees and Ants are social systems found
> so complex and well-order'd as to invite offhand
> a pleasant fable enough: that once upon a time
> or ever a man were born to rob their honeypots,
> Bees were fully endow'd with reason and only lost it
> by ordering so their life as to dispense with it;
> whereby it pined away and perish'd of disuse.

Perhaps, Emily Dickinson, the New England nun, saw a little more deeply:

> His labor is a chant,
> His idleness a tune;
> Oh, for a bee's experience
> Of clovers and of moon.

160

The term "as the crow flies," meaning in a straight direction, is a misnomer. Crows zig and zag, but bees fly in a straight line, and in many localities the shortest distance between two points is called the *beeline.* Indeed, the Beeline Highway connects Kansas City, Missouri, and Canon City, Colorado; and it is the shortest ground route between these two points.

Insofar as one knows bees have never put on a public demonstration against that egregious misnomer, "as the crow flies," nor have they expressed the indignation allegedly expressed by a gang of monkeys against Dayton, Tennessee. But Robert Burns may have neglected a vital talent in his celebrated poem, "To A Louse." ("Man's inhumanity to man makes thousands mourn.") Extremely little has been written from the rat's standpoint.

Of course, a few mice have always thought Robert Browning was a little heavy handed in his celebrated narrative, "The Pied Piper." In leading all of ancient Hamelin's rats to total extinction, the Pied Piper and Browning may have destroyed some capital musicians.

During the 1930's it was proven beyond all peradventure that mice can sing. There was a sweetly singing mouse in Lincoln, Illinois, that continued to slip into the canary cage in the home of Richard P. Steiner to sing duets with Steiner's canary.

Many laymen thought they smelled a dead rat, and several scientists said Steiner had confused an obstruction in his mouse's bronchial tubes with singing. In a word, the so-called singing is merely a whistling sound made by mice that have caught cold.

Nay, not so, declared the late Dr. Roy Chapman Andrews, director of the American Museum of Natural History. Dr. Andrews said he heard several singing mice.

To settle the argument, as well as to amplify American cultural tastes, a national radio hookup emanated from Lincoln, Illinois, with Steiner's mouse singing solos. (Inexplicably, he did not use "Three Blind Mice" for his encore.) Of course, many auditors said they smelled a rat, but many, many others thought the mouse sang as sweetly and truly as any canary they had ever heard. Although this concert came after Walt Disney's Mickey Mouse, the tremors and implications were audible and visible in Hollywood.

In American English the kibitzer is the officious oaf who "coffee-houses" a variety of games. He never plays these games,

161

but he exudes expert knowledge on how something should have been played after a player has erred. Nonetheless, kibitzer is derived through Yiddish from the colloquial German word, "Keibitz," the name the Old World gave to the lapwing, peewit, and green plover.

The lapwing attained immortality in Robert Burns's "Flow Gently Sweet Afton."

> Thou green-crested lapwing, Thou screaming forbare,
> Disturb not, I charge you, my slumbering fair.

This bird not only hangs around fields to supervise farmers at work, but he emits a shrill cry at the approach of any hunters. It was for this reason that card players in the 16th century coined "kibitzer" as a synonym for the officious and meddlesome person. Experts say that "kibitz" was imitative in origin and that it was suggested by the bird's ominous cry of alarm as it functioned as a gunless sentinel.

While the kibitz watches out for predatory hunters, the venerable scarecrow watches out for fields, birds, and the universe. Historians say the scarecrow's initial function was as a religious symbol, and not since Hannibal crossed the Alps with elephants has a scarecrow frightened any birds. It is the scarecrow's hand-me-down finery, his clothing, that frightens birds away via the unpleasant odors of the battered raiment.

At first his ridiculous, menacing stance may frighten some fledgling crows, but this passes as old crows fly to the man and use his crossed arms for a urinal. Inspired by this gesture the small crows come close enough to sniff out the scarecrow; and if the odor is not appallingly offensive, they fly and sing around, playing the feathered equivalent of "Here We Go Round the Mulberry Bush," singing it in crow idioms, of course.

The scarecrow is especially pathetic in autumn as he guards fields as denuded as a picked chicken. He reminds one of a sentinel still on duty when the war is over, a picket the brass forgot to call in. He stands there all dressed up in his shambles of Sunday-go-meeting best with absolutely no place to go. The woodpeckers bore holes in his ears for trinkets he will never wear.

Throughout his American history the scarecrow is to the wise crow what the uneven freight rates used to be to Southern politicians. The wise crow may protect his vocal chords in autumn, but come luscious spring and planting time he mounts the battlements as an impassioned Cole Blease or Tom Watson. The wise crow that needs a uniting issue can always thunder at and about the scarecrow. This is peculiar because the average crow, the run-of-the-mill voter, has known of the scarecrow's impotence since Cotton Ed Smith was a third grader. But just let the old fury fly from the top crow's throat, and his constituents profess to see the world's evil embodied in the delapidated scarecrow.

The magpie flies the way poets sing, and the mockingbird is Mencken with feathers, but when the crow leader starts whistling the ornithological equivalent of "Way Down Yonder In the Corn Field," all his followers chant affirmative hosannas. But to leave politics where they belong, one knows that old man winter will try to strip the ancient scarecrow and leave him naked in snow and sleet. A seasonal avalanche may bury his ancient carcass in drifted snow. And some irate, luckless hunter will shoot him in the back, just to say he has shot something. The lone hound, improvising a rabbit hunt, and seeming to run on snowshoes, will not give the scarecrow the time of day. And the scarecrow, that tragic comedian, stands out against the toppling darkness of winter as a humpback, immobile Don Quixote, shorn even of a windmill to menace or to pursue.

Off to one side from the birds, there must be a special place reserved for the cardinal, truly the aristocrat of the feathered creatures. The cardinal is the state bird in North Carolina, Illinois, and, perhaps, elsewhere. While his singing has never created any visible envy on Parnassus, he is the cavalier of the woodlands. North Carolinians used to love to boast, "First at Bethel, farthest at Gettysburg, and last at Appomattox." With equal justification the cardinal may boast: First in faithfulness, first in courage, first in durability, and first in dignified reserve.

For him all weather is good weather, and he will flash his magnificent redness amid snowdrifts as quickly and as easily as through summertime's erotic forests of enchanting greenery. He is likely the most persnickity and fastidious of all birds in his diet; and although he is not a gregarious bird, he will do continuous honor to the premises of the man who plants sunflower seeds.

George Whetsone, writing in 1578, was not thinking of the

163

cardinal, if indeed, he knew the cardinal at all, in his famous crack, "Byrds of a fether, best fly together." Robert Burton solidified the aphorism in his famous book, *Anatomy of Melancholy*: "Birds of a feather will gather together."

One will never find a cardinal leading the singing at Kiwanis, or at any other club. In the golden age of the club, he endures as the lovely antithesis of the club fellow. And unlike most of his feathered friends and remote relatives, he builds his nest for permanence. He and his mate live together like a true married pair, and this warm association does not terminate when their youngsters are capable of flight. Unless one puts a band on a cardinal's leg, it is almost impossible to tell when an old one has died and his domicile, his preserve, is inherited by another cardinal. Experts have noted that year after year the realm in the tree contains only the lord and his lady bird. Perhaps, much of his durability is ascribable to his having protective coloration throughout the year.

He eschews bird squabbles and stays away from crowds, especially crowds of excitable birds. His call seems to sound like "yea, yea, or nay, nay," especially in winter. Before the first crocus, nature's expendable skirmisher, comes to warm the frozen earth's innards with small quilts of yellow and blue, the cardinal is already sounding his clarion, his claxton, call. Some authority, perhaps, the late William Beebe, has suggested that he should have the same motto the U. S. Marines have, *Semper Fidelis*.

As aforementioned, Aristotle and many ancients thought storks and some other birds hibernated in marshes and mudholes during winter. As stated, this was before the migratory habits of birds were known. Today, this brings the interesting question: How do birds spend the winter when the grass and the plants are dead and the trees are shivering old ladies bereft of leaves? It is true that most of the birds fly south to a warmer climate. It is as Thoreau said about the wild goose: "The wild goose is more a cosmopolite than we; he breaks his fast in Canada, takes a luncheon in the Susquehanna and plumes himself for the night in a Louisiana bayou." Oliver Wendell Holmes, Sr. added: "A goose flies by a chart which the Royal Geographic Society could not improve." Many birds, such as crows and jays, lead the same existence the year around. Some of the northern robins fly a short distance to the upper South, for winter's food supply.

Conversely, the swallows and the warblers fly all the way to Central America to find a strange, exotic abode in bananas, mangoes, limes, and along the coral reefs.

With virtually every species of birds, sight is the chief sense. It is their remarkable eyes that enable them to find food and to elude their enemies. True, the owl and some of the night flyers have ears as keen as the Bionic Woman. Thus, the longer the day, the more the time to find food. Darkness is a natural enemy of most birds. This is true, especially during the long winter nights. The golden plover, of the icy north, breeds when the Arctic days are longest and the nights are short. They fly south after the breeding season, and many pass on to the tropics. While almost any bird has the sense and power to fly from the Arctic ice in winter, most of the animals stay at home, although the want of food prompts sorties near head taw.

Snakes don't charm birds in winter because they and the box turtle burrow into the ground to sleep throughout winter. Frogs and pond turtles, realizing fishes are frozen in the ice, remain immobile until springtime. (Field mice and bears desert the frigid, wild forests, and squirrels may be seen in winter on a day that is unusually warm and sunny for the season.)

All the fields with their summertime music are fallow, inglorious mute Miltons; the insects survive the winter quite well, and in almost endless ways. Many of these insects live through the winter in the adult stage, hidden in a warm retreat, and the same is true of butterflies, wasps, bees, and flies. A sudden warm winter day is a magic wand bringing the winged little creatures out of their snug retreats, and they fly around until the cold snap comes again.

Frequently, caterpillars transform to chrysalides near the end of summer, or in early autumn, and the butterflies, or moths, come out in the springtime. (The orange-tip butterfly, very small, parallels the crocus as a portion of nature's shock troops.) This beautiful butterfly flies in March and April, lays its eggs, and dies. The chrysalides remain inert, and they will fasten to the trunk of trees during the hottest portion of summer and again during the cold weather. Thus, two thirds of the life of this fragile creature are spent in sleep. Some other butterflies spend the entire winter as fully grown caterpillars, hidden in a loose cocoon. Then when springtime turns up the thermostat, these caterpillars turn into chrysalides, from which the butterflies come within a few days.

But life is a paradox. In the colder portions of the northern hemisphere there is a strange, wingless insect, the cranefly or daddy-longlegs, which reverses the normal habit of insects by living in summer as a grub or larva under decaying leaves, only to become an adult during extreme cold. It has been noted time and time again that if the sun shines brightly on an April morning, few of these strange insects are visible. But if the same afternoon turns cold, tremendous numbers come tumbling from all directions.

In America's insular eras two men might get really disputatious debating whether humankind was created by God and Adam or whether it was a product of evolution. Many folks denounced the flying-machine as an erratic, dangerous toy, and others hotly denied that tractors would ever displace mules. But on the first official day of spring, one could count, as one counted on the saints of his childhood, that fourth and fifth graders, all soaped and starched, would stand at the mandatory fifteen minute chapel break to sing:

The lilacs are in blossom,
The cherry boughs are white;
I hear a sound above me,
A twitter of delight;
It is my friend the robin,
As surely as I'm alive.
I'm very glad to see you—
Pray, when did you arrive?

This poem-song may sound naive today, even willy-nilly. But it is used to galvanize tremendous gratitude and gusto, and tender, protective custody. Children watched birds infinitely more than airplanes, and there were no jet streams leaving an indicting exclamation mark to the conquests of speed and space. This author sang the song often, amid boundless joy and rapt expectancy, and he knows several middle-aged and older men, as tough as shagbark hickory, who have, and still will, bust the noggins of any fancy-dan defamers.

The robin, or robin redbreast, of the Old World species of a small bird of the warbler clan, is a familiar New World bird of the thrush family. It was named by early American colonists for

166

the beloved redhead they had known in Europe. The robin redbreast of Eastern America is around ten inches long, or four inches longer than its European counterpart. The American robin's back is olive gray, and the head and tail are darker. The white throat is banded with black, and its breast is chestnut red. Its early return each spring, with its sweet, cheerful music, and with its destruction of pesky insects, makes it almost revered in many American homes.

"One robin doesn't make a spring" has been an irrepressible cliche for centuries; and while the robin does not seem to be mentioned in the Bible, the story of the robin and spring is ascribed to Aesop, who is supposed to have lived 620-560 B.C.; and it has been proverbial since Aristotle said, "One swallow doesn't make a spring." Many writers have lifted the phrase, in one way or another, but it goes back to Aesop's story about the man who saw a robin (or a swallow, perhaps) near the end of winter and sold his coat in the belief that spring had come. In a day or two he was the victim of a heavy, killing frost. Aristophanes used the phrase, or the essence, in a play, and it seems likely that Aesop made up the fable about the robin and his coat to illuminate and to enhance a cherished, well-established proverb.

The familiar nursery ditty, "Who Killed Cock Robin," was printed first in 1744:

Who killed Cock Robin,
'I did,' said the sparrow,
I killed Cock Robin
With my little arrow.

Some scholars think this enigmatic nursery rhyme refers to the political demise of Robert Walpole in 1742. But others believe the rhyme is much, much older, and these researchers think it is a recondite allusion to the death of Balder, the good and handsome Norse god, and the favorite of all the other gods, save Logi, god of evil. According to the account, Balder's mother, much in the manner of Achilles' mother, sought to give him every known protection. Hence, Balder's mother extracted from every living creature and thing a solemn promise to keep Balder in protective custody. However, she overlooked the mistletoe, and Logi fashioned an arrow from mistletoe, crashed a

167

god's banquet, and killed lovely Balder with the arrow.

(But mistletoe undergoes a complete transformation from Norse mythology to the druids. The druids believed that the mistletoe had numerous curative powers, and that it was a symbol of peace. Hence, when two antagonistic warriors met beneath mistletoe, or the oak on which it grows, they threw aside their arms; and to prove their peaceful intentions, they embraced under the mistletoe. Sir James Frazier talks of this in his indispensable work, *The Golden Bough*. Beyond peradventure, it was the embracing beneath the mistletoe which culminated in the charming custom of kissing under mistletoe at Christmastime.)

No simile is used more extensively to demonstrate accuracy and swiftness than "Like a bee martin to its hole." Unglamorously, perhaps, bee martin and bee bird are merely popular terms for the American kingfisher. This species subsists on insects, captured on the wing, but the bee martin has acquired an unsavory reputation with farmers who believe its diet is chiefly composed of honeybees.

However, the U.S. Department of Agriculture says the martin's predilection for honeybees is preposterously overrated, that beekeepers have little economic fears from martins. Government officials examined the stomachs of kingfishers, from all parts of the country, and only twenty-two of these bellies contained the remnants of honeybees. Scientists insist that for every honeybee a martin eats, this species of birds kills a thousand dangerous insects. There is always the popular notion that the flowerlike crest of the kingfisher attracts bees, lures them within reach of the bird's bill. In a word, there is the lingering nonsense that the bee martin had radar long before World War II.

Just as a special chair used to be reserved for the village patriarch at formal meetings, there must be a special place, just over the fence for the bluebird. The bluebird, the lullaby, and the genuine love song almost face distinction. For some time amateur ornithologists have warned about the increasing paucity of bluebirds, and by now this doleful admonition is corroborated fully by *Audubon's Field Notes*. Bluebirds along the Atlantic seabord are down to less than twenty per cent of their normal population. Severe storms and insecticides are the chief villains, but any ordinary observer knows that the predatory

168

sparrow has a diabolical talent for usurping the nests of bluebirds. Of course, in the light of the energy shortage and the many world-ending bombs, the death of a bluebird is hardly a wanton feather in a hard wind. But whether man is in orbit, on the moon, or in a survival cave, he has to have certain basic symbols to give pertinence and drama to what he does. He must have words for his music and music for his words. For man is never so much the sum of his own mistakes as he is the vibrant product of his own implications. He casts his own shadow and no amount of beauty aids can alter that shadow.

The bluebird (North American thrush) is not indispensable in fighting inflation, and no new housing developments of factories will be turned away for the lack of these tiny delights, and neither shall inflation lower or business boom because of an increase in bluebirds. But the bluebird is inexorably tied to young love, to tender, mutual passion, to unsullied daydreams, and to the endless melody which keeps man marching onward. The bluebird is a magnetic talisman for youth and ardor. Of course, man may conquer all there is of space without any help from the bluebird, but the thoughtlessly cruel extinction of this precious little warbler will leave a hole in our dreams and hopes as big as the sky is big when the whole sky is a soft sandpile trimmed with a blue no artist has ever quite caught.

The Elephant Walk

The Bible doesn't mention the elephant, but from the repeated references to ivory, one assumes some sort of elephant existed in the Old Testament era. Hannibal (247-183 B.C.) used some elephants to transport his army across the Alps. (At the age of nine, Hannibal, the famous Carthaginian, was forced by his father to swear eternal hatred for the Romans.) While many people think a vast number of elephants made the trek over the Alps, Hannibal seems to have had around forty in his transport command.

The elephant is the longest liver among all the known animals, and when one is caught it is relatively simple to train him for the circus and other such enterprises. The first elephant to be displayed in America was exhibited near the end of George Washington's second administration. It was brought from India to New York City in 1796, on the famous warship *America*. This elephant, four feet tall, was sold for $10,000. She was exhibited from New York to Charleston, and the phrase "to see the elephant" emerged from these exhibitions. The famous Elephant Hotel at Coney Island was burned in 1896. This hotel contained thirty-two bedrooms and several parlors and bars. A "howdah" on the back of the hotel served as a dining room, and the whole structure was shaped as much in the form of an elephant as a building can be so shaped. And by the days of the gold rushes, "to see the elephant" was popular along the Oregon and the Santa Fe trails.

The longest tusk of record measured eleven feet and one-half inch in length. This tusk and its mate weighed twenty-two pounds. These tusks were taken from an elephant of the Sudan species (*Loxanodonta africanus*). The elephant was shot by an American hunter in the 19th century, and the shooting occurred near the border of Ethiopia.

David Livingston, the famous African missionary, the man

"found by E. M. Stanley," saw African elephants lift their young from the ground on their gigantic tusks and "carry them a considerable distance." The average newly born African calf weighs two hundred pounds and is about three feet high. The baby elephant sucks its mother with its mouth. Two teats between the female elephant's forelegs supply the baby with all of the nourishment it requires. When the calf sucks his mother, it doesn't seem to know what to do with its own trunk. According to Frank "Bring 'em Back Alive" Buck, it develops the habit of hanging its trunk out of the way while it feeds. And despite the popular fallacy, elephants do not drink through their trunks. They drink with their mouths, and the use of the trunk in drinking is confined to taking water up and squirting it into the mouth.

If precise knowledge of the elephant's breeding habits are cloudy, the gestation period may range from eighteen to twenty-two months. However, the late Raymond Ditmars, Curator of Mammals at New York City's Zoological Park, said that the average period of gestation among Indian elephants is six hundred forty-one days, or more than twenty-two months. When captured young, virtually all Asian elephants are easily trained for show or service or circus. Conversely, the African elephants are much less tractable and are much harder to train.

The elephant's fabulous capacity for remembering probably rests on reports such as this. Typical of the elephant's extended memory is the story that used to be printed in most of the elementary school books. A circus was parading through a small town and as the elephant passed a tailor sewing in front of his shop, the tailor pricked the elephant's trunk with his needle. Several years later when the same circus returned to the same town, the elephant filled his trunk with slush from a mudhole and squirted it on the same tailor who had pricked him some years before.

Many elephants chew tobacco. (Apparently, none has signed a testimonial, and there is nothing comparable to Brown Mule Chewing Tobacco.) Most experts say elephants like to chew tobacco. Many seem inordinately fond of chewing tobacco if the stuff is given to them in small portions. Apparently they like tobacco because of the licorice and sugar contents.

The assertion that elephants create their own burial ground seems to be a myth. Albeit, several English hunters have

171

reported that natives have brought them tusks from "secret places." Long before Joseph Conrad and others wrote about Africa, hunters imagined an Eldorado in shape of a huge elephant dying place. Apparently very few elephants die of old age, and most of the deaths are brought about by man. As is common with many other wild animals, elephants do attempt to hide when they feel death approaching, and elephants usually die singly and far from settlements. Elephant fossils are found in terrain once covered by water. In many cases the dying elephant seeks surcease in a river and is carried out to sea after death. Climatic conditions in Africa and in southern Asia cause the carcasses to decay rapidly, and the natives, carnivorous animals, swarms of insects, and carion birds make quick work of the dead flesh.

Dr. William Mann, late director of Washington's National Zoological Park, said that in 1926 his competent guide took him to the precise spot where an elephant had been killed only a year before. All that remained was a portion of the skull and two widely separate bones. But Teddy Roosevelt, in *African Game Trails*, alluding to burned over land in the Lado, wrote: "Here and there bleached skulls of elephants and rhino, long dead, showed white against the charred surface of the soil."

In the *Voyage of the Beagle*, Charles Darwin wrote: "The guanacos appear to have favorite places to die. They lie down on river banks. On the banks of the St. Cruz in certain circumscribed places, I counted between ten and twenty heads. But, thus far, no explorer has located the mother lode of ivory which would be seen and found in the alleged burying grounds if the elephant actually existed."

Many people are baffled that such an enormous beast can lie down with relative ease. Until 1646 when Sir Thomas Browne published his *Vulgar Errors*, there was the common belief that elephants had no joints. In *Troilus and Cressida*, Shakespeare had written, before Browne, "Elephants are peculiar among quadrupeds in that it has joints, but none for courtesy; his legs are long for necessity but not for flexure." Actually an elephant lies down as a man does. It kneels, with its knees touching the ground. Those stout, pillar-like legs enable the elephant to support his prodigious weight, to sleep while standing and climb and descend declivities with remarkable ease. Despite its tremendous weight and heavy legs, the elephant can lie down when it wants to lie down. But few seem to want to lie down, save to wallow. The Asiatic elephant often lies down to sleep, but the African species never lies down, save to roll. The late Frederick Selous, British author and hunter, said he had seen several thousand elephants sleeping while standing, and he had never seen one lying down to sleep or to rest.

Because of their whopping girth, there is a natural tendency to overestimate an elephant's height. The largest elephants seem to be the African males, and a specimen more than ten feet tall would be regarded as untypical. Actually, no one, the afore-mentioned tailor included, has been able to measure a live elephant, and this is hazardous to do with a dead elephant because the position of the dead feet is a puzzle. As the legs lie prone and relaxed when tranquilized or in death, it is impossible to know how much to push it up into the shoulder in order to place it just as it was in life. (Thus far, no penny, or even public, scales have been made to weigh elephants.) Not just incidentally, Jumbo, the well known elephant that P. T. Barnum bought from the London Zoological Park weighed six tons and was ten feet and one inch tall. It has been determined by scientists that the circumference of the elephant's forefoot is equal, roughly, to one half of the animal's height.

In *The Lamentable Tragedy of Locrine*, written about 1595, an anonymous poet asks:

Have you not seen a mighty elephant
Slain by the biting of a silly mouse?

But the alleged fear of elephants for mice seems to be yet another cherished delusion. Zoo keepers and circus attendants all assert that elephants show little, if any, emotion when rats run through their cages or in the hay they eat. Some folks with a penchant for the maudlin have taken a rat in a sack and pitched it to the elephant in the cage. In every known time the elephant has ignored the rat, as he continued to eat the peanuts thrown to him. Indeed, most experts agree that the elephant's chief fears are of dogs and men. As the late naturalist Carl Adkeley put it: "If a mouse ever ran up an elephant's trunk, the mouse would soon be in the next county."

"White elephant" exists today chiefly as a metaphor for continuous bad luck. The so-called white elephant is merely the

173

albinistic Indian elephant, in which much of the habitual dark pigment is missing from the skin. Nonetheless, some etymologists say the phrase derives from some white elephants once presented by the King of Siam to the members of his court. Because the white elephant was sacred, the courtier could not work him; and the gift usually meant poverty for the recipient. But in many parts of Asia and Ethiopia the white elephant is not merely the symbol for purity but is believed to contain the soul of a dead human, in some cases the soul of an ancient god. In several Asiatic countries there was the old custom of a white elephant's being baptized, worshipped, and kept as a sacred beast. (The American Plains Indians had the same reverence for the albino buffalo.) Ava, King of upper Burma, was heralded as "The Lord of White Elephants and Twenty-Four Umbrellas."

The Siamese came up with a new wrinkle about the white elephant: Moye was standing on a river bank when a rainbow encircled her and the result was that twelve years later she gave birth to Fo-Hi. During the sacred time of Moye's pregnancy, she dreamed that a white elephant was in her belly, and that is why the Siamese used to refer to white elephants as "Lord," and each white elephant was attended by an eminent person of high station.

The hard luck omen may have begun when P. T. Barnum bought a giant white elephant for around $200,000, and this turned out to be a bad investment.

It is virtually impossible to estimate the longevity of elephants that live in a wild condition. But there doesn't seem to be any evidence that an elephant, wild or trained, has lived beyond seventy or seventy-five years. A rule of thumb for the elephant's longevity is to multiply by four or five the number of years the animal takes to reach maturity. Elephants begin to show the ravages of old age at sixty to sixty-five years.

An elephant's tusks are really his elongated incisor teeth, and they are singular in that they continue to grow so long as the animal lives. That is why the tusks of an old elephant appear to be about the same length no matter how much they use them. But these teeth are never shed; and if they are broken off or extracted, they are never replaced. (Even if an elephant can't order a set of Roebuckers, or false teeth, his first teeth are milk teeth, the same as a human baby's.)

As aforementioned, Hannibal used some elephants as transports when he crossed the Alps. Pyrrhus, of Epinus in Greece, defeated the Romans at Heraclea and Asculum, in Italy. In 280 B. C. Pyrrhus agreed to help the Lucabians in their war against Rome. The Romans and Greeks had never fought each other before, and in the war Pyrrhus used elephants as cavalry and as transport animals. When Rome failed to sue for peace, Pyrrhus fought them again, but he lost heavily of his own men. According to Plutarch, "When they had all quitted the field, and Pyrrhus was congratulated upon his victory, he observed, 'Another such victory and we are undone'." Thus came the origin of "a Pyrrhic victory." (Not just incidentally, Plutarch says that Pyrrhus had no regular teeth, "but in place of them a continuous bone." Pyrrhus was killed by a tile that fell on him from a building in Argos.)

The elephant has enriched our language with words and phrases such as white elephant, elephant apple, elephant root, elephant fish, many Elephant Rivers, elephant grass, elephant shrew (or jumping animal), Elephant Isle in India, elephantine, elephant papyrus (now obsolete), and elephant's ear (a begonia).

And there is always the late Carl Sandburg's quiet, but impassioned plea for tolerance in his once famous poem, "Elephants Are Different to Different People," in which three blind men feel an elephant. Each comes up with a different feeling and description, but these differences were not allowed to spoil a sweetly singing summer afternoon.

Another popular story illustrative of the elephant's prodigious memory concerns the man who removed a large thorn from an elephant's foot. Many years later the circus played the hometown of the good Samaritan, and amid much trumpeting, the elephant, stepping from the walk-around parade in the tent, picked his benefactor up and moved him from the general admission section to a $5.00 box seat. (This tale smacks somewhat of Bernard Shaw's drama, *Androcles and the Lion*.)

In *Paradise Lost*, Milton has this to say:

Th' unwieldy elephant,
To make them mirth, us'd all his might
                    and wreath'd
His life proboscis.

175

Saki (H. H. Munro, writer-soldier killed in World War I) has this maxim in his story, "Reginald On Besetting Sins": "Women and elephants never forget an injury." It was J. G. Saxe (1816-1887) who left this object lesson:

It was six men of Industan
To learning much inclined,
Who went to see the Elephant
(Though all of them were blind):
That each by observation,
Might satisfy his mind.

According to tradition the camel of the prophet Manomet covered the entire journey from Jerusalem to Mecca in four mighty bounds, and for his incredible service Manomet reserved a special place in heaven for the camel, along with Alborak, the prophet's dog, and Ketmir, the dog of the seven sleepers.

If most of the camels Americans see are in circuses and at zoos, two species have been domesticated since prehistoric times, to be used as riding animals and beasts of burden in the deserts of the Old World. Although scientists have tried unceasingly to give the camel a proper ancestry, no wild species of camel has been found, save for one small two humper, which inhabits (or inhabited) central Asia, and northward to Siberia.

The Arabian camel (*Camelus dromedarius*), popularized in the movie *Lawrence of Arabia* has one hump upon its shoulders. The hump is composed of muscles, flesh, and fat; and in times of famine is reabsorbed to a large extent. If the camel rests three or four months, the hump comes back again. This type of camel is used from Mongolia and northwest India, throughout south central Africa, and on through the entire region of ancient Asia Minor. If its original home remains a mystery, it adjusts well to a sandy region. The callous pads on its feet are repeated upon its chest and the joints of its knees, on which it rests, kneeling or lying down.

Its long eyelashes protect it from the sun's glare, and its wedge-shaped cutting teeth are particularly suitable for the short grass of the desert. The ability to close its oblique nostrils enables the camel to be protected against dust storms. But its most remarkable feature is its stomach, the interior of which has no villi. Both compartments of the paunch contain a number of cells, or pouches, in their walls, each of which may close and separate from the remainder of the paunch. These are filled and closed when the camel drinks water. This gives it the means to store more water than is required for a specific journey. On waterless terrain, the camel draws gradually the water required for the trip.

The camel's senses of sight and smell are uncanny, and this enables it to discover the existence of water at a great distance. This made the camel an important factor in the colonization of the countries that lie south and east of the Mediterranean, the Black, and the Caspian Seas. The camel was indispensable in the colonization of arid areas.

The Bactrian camel, though smaller, is heavier, and by dint of its cloven feet and longer and finer hair, is better adapted to a cooler and rockier terrain. Its basic habitat is central Asia. Like the southern, one-humped species, it has marvelous endurance, in summer as well as in the cold of Hindu-Kush and Mongolia. The British used this camel successfully to move military supplies in northwestern Asia. Some camels are bred for the saddle and others are bred to wear harness and to pull as a draft animal. The Arabian species can pull twice the load pulled by a stout mule, and it is not unusual for the Bactrian species to carry half a ton of weight upon its back. Some desert caravans have employed as many as a thousand camels at one time. These camels will move steadily at a pace of two and one-half miles an hour. When bred deliberately to be ridden, camels have been known to carry a rider one hundred miles in a day's time. They move with a pacing motion, lifting the feet on the same side successively.

The camel served the nomadic tribes of Arabia and the Sahara in ways other than as riders and haulers. Their long hair provided the hair that was woven into coarse fabric for tent covers, ropes, and even the finer shawls and rugs that fetched such a high price on the public market. Its milk and flesh were used for food, and when one died, its bones were used as fuel in lieu of absent wood.

For a long time the British Army maintained a Camel Corps in Egypt and in northeastern India, doing the service normally done by the cavalry horse.

Following the California gold strike of 1849-1850, many camels were imported because of a shortage of mules. This was a miserable failure. The camel, by nature, is truculent and ornery; and the miners simply could not manage the dromedary. The U.S. Army, undoubtedly thinking of the British Camel Corps, put some cavalrymen on camels, as a substitute for the cavalry horse, but the contrary camel was as big a bust as it had been in the gold fields.

The story of the camel would be incomplete devoid of Camel Cigarettes, the most popular cigarette manufactured in the pre-filter days.

In 1911 when every cigarette manufacturer was pushing several brands, R. J. Reynolds of Winston-Salem, N.C., decided upon a "single leader." Many unnamed cigarettes were manufactured, and R. J. Reynolds and his associates decided to use the blend in Sample 29, but no name was given to this brand. Then Reynolds took his young sons to a circus. Much impressed by the camels he saw, he said to his sons, "A camel can go a long way without water." The children agreed, and Reynolds decided not to "water" his new stock, as some of his associates had insisted.

In what may have been the first "teaser advertising," Reynolds decided to put the Camel on sale for a brief period in one American city only. Indianapolis was chosen, and for two weeks the billboards and street car ads carried the news that on such and such a day there would be more camels in Indianapolis than in the entire history of Arabia and Egypt. When public curiosity was at the bursting point, Reynolds introduced his new brand, Camels, at ten cents for twenty cigarettes.

If a housewife called a dairy and asked for a gallon of camel's milk and two pounds of camel's butter, the fool-catcher would likely come for her with his net. Even so, experts say the camel's milk is "delicious, wholesome, and contains considerable butterfat." But a camel will not yield much butter because no matter how long it is churned; the fat globules are so small that they cannot be separated simply by agitating the milk by conventional methods.

For those of us who lack any extraordinary dexterity, milking a camel could present more problems than putting Pampers on quintuplets, simultaneously. However, many historians believe the idea for churning a cow's milk for butter was suggested originally by the occurrence of this substance in the leather bags of milk carried across the desert on camels' backs by Arabs.

Even today some of the Arabs made butter (which Americans find a little rank) from camels' milk by pouring the cream into a goatskin sack and shaking it continually until butter is formed. Another Arabic expedient is to milk a camel, put the milk in a goatskin, and have the goatskin thrown back and forth between two men mounted on speeding camels. Whether or not this butter evenuates in a TV commercial, the trick of making butter by throwing the goatskin back and forth is an improvement upon some of the rodeo stunts one sees.

The Danebrog Was A Powerful Charm

One of the most important charms of the "modern" world was the Danebrog, or Danish national banner, woven in a single night, according to legend, by three sisters, all descendants of the god Odin. A wonderfully realistic and lifelike raven, Odin's favorite bird, was in the center. If the raven held its head and bill upright, the Danes were sure to win any battle fought. By observing the raven, the Danes won twenty-seven victories within three years. Whenever the raven drooped, the Danes stayed in camp. If the bird dropped its head once a battle had started the Danes withdrew immediately.

Alfred, king of the Anglo-Saxons, determined to possess this magical flag, and he won it after a three-hour battle. Apparently, the same fortunes attended the attitude of the raven after it was possessed by Alfred. It seems true historically that the Danes were models of courage and boldness only so long as the raven superstition fired their spirits.

In Proverbs there is a passage that seems to have small vibrance today, one in which the Biblical writer talks about ravens: "The eye that mocketh his father and despiseth to obey his mother, the ravens of the valley shall pick it out, and the young eagles shall eat it."

One of literature's most ominous stanzas occurs in Edgar Allan Poe's (1809-1849) "The Raven":

And the Raven, never flitting, still is sitting,
      still is sitting,
On the pallid bust of Pallas, just above
      my chamber door;
And his eyes have all the seeming of
      a demon that is dreaming.
And the lamplight o'er him screaming throws
      his shadow on the floor;

And my soul from out that shadow that lies
      floating on the floor
Shall be lifted—nevermore.

"Quoth the raven, 'Nevermore',," is known by almost every literate person, whether or not he has read Poe's poem.

Just as ominous and just as redolent with implications of doom are Shakespeare's lines from *Othello*:

O, It come o'er my memory,
As doth the raven o'er the infected house,
Boding to all.

The raven is the first bird mentioned in the Bible, and reference is to the pair alleged to have been put on the Ark by Noah. The raven is a typical species (*Corvus coras*) of the crow family, of which of all passerine birds the raven is the largest. Even so, its size is variable, but generally it is around two feet in length and four feet in expanse.

Its plumage, feet, and bill are all black, the former with rich purple and violet lusters; albeit, the young and the females are much duller. Two sub-specific species are found in the United States, and the raven is most abundant in rocky areas, near bodies of water. Ravens are usually seen alone or in pairs. This bird can fly at a tremendous height for several hours at a time. Carnivorous by preference, it eats small animals and even dead fish. The European variety is known to destroy rabbits and even lambs. It disgorges bones, feathers and other indigestible matter in keeping with some other birds of prey. Wary and cunning, a raven is rarely ever caught in a trap or shot by a hunter.

But it is easily domesticated, and it can be taught to imitate the human voice. When domesticated, the raven responds remarkably to kindness, and it will follow its master around as if it were the family dog.

Despite anything he may have said, Poe must have been influenced by Grip, the raven in Dickens' novel of 1841, *Barnaby Rudge*. Poe did not write "The Raven" until four years later, in 1845, and there is an extant copy of Poe's review of *Barnaby Rudge*. The Poe review says: "Its (the raven's) croakings might have been heard *prophetically* in the course of the drama. Its character might have performed, in regard to that of the idiot, much the same part as he does, in music, the accompaniment in respect to the air. Poe also is indebted to Elizabeth Barrett Browning for the interior rhyming of "The Raven." Mrs. Browning had used the same device earlier in "Lady Geraldine's Courtship." Indeed, Poe dedicated the poem to Mrs. Browning, whom he had never seen. Gall Caine quoted Dante Gabriel Rossetti, the English poet, as saying that Rossetti's "The Blessed Damosel" was inspired by "The Raven." "I say that Poe had done the utmost it was possible to do with the grief of the lover on earth, and I am determined to reverse the condition and give utterance to the loved one in heaven."

In his "The Philosophy of Composition," a long essay, Poe attempts to explain the nature and inspiration of "The Raven." He says that the death of a beautiful woman has to be the most dramatic and hauntingly tenacious of all poetic themes. But since the explanation came after the fact, many scholars think Poe's explanation is somewhat contrived. There are even suggestions that he wrote "The Philosophy of Composition" to annoy the pastoral poets of New England. One may forget that poor Poe's parents were traveling actors, that Poe was born in Boston, and he always referred to Boston as "the frog pond."

Today's pedant is likely to find the poem contrived, too, that in lieu of the charted course and inspiration Poe outlined, the poem has the air of the expenditure of much midnight oil.

In his "A Fable For the Critics," (1848) James Russell Lowell seems to have thought he exhausted observation with his lines:

There comes Poe, with his raven, like Barnaby Rudge;
Three fifths of him genius and two fifths sheer fudge.
Who talks like a book of iambs and pentameters,
Who has written some things quite the best of their kind,
But the heart seems, somehow, all squeezed out by the mind.

That's mostly malarky, and it reminds one of the bromide, "Beauty is only skin deep," which endures as a skin deep maxim, only.

Another talking bird, the parrot, habituates sub-tropical areas of both hemispheres. It has four toes, two facing forward and two facing backward; and while it is adept at climbing, perching, and holding food as it eats, it is a poor walker. The parrot owns a strong, hooked bill; and its upper mandible is hooked onto the bones of its head.

Many learn to imitate the human voice. The male is an attractive color arrangement, with green plumage, with red on the head, shoulders, and thighs. The parrot is partially insectivorous, but the *kea* parrot of northern Australia acquired the habit of attacking sheep. But experts say if a parrot is given the proper treatment it may live for a century. Indeed some domesticated parrots have been known to live for a hundred years, to be possessed by three generations of the same human family.

Many curious people ask for the longest sentence ever put together by a parrot. This is difficult to ascertain, and the length, obviously, is predicated upon the vocabulary and the patience of the trainer. And, of course, parrot talk is mostly imitation of sound and it is devoid of reason or thought. The parrot's longest sentences are mere words strung together. And it must be remembered that parrots learn "to talk" only in captivity. Most birds are able to move just one mandible of the beak, although both of the parrot's mandibles are movable.

The parrot and the other talking birds have no lips and their "speech" is produced in the throat, almost the same way that a ventriloquist talks. A parrot can learn to speak one language as well as another, and carefully trained parrots are known to have acquired vocabularies of several hundred words, even if most of the specially trained parrots emit disconnected ejaculations. However, many are taught to repeat verses of songs, and a Parisian writer took an oath that he heard a parrot speak the Lord's Prayer, without making a single error. In his *Cage and Chamber Birds*, J. M. Bernstein writes of a parrot, a gray parrot, that could repeat the Apostles' Creed without a slip. And it is a recorded fact that on several occasions the testimony of parrots has been given a restricted legal recognition in court trials.

The Tragedy of the Twilight Owlets

It is told that the sadistic gunfighter, John Wesley Hardin, began as a beautiful, blue-eyed, curly-headed baby boy. As an adult he was asked how many men he had killed. He scratched his head, scribbled on a sheet of paper, to ask: "Counting Mexicans?"

People used to say that one who wanted perpetual youth and innocence in a small child should put salt into his shoes, that this would keep him from growing up. Apparently, this cherished chromo was neglected for John Wesley Hardin and for the twilight owlets, too. The transformation of twilight owlet into full grown owl, if much less lethal, has parallels with Hardin's infamous saga. In common with the oldtime road agent, the owl sleeps in thickets by day; and he goes out at night to forage. The night owl's blazing eyes could pass for the headlight on a through locomotive. Unlike most other birds the owl's upper, not lower, lid is used in closing his eyes. Again, the owl is unusual in that it has an outer ear, much as mammals have.

The mystery surrounding their nocturnal·habits and their lugubrious hoots have made owls objects of superstition for many centuries among many people. The owl was such an ill omen among ancients that many folks thought its appearance near a sick room meant sudden death. Among the Hindus the crow (night) and the owl (day) battled for supremacy. The owl is almost as sacrosanct in many of the traditions of the American Indian. The Kootenny tribe believed that the owl flew away with their young, but via a ruse, the owl was slain, and the coyote burned the owl's corpse, but phoenix-like, the owl's spirit arose from the ashes as a huge swarm of deadly mosquitoes.

Alive, the owl's cry runs a morbid range from moronic hooting to maniacal laughter. This shrill laughter sounds, for all the world, as if a human being, about to be gored, has been caught in the owl's trap.

184

If every author is permitted a couple of deep-seated antipathies, the owl impresses us as a stupid stick in the mud, an incessant croaker of harrowing gibberish, a bundle of feathered diffidence waiting for a helpless insect to deliver itself up as a welfare check. But the owlet, especially at twilight, is almost as charming as the owl is repulsive. Nonetheless, the cute little owlets grow up to become owls. This is the same sort of transformation that occurred in the life of Blackbeard. As a boy he had yellow curls. He helped his mother with chores, whether requested to help her or not. He sang in a boy's choir, and he learned his catechism letter perfect. And you know the remainder of the story.

When early summer is really lined with silk and satin after supper, when the color curling from the woodlands is a sort of greenish blue, the owlets practice flying in the hit-or-miss fashion that the Wright boys got their crate off the ground at Kitty Hawk. There is more of prayer than hope in these first flights. There is tremendous excitement among the owlets. There is fear, too, because a few fall on their bellies or prats in crash landings. Then you can almost swear they are honking about the "Little Engine," cooing, "I think I can, I think I can."

One likes to believe the pull of unsullied youth and ambition kicks up the uproarious mischief of exploration among the owlets. They certainly put on a marvelous show, and a most innocuous one. And the poet in one tries to push down the inevitable truth that these small delights will grow into big chunks of bums on the wing. Yet when the darkening woods hold a cargo of fragile delight and one returns to one's home, one rubs his rabbit foot so he will not concentrate on: Like father, like son, and all too soon, too soon.

In Diogenes Laertius' *Lives of Eminent Philosophers*, written sometime between 200-250 A.D., appears the bromide, "Like sending owls to Athens, as the proverb goes." The owl, sacred to Athena, was protected in Athens, and thus was most plentiful. Later on in history, this ancient proverb would be altered to "sending coal to Newcastle," or "sending salt to Dysart."

Macbeth spoke for many of us with "I heard the owl scream and the crickets cry." School children of a former era had to say parts of Gray's "Elegy" by heart, including always, "The moping owl does to the moon complain." Tennyson left an excellent word picture with:

185

Alone and warming his five wits,
The white owl in the belfry sits.

No brief sketch of owls is complete without some portion of
Edward Lear's "The Owl and the Pussycat":

The Owl and the Pussy-cat went to sea
In a beautiful pea-green boat,
They took some honey, and plenty of money,
Wrapped in a five pound note.
The owl looked up to the stars above,
And sang to a small guitar,
'O lovely Pussy, O Pussy my love,
What a beautiful Pussy you are.
You are,
You are,
What a beautiful Pussy you are.'

This is bound to have been one of the most incongruous trips
within the entire history of whimsy-whamsy, and it routes
Charles Dudley Warner's "Politics make strange bed fellows."
Lear (1812-1888) died long before Hollywood emerged, but his
engagingly anachronistic pair may have had some effect,
eventually, on the creation of the animated cartoon.

No Peace For Doves

The mourning dove, named amid savage sadism, is not as big as a minute and his life span is hardly any longer. But it was only in recent years that hunters deigned to waste expensive shotgun shells upon a mouthful of meat. Now it seems as if every community's hunters have made an inviolable pact dedicated to the liquidation of the tiny mourning, or morning, dove. The enormous firepower expended in a single gleaned field is sufficient to make a drowsy ex-soldier think a Panzer Division is just up the road.

This excessively one-sided "sport" seems to have irrepressible appeal for endless numbers of men who do not want to spend the energy and ingenuity to roust out quail or rabbits. Shooting doves is a sort of reverse re-enactment of the lions and the Christians. The Christians with the high-powered shotguns foregather at appointed times, at appointed fields, to wait for the doves to fly along as accessories to massive suicide. To add insult to lethal injury, the dove is not even given the break a con man gives his pigeon. Many dove hunters sit back-to-back so that the deadly enfilading firepower can go in both directions simultaneously. Thus any route is, literally, a dead end street for the doves.

Concurrently, the dove supper is becoming as popular as whiskey to men suffering monumental hangovers. The dove, prepared about the way a quail is fixed, is so small a large sack full is required for a single supper. And the devotees, especially the hunters who entertain many guests, complain frequently the meat on a dove is hardly worth the cost of a single shotgun shell. That testy complaint is the habitual requiem for the mourning dove, but the thousands and thousands killed each year ought to slake the hunger of a few gnashing teeth, and also of many shotguns. But at least this tiny, winged morsel is named properly. "Mourning" is appallingly apt. Never within the

187

history of so-called recreation have so many wings provided so much "sport" for so many men, and all in such a furtive autumnal interlude.

The Writ says that God's eye is the sparrow. Somehow it seems more to the dove's point if He kept his eye on two-legged bastards who go bang-bang-bang at the doves.

Birds of Paradise

Birds of Paradise, or Paradisaedae, are found in New Guinea, northern Australia, and the adjacent islands. The species contains a large number of birds, of which the male is heralded for his brilliant plumage, although the Birds of Paradise are closely related to the common crow. These are forest birds, ones that spend much of their time in treetops; and ornithologists have counted around fifty different varieties.

They do not sing but they emit sharp, shrill whistles at sunrise; and natives of their habitat call them "Birds of the Sun." The female is comparatively drab compared to the male. The dissimilarity between males and females is a protective arrangement designed to keep the females from lethal observation while they are sitting defensely on their nests. The females would be discerned easily and killed if they had the distinctive, brilliant colors of the male. By the Darwinian process of natural selection the young birds and the females, inexperienced and helpless, would be placed in jeopardy if they had the coloring of the males. The drabness of the female protects them from such birds' predators as monkeys, lemurs, civets, and snakes. Indeed, when the somewhat homely female is breeding, the brightly bedecked male mate stays some distance from the breeding nest in order to obviate the dangers of sundry hunters. Most of the breeding is done at sunrise, and natives call such breeding by Birds of Paradise "dancing parties."

When Magellan circumnavigated the globe in 1523, he brought a few Birds of Paradise to Europe. Apparently the climate and terrain were incompatible with their natures and they died out.

Magellan had two dead Birds of Paradise, given him on the island of Battchian, as a token of regal favor. As was the custom of the island, the dead bird's feet and wings were cut off, apparently, in preparation for cooking. But when Magellan exhibited these two birds in Europe the long lasting, absurd legend that Birds of Paradise were wingless and footless took root. It was natural for an unlettered public to endow a wingless and footless bird with magic powers.

High-Flyer

It was Ralph Waldo Emerson (1803-1882) who wrote the once famous poem called "Fable":

> The mountain and the squirrel
> Had a quarrel,
> And the former called the latter 'Little Prig.'
> Bun replied:
> 'You are doubtless very big,
> But all sorts of things and weather
> Must be taken in together,
> To make up a year, sphere,
> And a spear.
> And I think it no disgrace
> To occupy my place.
> If I'm not as large as you,
> Then you are not so small as I,
> And not half so spry.
> I'll not deny you make
> A very pretty squirrel track;
> Talents differ; all is well and wisely put,
> If I can not carry a forest on my back,
> Neither can you crack a nut.'

There are numerous members of the squirrel family (*Sciupadea*) all of which have slight bodies and long tails, and well developed clavicles. But few native American mammals are more fascinating and beloved than our gray squirrel, sometimes called the cat squirrel. It abounds in hardwood forests from Canada to Florida and as far west as Minnesota. This species ranges to twenty inches in length, of which the tail is half. Its active aboreal habits and antics and its engaging appearance make this species of squirrel an enduring symbol for innocent frolicsomeness.

191

The fox squirrel, found in the southern forests, is fourteen inches long, and half of that is his tail. Its color is a rusty gray or clay color, and unlike many of its cousins it does not hibernate or store up food.

The ground squirrel has a pair of large pouches. Its hair is dense and a hairy fold of skin runs along each side.

The flying squirrel has no pouch, but the fold of skin along its sides form a crude parachute which, when extended, supports the squirrel on its flying leaps. The long tail acts as a sort of rudder, and it assists the dense, fine fur that is spread along the squirrel's sides. Undoubtedly, close observation of the flying squirrel contributed to the notion of manmade parachutes, just as gulls are said to have given Leonardo di Vinci the idea for the flying machine.

Housewives who look out the kitchen window at a squirrel emulating a circus high-flyer, or nibbling here and there as if it were a connoiseur of fine wines, call the little dab of fur and dexterity "cute." But the squirrel has a vicious set of teeth; and when it feels its life is really endangered, it bites and scratches to beat all hell.

The word endures when a hot-rod car driver squirrels, or weaves, from side to side; and throughout this century to squirrel money means to cache it. The railroad employee who climbs to the top of a boxcar is called a squirrel, and a squirrel may be a psychiatrist or one who suffers aberrations (a nut). Blockade whiskey was called squirrel in many rural and small-town sections because the drinker was said "to jump about like a squirrel."

Short Shrift For Pelicans Et Al

Ploffskin, Pluffskin, and Pelican jee.
We think no birds so happy as we!
Plumpskin, Ploshskin, Pelican jill!
We think so then, and we thought so still.

Edward Lear, the original limerick writer wrote that, and even better is the late Dixon Merit's:

A wonderful bird is the pelican!
His beak holds more than his belican.
He can take in his beak
Enough food for a week
But I'm damned if I know how the helican.

That ditty is supposed to have been one of Woodrow Wilson's prime favorites.

The pelican is one of the most singular looking of all animals. It has a long flattened beak, with a huge pouch under its lower mandible. Its waddling gait is enunciated, made even more ludicrous looking, because of its short legs and massive body. But airborne it has the grace of a running fawn, and its wingspan measures out to eight feet while it is flying. Almost apropos to nothing, or so it seems to the human observer, it dives straight down, in the manner of a World War II fighter plane, to land upon water with a splash and catch the fish it has sighted from far above the water.

The mother feeds her young by opening her beak widely as the young plucks a small fish from her pouch or crop. This unusual procedure led ancients to assume that the pelican fed her young with her own blood. Thus the pelican became the symbol of mercy in ancient art, and the habitual compassion of the pelican was reinforced by the psalmist: "I am like a pelican in the wilderness."

It is hard to think of the kermes as an animal, in any known category. It is a nodelike insect, about the size of a pea, and it is found on the kermes oak tree. Today, as in prehistoric times, the dried bodies of the female are treated with vinegar to make a scarlet dye that will never bleach or fade. This, obviously, is the scarlet alluded to so often in the Bible. Scholars think its permanence is what Isaiah referred to when he promised, "Though your sins be as scarlet they shall be white as snow." (Isaiah 1:18) This scarlet dye was expensive and only the very wealthy could afford to use it, could afford garments of scarlet. However, there is an inconsistency because soldiers were often dressed in scarlet. It was a scarlet robe the Roman soldiers placed on Jesus (Matthew 27:28).

When the ancient Egyptians found cracked red clay in their desert, they equated the red dirt with evil; and one of their evil gods was depicted as red. Sin and scarlet tie together, obviously, in the early paintings of Cain and Judas. All of the early Cain and Judas artwork depicted them as having red hair and red complexions.

Kangaroo is the popular name for several of the species of the various herbivorous marsupials, of the family *Macropodidae*. This animal is found in Australia and adjacent regions, and it is believed that "kangaroo" probably came from a word known and used in Queensboro and confined to local usage.

Its ancestry is ancient and obscure. One theory ties the animal's name to the ventral pouch, which covers the mammary glands in which the young are nourished and protected. The babies are about one-half the size of a mouse at birth, and they are dropped from the mother's womb. Actually, at birth the babies are minute, undeveloped fetuses. With her lips the mother reaches down and places the mites, one by one, into her pouch; but even after the babies have developed sufficiently to walk and to explore on their own, many return to their mother's pouches to sleep and be protected. This process is likely to continue for several weeks.

The kangaroo court is a sham trial. The term, of unknown origin, seems to have originated in prisons and aboard pirate ships on the Spanish Main. The kangaroo court seems to have started in Australia, and frequently it took on the dire shadings of vigilantism.

There is also the kangaroo rat, a long-tailed rodent, said to leap; and the kangaroo vine is a trailer or a creeper. Kangaroo Island lies in the Indian Ocean, south of Adelaide.

The locust, the plague of the Middle East, is a species of the grasshopper. Around two inches long, it is a reddish brown, with a wingspread of five inches. They come on prevailing winds in the late summer or early fall. The destruction of the locusts is as devastating today as it was when the plague of locusts visited Egypt (Exodus 3:4).

Mosaic law and dietary law allows the eating of locusts, and John the Baptist subsisted on locusts, flavored with honey, when he was in the wilderness. It is possible, however, that some Biblical writer or translator confused the locust with the fruit of a carob tree, an evergreen that grows as high as fifty feet. It bears large thick pods, used by men and animals for food.

Lobster was an extreme delicacy with the Egyptians, but it is not mentioned in the Bible because the Jews thought it was "unclean."

The Egyptians made pets of the swift gazelle, a member of the antelope family. One of the fastest animals in the entirety of history, it can leap as high as three feet in the air, even as it runs at breakneck speed. It is one of the most timorous of animals, and it usually travels in herds of thirty or forty. The gazelles are difficult for big game hunters to bring down, save when driven into narrow, bottlenecked valleys.

The giraffe, a camelopard, the tallest of the known animals, even if unsigned by a basketball team (*Giraffe camelopardalio*) comes from a family of ruminants (usually animals with even toes and horns). The giraffe is a native of Africa, in brushy plains or open forests, but unlike Abou Ben Adhem, its tribes are decreasing rapidly. (As yet there is no international movement "To Save the Giraffe.")

This strange looking animal's head usually stands eighteen feet from the ground, and yet its movements are the epitome of gracefulness. Both sexes have horns, or protuberances, between the ears, and these horns are far different from horns of other animals. Each horn is connected to the skull by a suture, and the horn is covered with skin and hair. Even though the giraffe may be called an innocuous animal, one that seeks safety constantly when cornered, it fights with reckless abandonment and with its hind legs. Several big game hunters have reported that they have seen a giraffe give a lion wotfer with his rapidly

195

flailing hind legs, and in these bouts it is the lion that has hollered for the calf rope or has thrown in the wildlife equivalent of the towel.

Everyone to his own taste, the old lady said when she kissed the cow, but many people find the giraffe's meat excellent food, and the skin makes excellent leather for several oddments. Nonetheless, broiled giraffe hardly ever appears on an American menu.

There is a common saying that the giraffe has no voice, and that it is the only four-legged mammal that does not make some vocal sound characteristic of the species. The late Dr. William M. Mann, curator of the National Zoological Park said, in 1931, "I have never heard a giraffe make any noise and it is virtually voiceless, but there is evidence that it does occasionally utter a feeble sound characteristic of the species. Even so, a few zoo keepers say they have heard giraffes make feeble noise to attract attention when their young were menaced. In 1936 the game warden of Kenya reported that the larnyx in the giraffe is poorly developed, and members of the species utter a sound when endangered or hungry, but this is a low series of snorts issued staccato and often unheard by humans.

Despite its neck's great length the giraffe cannot reach to the ground to graze. Its neck is only seven vertebrae, the usual number in mammals, but the giraffe's neck has limited flexibility. (The flexible necks of most birds contain fourteen vertebrae, or twice the number of a mammal.) Thus the giraffe never feeds on grass, and it can go a long time without water. In order to bend its head to the ground to eat grass and to drink water it has to assume an awkward position, by lowering its entire body. Chiefly, it feeds upon the leaves of trees by browsing on the lower limbs. It is an extremely timid animal, and it must take caution in its wild state because of the position of its eyes which project far from the skull and give the animal the peculiar advantage of being able to see behind without turning its head.

"Puss In Boots"

Someone with a penchant for platitudes said the chief difference between a dog and cat is that the dog thinks he is human but the cat disdains humans because they are not cats. Albeit any subtle nuance in the vagaries of animals is not implicit in Mark Twain's famous crack, "A cat that has sat on a hot stove will never sit on a hot stove again, or a cold one for that matter."

If the dog is usually an irrepressible sycophant, aping man and trying constantly to stay in man's affections and good graces, the more a human tries to pet a cat, the more he is likely to disobey, to spurn his gestures of good will until the cat is in a mood for human affection. The cat is the original diva, the grande dame.

Several authorities say the first reference to a domestic cat came in 2100 B.C., in Egypt, naturally, where cats were revered. Soon after the original reference to cats the courtier to the mother of a Pharoah was given a nickname that translates as "Pussy."

The endowment of the cat with nine lives started along the Nile, and the nine lives tied to mystical thoughts and to realistic observations. The cat, one of nature's most tenacious creations, takes excellent care of her health. When she falls, it is likely to be on her feet; and her feet, nicely padded, are excellent shock absorbers. Unlike many dogs, she takes few foolish traffic risks; and although she is adroit at catching rats, she knows how to escape her own capture by predatory animals. Everyone is familiar with the picture of a cat climbing a tree to escape menacing dogs. If one looks at such a cat closely, one is impressed tremendously with the cat's all-seeing, vigilant eyes; and one compares the cat with the coon that is treed. The coon may quiver, and in his state of alarm he may jump from one hiding place to another. Conversely, the cat remains on her lofty

197

perch until the dogs leave; and even as they bark maniacally at her, she looks down upon them as condescendingly as if they were so many babies yelping because their diapers are wet.

(Nine was a mystical number among virtually all ancients, and it possessed supernatural powers. Egyptian astronomers divided the world into nine spheres, and the Greek lunar year contained nine, not twelve, months. The River Styx was said to encircle hell ninefold. Odin, the Teutonic god, gave Freya (for whom Friday is named), the Norse goddess of love, dominion over nine worlds. And Jesus died on the ninth hour. In several places in the world, the killing of a cat is certain to bring bad luck since he has nine lives.)

To exclude Morris, deceased, the beautiful cat that sold his birthright for a mess of TV pottage and catnip for his master, the three most celebrated cats in history may be the grinning Cheshire cat, the Kilkenny cat, and Dick Whittington's cat. The ancient British county of Cheshire was noted for cheese and fiery independence. For five hundred years after the Norman Conquest of 1066, Cheshire managed to maintain its autonomy. Politically independent from the remainder of the realm, it maintained its very own parliament, magistrates, and its own system of taxation. Magistrates appointed by a king of England had no authority in Cheshire, but it seems likely that few, if any, tried to be authoritative in Cheshire.

The delicious cheese was shaped and sold in the form of a grinning cat's face. While many etymologists and historians accept the cat-like cheese as the origin of the Cheshire cat, there is also the theory that because Cheshire's population was so sparse, the county became a haven for men on the lam. When crime ran rampant under Richard III, the king appointed one Caterling, of Chester, as Forest Warden for the county. Caterling was given the legal authority to hang highwaymen who took refuge in the dense forests of Cheshire. Caterling, as vain as he was brutal, hanged at least one hundred alleged highwaymen, and he always attended the hangings; and spectators said he grinned sardonically throughout each poor devil's torture on the rope. Shortly, "Grinning like the Cheshire Catterling" became a pat phrase. In time Caterling, as a personality, was forgotten, but the phrase endured and Caterling was shortened to "cat."

And Eric Partridge produced yet another theory. He said that a cat that liked cheese was called a "cheeser cat," and people

198

equated personal pleasure as being "as happy as a cheeser cat that had just feasted on delicious cheese."

Several legends relative to the famous Kilkenny cat run close parallel to one another. The one accepted by a majority of linguists and folklorists says that during one of the innumerable Irish rebellions, Kilkenny was garrisoned by some Hessian mercenaries who amused themselves sadistically in barracks by tying two cats together by their tails and then throwing them across a clothesline to watch them fight.

When the Hessian officers heard about these bloody contests, they resolved to put an end to the cruel sport. The lookout, ever alert for an officer's footfalls, failed to see an approaching field officer; but one of the troopers watching the fight saw the officer, seized his sword, and cut the two tails. The cats made their escape; and when the officer saw two bleeding tails, he demanded an explanation. With the most cavalier nonchalance the soldier explained that the two cats had been fighting and had devoured each other, save for their tails. (One is reasonably sure the late Eugene Field had the Kilkenny Cat in mind in the poem in which the calico dog and gingham cat devoured each other.)

Legend tried hard to make a destitute foundling of Richard Whittington (1359-1423). Actually he was the son of a Gloucester knight. He set up as a mercer in London and he served as alderman, as sheriff, and as Lord Mayor of London, in succession, and he was elected, or appointed, Lord Mayor three different times. According to the endless legend, he sent his cat on a ship going to the Barbary Coast where the cat was sold for a fabulous price.

Apparently Whittington, a man who refused to discuss the source of his wealth, palmed off this story himself. The legend is embellished additionally by the myth that just as the destitute Whittington was about to catch the same ship as his cat, he heard London's Bow Bells chiming:

> Turn again, Whittington,
> Lord Mayor of London.

Whittington acquired a large fortune via sharp trading and by inheritance. He made large loans from his own funds to Kings Henry IV and V, and the latter put Dick Whittington in charge of the finances essential to complete the building of Westminster Abbey. When he died he left a large sum to sundry London charities. But he endures today solely in the phrase "Dick Whittington's cat." For a long time young Englishmen, trying to establish themselves in the worlds of commerce and finance, were enjoined, facetiously, "Well, find a cat such as the one Dick Whittington sold."

"No (or not) room to swing a cat" may not refer to cats at all. True enough, some were swung by their tails by sailors who believed cats were the reincarnation of witches, or certainly the companions of witches. The "cat" referred to so often must have been "the cat o' nine tails," the thonged whip used in the British army and navy for disciplinary purposes. The tie to the cat endured in the obvious fact that the torn flesh of the sailor looked as if it had been scratched by a ferocious cat's claws.

Then again, sailors used to sleep in swinging hammocks which the British called "cots." Once on land for liberty many used the same sleeping room, with the concomitant comment that the room was too crowded to swing a cot, and through indistinct articulation, the *cot* became a *cat*.

The belief that one will encounter dreadful luck if a black cat crosses his path goes back to Egypt, wherein the black cat was almost deified. The cat was sacred to the goddess Isis; and the goddess Bast, or Pasht, the daughter of Isis, was depicted in drawings with the face of a cat. The black cat was endowed with such powers that anyone who killed a cat, even accidentally, was put to death. Cat cemeteries were found by archaeologists, and a shipment of embalmed cats was sent to England.

Then during the Middle Ages the European black cat was a witch or an associate of witches. The belief that a witch could turn herself into a black cat was prevalent in Europe throughout the Middle Ages. There is the old story of a father and his son in Lincolnshire, England, who met a black cat. Thinking that she was a witch in disguise they pounded her with rocks and sticks. The next day when they saw the "real witch," in human form, her face was lacerated and she died soon afterwards. And such is the stuff of enduring legends.

"Letting the cat out of the bag" goes back to marketing methods at British fairs. A customer would buy a small pig; but when he got home, it was a cat that jumped out of his sack.

Apparently this ties closely to Coke's *caveat emptor*: If the purchaser examined the contents of the sack before leaving the fairgrounds, the seller had to replace the cat with a small pig. But if he waited until he got home, he was stuck. From this the legal phrase, "Let the buyer beware," seems to have emerged.

Among the "cat" catch phrases prevalent during this century are "cat house" (meaning a brothel), "the cat's pajamas and the cat's meow" (used as accolades), "cat around" (to loaf or to seek sex while walking the streets or in a bar), "catamaran" (one who loves to be disputatious), "cat beer" (army jive for milk), "cat plant" (an oil or gasoline refinery), "cats and dogs" (cheap stocks), "cat's eye" (a marble game played by small boys), "cat's paw" (a pawn or a dupe), "the cat's whiskers" (which is replaced in recent years by the constant misuse of "neat"), and "cat and mouse" (a game or deal played by two people with consummate caution).

For a long time San Salvador, the smallest and most dense of the Central American republics, was known popularly as Cat Island because of the extraordinarily large number of cats encountered by Pedro de Alvarado, who was sent from Mexico to San Salvador by Cortez. (San Salvador means "The Savior.")

There is the story, not believed to be apocryphal, of the early 19th century New England skipper who sought a loan from a Boston banker. The banker said, "But you have no cargo to sell." The skipper, looking from a window to the solidly frozen St. Charles River, said he could cut and sell ice to the thirsty folk in Latin or Central America. The loan came forth, but it was more in the terms of a wager.

When the skipper returned, having sold his ice, the same loan-bet was made about a shipload of cats. According to the story, the skipper and his crew went around Boston and environs catching stray cats until the ship's hull was filled with rasping meows. He sold the shipload of cats to the governor of a Central American state which was plagued by rats.

There is little known about the civet cat, the name given pretty generally to an Old World animal that resembles the mongoose. This species, two to three feet long, is the source of the commercial civet used as a perfume. And civet cat is applied, also, to the small, spotted skunk, of the genus *Spilogale*. In the American southwest civet cat is the regional name for the cacomistle, or ring-tailed cat, a carnivorous animal that is related

201

to and resembles the raccoon.

"Who'll bell the cat?" is ascribed to Aesop; but apparently the phrase was not used until Piers Plowman (1362-1399). We misuse it today frequently as if heroism conquers all difficulties. But an earlier connotation was, "It is easy to impose impossible remedies." The cat's imperial ways were put into proper focus in one of John Heywood's *Proverbs* of 1564: "A cat may look upon a king." And this may be what Lady Macbeth meant when she said she had to wait to see her husband, although the cat needed no official permission to enter Macbeth's chambers.

It was Montaigne, prince of essayists (Michel Eyquem Montaigne, 1535-1592) who declared truthfully, "When I am playing with my cat who knows whether she have [sic] more sport in dallying with me than I am in gaming with her?"

> Hey diddle, diddle
> The cat and the fiddle.
> The cow jumped over the moon;
> The little dog laughed
> To see such sport
> And the dish ran away with the spoon.

This popular nursery rhyme was first printed around 1765, although there are references as early as 1569 which seem to point to the rhyme. This is almost singular among the best known nursery rhymes in that it appears not to have been based on an actual event. (Many nursery rhymes, satirical when printed, are garbled by the processes of time and the original subject is completely lost.)

Normally we render Charles Kingsley's dictum from *Westward Ho* as "There is more than one way to skin a cat." Kingsley actually wrote, "There are more ways of killing a cat than choking her with cream." Our platitude states the palpably obvious, but Kingsley's phrase implies that someone has accomplished a relatively simple chore in a foolish, expensive manner, and one which may not accomplish the stated and intended object.

Tabby, as a general name for cats, is derived from the Old French *atabi*, via the Arabic *attabi*, a rich watered type of silk manufactured, originally, at Al-attabuya, a suburb of Baghdad. Tabby was applied to brindled domestic cats because their fur

202

seems to have suggested watered silk. *Tabby* is used also to mean an old maid. Hence, *Tabby* endures just as *Bossy* endures as a general name for a cow and *Dobbin* for a horse.

The Indispensable Fly

When early summer begins to fling red pepper by the boxcar load, that psychopathic bum and pestiferous freeloader, the fly, takes up residence in every home as a non-paying hot weather guest. The man who has lost faith in all other verities can count upon the fly as he counted upon the saints of his innocent childhood.

And if Noah took two flies on his Ark, he could certainly envision the day when the housefly would have voluntary ingress to all buildings that would defy second story artists, termites, and the Big Bomb. And surely Job must have known that for sheer, damnable exasperation, the fly was ellipitical in the pestilences that struck him.

Fortunately, though, the fly, a real democrat, plays no favorites. He had just as soon aggravate a saint as a solicitor for a charity campaign. Indeed, he unites all of humanity when other magnets turn into soap bubbles. In summer mankind is lawyers, doctors, merchants, bankers, mechanics; and the fly survives only during those vacuous hours when mankind is not pitting his strength, skills, and ingenuity in the timeless battle against him. As the dumbest bullfrog in the pond must know, mankind's chief talents are hung on the line to try to outfox that fly. Emily Dickinson wrote, "When Papa is on the sofa, the whole house is filled," and one fly seems to dominate an entire household as the wicked Pharoahs bullyragged the hapless Israelites.

One of our favorite passages in literature comes in Lawrence Sterne's (1713-1868) *Tristram Shandy*. Amid laborious expenditure of energy, Uncle Toby catches a fly, raises the window, and gives the fly the run of the outdoors. His nephew asks Uncle Toby why he did such a strange thing, and Uncle Toby answers, "The world is big enough for that fly and me." (Aaron Burr, a devotee of Sterne's, said, towards his last, "How different my life would have been if I could have emulated Uncle Toby and realized that the world is big enough for me and Alexander Hamilton.")

There are innumerable types of fly killers today, just as there are multiple choice plays in baseball, or being a cop, or a kidnapper. But two classic types will suffice for summary explanation. As the fly buzzes and spews maniacally, one man pretends to be lost in his newspaper or his book. The fly is supposed to think the man is unaware of his minute buzz-bombings. However, beneath this pose of utter unawareness the man thinks of nothing but luring the fly within striking distance. For that fly is a tiny black bear on the wings of Satan, and the man feigning indifference in his chair is actually pouring out invisible honey.

Sometimes he secrets a swatter behind his back or under his hindquarters. Periodically he reaches to touch the swatter the loving way an indigent fondles a bale of cash he finds under the rock upon which he has been sitting and loafing. Yet when he fires his heavy artillery, there may be more busted vases than dead flies. The garbage collector can almost count the town's fly population by counting the broken vases and other bits of smashed crockery in the town's garbage cans.

The second type of killer is much more sadistic. He grins and shows more teeth than ten Halloween pumpkins. He seeks flies as Teddy Roosevelt and Ernest Hemingway stalked big game. He is a bounty hunter and a lethal claims' jumper. When he sees a sun-crazed fly outside the window, he turns from placid, buck-toothed freeholder into Mr. Hyde operating with a Browning automatic rifle. Opening the window may seem too obvious, but he leaves a wide crack in the screen door. The freeholder lies in wait, like the road agent of old, to bash the gullible fly's head as it oozes into the treacherous paradise the man has devised for it. When such a man makes a kill on the rise, one expects to see him photographed with one foot on the carcass, folded newspaper on the shoulder, in the manner that Teddy Roosevelt posed with the moose he had just killed.

Some of the more inverterate stalkers have been known to sprinkle a little sugar just inside the doorway. The fly goes so insane doing back flips to get to the sugar, one has a harrowing picture of the heroin addict who is dying for a fix. The poor fly is exactly like the addict who is within arms' reach of the fix but it keeps eluding his grasp. Finally, the man opens the door and other flies are lured into the sweet smelling trap. And after a really big safari, one almost expects to see this man send for a taxidermist to mount the dead flies that pile up near the baited doorway.

But if one thinks about this seriously, he knows it is well that old Noah did not take a swatter or any flypaper on his fabulous voyage. Before the Ark completed its shakedown and before the first cat got as seasick as a dog, those two flies would have been *corpus delictied*, most likley. And today there would be a hole as big as the Dead Sea in every summertime's heartland. If it were not for the perennial visitations of the housefly, man's ingenuity would likely become so inept a cub scout could whittle a better specimen of aggressive agility from a piece of bark with a Barlow knife.

The large compound eyes of the horsefly are located most conspicuously on its head. Many people think the eyes of this pesky insect consist of small yellowish specks or scales on tiny stems under the wings. This, it is contended, is proved by the fact that when these clublike appendages are removed, the horsefly loses its equilibrium and flies erratically. As a matter of fact, the specks or scales are aborted underwings, called calypters or squamae, by entomologists. Similar phenomena exist in other insects. The common horsefly has five eyes located on the upper front of its head. Because of its five so-called eyes, many people compare the horsefly's sight to the giraffe's with his protruding eyes that enable it to look forward and behind simultaneously.

Not just incidentally, two of the most popular songs of the 19th century were "Shoo, Fly, Don't Bother Me" and "Flies In the Buttermilk."

In Defense of Frogs

Many people are wantonly callous about bull and toad frogs, and they are completely unaware of the charms and spirited services of bull and toad frogs. If they bother to think at all, they may remember Mark Twain's story about the champion jumping frog that was crammed with bird shot. Poets go off their rockers chanting madrigals about robins trilling, creeks playing kettle drums, trees crooning poignantly in the late autumn wind, or meadow flowers doing a ballet while the spring wind plays a silver flute.

Hardly anyone makes up lyrics about frogs, but to those with two inner ears, the booming of the bullfrogs is more ominous than heavy cannons firing along the bay. And this rollicking basso is a summons to the reality of any season. Birds may sing chipped fragments that are as incomprehensible as the late Gertrude Stein; but the big bellied frog, the stout lunged baritone, sings the way bugles blow, the way that eagles fly. Meanwhile, the lark, the dove, and the pine tree are canonized, and the frog may be ugly as Old Testament sin, but his garbled hosannas herald the truth that fervor can win over patched trousers within a single week. (The unholy neglect of the frog by lyricists may be ascribable to some old idiot's assertion that handling a toad will put warts upon one's hands, or it may be that some incipient poet was badly frightened by the jumping of detached frog legs. Anyway, each community used to have an old lady who specialized in removing warts. She never revealed her private magic; but she counted the warts with a special broom straw, asked the person if he believed she could remove his warts, and, according to local mythology, the warts vanished in three days. Our founding fathers stole a dishrag and hid it in a stump of a tree. Another cure-all was to tie as many knots in a string as there were warts on the hands. Yet another was to rub the warts with beans, peas, or stones and throw these away

207

along the roadside. After the peas, etc. were thrown away, the warts disappeared alongside the same roadway. Two thousand years ago, Pliny, in his classic *Natural History* wrote: "Lie on your back along a boundary line on the twentieth day of the moon, extend the hands over the head, and with whatever thing you grasp when so doing, rub the warts, and they will soon disappear.

Scientists say there are more than one hundred species of frogs and toads. These and not "Chloe," are the real laureates of the swamplands. Scientists say some frogs are innate directors, guiding musicians without a baton, bringing from the murky darkness, in fee simple, the same deep, rolling magic a symphony director or a choir director gets paid big money for doing. Before spring races hither, let us remember to attune to the voice of the turtle (dove), but let us not forget the much aligned basso profundo of the branch head.

But even when spring has eaten her delicious lollipops and has hidden her fairyland in the sky's far pastures, or even when July is a mad dog snapping his leash and chasing his own tail in a furious circle, the frogs conspire with the lily pads to help us retain our sanity amid the anguished torpor of Dog Days.

Anyone with a single inner ear has heard a lone tree frog, unseen by him and by scores of other tree frogs, heist a tune, and almost immediately there is a rousing acapella concert. When the leader stops, the choir invisible stops; and when he pitches another tune, the hidden tenors and sopranos chime in.

Meanwhile, the green frog that leases the lily pads for the summer casts a spell of sheer ingratiation. It is as if a water ballet were being made of "Beauty and the Beast." Green, he may be, and mangy, too, but he's an atomic submarine singing the basso parts in a Wagnerian opera. He dives down so far and stays so long beneath the muggy water one thinks he must have been torpedoed; but just as one is about to make a short memorial speech, the green monster floats up, with all of the offhanded aimlessness of a piece of green flotsam.

Harsh music critics say he cannot sing but one song. But no one since Miriam found Moses in the bullrushes has ever injected so much passion and lyricism into "Knee-deep, knee-deep." The metallic echoes of it seem to set the church bells to chiming. Water lilies are cool poems on stainless parchments, and the bullfrog is a court jester. If neither elevates any stocks on Wall

Street, they always manage to bring the fretful, peevish summer weather back its soul and its grace. And anyone lucky enough to understand the saga of the bullfrog and the lily pad spends his wealth one golden coin at a time. Indeed, the real devotees save some of it to melt the ice that tries to make a Silas Marner of nature during winter's harsh inundations.

Although "frog" is used humorously and even derisively to mean a Frenchman, the term contained no original denigrations. Paris began as a quagmire and it endured more as a quagmire than as a city, for several years during its formative period. Frogs live and breed in quagmires, and that is precisely the reason that residents of Paris were known as frogs from the outset. Gradually the term absorbed a degree of culpability, as it was extended to the entire French nation by people who did not know any better.

" 'Twixt Plated Decks"

It is unlikely that any piece of folklore is more widely known than the race between the tortoise and the hare. While this story is ascribed to Aesop, it has turned up in one fashion or other, in several European languages. Actually turtle, tortoise, and terrapin are members of the reptilian order of *Testudinato chiloria*.

The word *turtle* is applied to marine mammals and to some of the freshwater species. Most of the ones that live in ponds or marshlands are called "water tortoises," and the terrestial breed, regardless of size, is tagged "land tortoise." The diamond terrapin comes down from the Algonquins, and the name is applied recklessly to any of its North American double first cousins.

The snapping turtle, a creature of dry land, is said to hold on to a human until Judgment Day, although in some accounts violent thunder makes the turtle relax his grip and scoot away.

Female turtles come out on star struck nights to lay their eggs. When retreat is wise, many of these turtles turn with their plated bellies up. In this position they are unable to move, but such turtles have been known to live in this clumsy position, and without water or food, for several weeks hand-running.

Turtle was applied to *dove* long before it was construed as a reptile. The word is believed to have acquired the latter sense through the assimilation of French *tortue*, from the Latin *tortus* (meaning crooked). In Spain *tortuga* is applied to turtles and tortoises. Columbus named an island off the northwest coast of Hispaniola *Tortuga Island*. Columbus thought that the island greatly resembled a humped turtle, asleep on the sea. (Dr. Mudd, who set John Wilkes Booth's broken ankle was imprisoned at Dry Tortugas, then one of the lesser known Florida keys.) It was Ponce de Leon in 1515 who gave a series of springless islands off Florida the name Dry Tortugas. Although drinking water was virtually unknown, these islands abounded in turtles. In a general way, a turtle, a tortoise, or terrapin may be described as a reptile with its skeleton on the outside of its body.

The giant turtle is one species of animal life whose span may be greater than man's. There is irrefutable scientific proof that giant Galapagos turtles have lived one hundred and fifty years, and scientists have estimated the age of several turtles to be as much as four hundred years. While the turtle's prodigious longevity is true, beyond all peradventure, many pranks have been associated with the astonishing old age. Captain James Cook is supposed to have captured a tortoise on the Galapagos Islands in 1773. Cook carved "1773" on the turtle's back and turned it loose. For almost two hundred years newspapers reported that someone had reported seeing the 1773 turtle.

A tortoise on St. Helena used to be pointed out, given immense deference, because it was the only living thing that ever saw Napoleon. (Victor Hugo explained the ghastly change of events in Napoleon's life by saying, "God was bored with him.)

According to an old proverb, the turtle contains seven kinds of meat. But this appears to be just another way of saying that the flesh of a turtle is tender, palatable, and wholesome. Thus it has the qualities of chicken, venison, beef, pork, mutton and other meats. It is unlikely that epicures would agree on just what seven varieties of meat the turtle's is supposed to resemble.

The green fat of the turtle is justifiably celebrated for its succulence. The last time a head count was taken, Chinamen bought eighty per cent of all the turtles sold at New York City's famous Fulton Fish Market. Epicures have declared turtle soup an inordinate luxury for several centuries.

During the American Revolution, a French naval officer named Blanchard described in his journal a "turtle party" given at Newport in 1780. Blanchard says this kind of supper had a "great vogue in America." He said that the purpose of the party at Newport was "to eat a turtle weighing four hundred pounds which an American vessel had just brought home from one of our islands in the West Indies. However, the meat did not seem very palatable to me; it is true that it was badly cooked."

For centuries many people have believed that when a turtle gets sufficiently hungry, it will suck a cow's teats for milk. This is a fascinating nuance that seems to be bereft of any foundation.

The Insect Barons

If boys did not go out and catch a few lightning bugs and ticks, summertime would stump her toe and have stone bruises for three months. Thus far, few things in science are so thrilling and fascinating as a child's personal discovery of various summer insects. All the electronic miracles of the age are routed by the child's personal discovery of the bugs that blink off and on, as if the headlight on a locomotive were batting its eye.

The old medicine bottle is filled with many genies when a child goes out in the velvety summer night to catch lightning bugs, to hold them in protective custody, and then to let them fly away. For some children the magic bottle is the light in Boston's Old North Church, and others are flagmen waving through trains of night birds down the main line. Some are Greek marathon runners, handing the sparkling torch to a brother or a playmate. The possibilities are as numerous as they are enchanting, but the best part is that these flying golden nuggets are completely unknown, far out in limbo, until they are discovered by a new set of tykes each summer.

And children a little older still pluck long, stiff blades of grass to burrow into a doodlebug's hole. Some others burn a piece of old newspaper although the doodlebug is not hurt, as they chant:

> Ladybug, ladybug
> Come out of your hole;
> Your house in on fire
> And all your children are gone.

Originally "ladybug," or "ladybird" in England meant "Our Lady's Bird," or a reference to Jesus's mother. Experts say this rhyme is of "great antiquity," and parallels are to be found in almost every European language. It is also thought this child's jingle is all that remains of an. ancient incantation, a charm against witches and demons, or perhaps a chant to the goddess Freya.

Today the doodlebug is hooked in the manner of an unwary fish, and it is not uncommon to see a boy (what we used to designate as a hobbledehoy) going around with a doodlebug in a bottle. (It can be a jumping beetle.) As cunning as Tom Sawyer and as racy with sporting blood as Penrod, the boy carries his tick or beetle around to jump against other local champions. This boy, who emulates "Bet 'em a Million Gates," has all of his associates' bright baubles one day, and the next day he is out hunting a new bug or frog to recoup his lost fortune. And it was ever thus. If harmony and environment are to run deeply, it usually finds marvelous fulfillment in the inquisitive minds of unsullied children who are the temporary monarchs of the summer night and the exalted sovereign of the moon and the scented breezes.

"Pigeons On the Grass, Alas"

Many years ago Gertrude Stein wrote "Pigeons on the grass, alas," and Vaughan Williams wrote a first-class musical composition, a tone poem, after "Pigeons on the grass, alas." Although doves and pigeons are virtually synonymous, when used without modification the two words are coextensive in application. Every dove is a pigeon and every pigeon is a dove. Dove comes from a Teutonic root of unknown origin and meaning, while pigeon is derived through French from a root that means "little bird." Pigeon is now the better known of the two words. In plain prose dove is applied to the smaller and wilder species to distinguish them from the larger, tamer bird, the pigeon. Thus we talk about mourning doves, stock doves, ground doves, scales doves, rock doves, wild doves, and turtle doves. Conversely, we talk about wood pigeons, homing pigeons, pouter pigeons, passenger pigeons, tumbler pigeons, and wild pigeons. Writers, especially poets, lean to *dove* for its graceful and tranquil sound.

Two centuries ago the passenger pigeon, a migratory bird slightly larger than the turtledove, was likely the nation's most plentiful bird. Audubon reported seeing great flocks of passenger pigeons, and they flew in such compact formations Audubon said they shut off the sun. When the flocks, estimated at "from one to two billion," settled on a forest for the night they broke the trees. Audubon calculated that such a flock required nine hundred bushels of feed each day.

During breeding season hundreds of passenger pigeons nested in the same tree. Their cooing was so loud the report from a gun could not be heard. In 1857 an Ohio game commission reported that the passenger pigeon needed no legal protection: "Wonderfully prolific, having the vast forests of the north as its breeding grounds, traveling hundreds of miles in search of food, it is here today and elsewhere tomorrow, and no ordinary

214

destruction can lessen them or be missed [sic] from the myriads that are yearly produced." Yet, in less than sixty years all the passenger pigeons were gone. The bird had become extinct. Authentic records reveal that the last one was sighted in 1898, although three in a wild state were reported but without official corroboration. The last known survivor was a captive bird that died in the Cincinnati Zoo in 1914. When the passenger pigeon's mate had died in 1910, one thousand dollars was offered, for another, but none was ever found.

Many theories attempt to account for the extinction of the passenger pigeon. It is probably not true, as some surmised, that the pigeon vanished, presto, at the apogee of its American population. Some woodland experts believe that these birds, numbering several billion, went into a massive migration to some unknown land. Again, they were killed by forest fires or large pieces of hail, and here and there someone wrote that they must have been blown out to sea, where they drowned. One expert believes they were destroyed by a chicken mite brought over from Europe. This man reported that in the 1870's and 1880's he found thousands of dead squabs at the bases of trees in which passenger pigeons nested.

Many factors probably contributed to the extinction of the passenger pigeon. Early settlers shot them by the thousands, and millions of bodies were shipped to markets. (In 1879 they were selling on the Chicago market from fifty to sixty cents a dozen. A good pigeon hunter could make ten dollars a day when ten dollars was a chunk of money.)

The last large nesting of passenger pigeons occurred near Petrosky, Michigan, in 1878. The nesting area was around forty miles long and several miles wide. Indians and American boys captured thousands at a penny a piece.

But since the passenger pigeons were communistic in their habits, the species may not have been able to adjust to a new and alien environment. (The destruction of the great forests of the mid-north would be a powerful agency, also.) But as civilization encroached upon the wildness, the birds disappeared. The common turtledove and the band-tailed wild pigeon of the Pacific Ocean area have some superficial comparisons to the passenger pigeons. Fortunately, for history and for science, a few of the passenger pigeons were stuffed and are on public exhibition.

Crocodile Tears

The legend that the crocodile cries and sheds tears to entice victims is among the oldest myths. Ancients believed the crocodile could emulate precisely the signs of a distressed human, and they believed the crocodile cried when it ate its victim.

There are secretions in the eyes of crocodiles, to keep them moist, just as there are in all animals, but they do not have tear glands. Nonetheless, scientists say the eyes of crocodiles and alligators emit a watery liquid when they attempt to eat something that is too large to swallow.

The earliest account of the crocodile's emitting the cry of a distressed human may have come in *The Voyages and Travels of Sir John Mandeville*, written in French in 1371 by an unidentified author. And there are numerous allusions to this Uriah Heep-like performance by Elizabethan writers and some who came afterwards. Francis Bacon, in an essay called "Of Wisdom For A Man's Self," wrote: "It is the wisdom of crocodiles that they shed tears when they devour." And this colloquy occurs in Shakespeare's *Anthony and Cleopatra*, during a drunken bash aboard Pompey's galley, off Minsnum:

Lepidus: What manner of thing is your crocodile?
Anthony: It is shaped, sir, and as long as it hath breath; it is just so high as it is, and moves with its own organs; it lives by that which nourisheth it, and the elements out of it transmigrates.
Lepidus: What is the color of it?
Anthony: Of its own colour, too.
Lepidus: It is a strange serpent.
Anthony: 'Tis so. And the tears of it are wet.

216

In *Othello* the jealous Moor says to the weeping Desdemona:

If that the earth could teem with woman's tears
Each drop she falls would be a crocodile.

And in *Henry VI*, Queen Margaret says:

Henry, my lord, is cold in great affairs,
Too full of foolish pity, and Gloucester's show
Beguiles him, as the mournful crocodile
With sorrow snares relenting passengers.

Killer-Sharks

Much fulsome adoration attended the two movies *Jaws* and *Jaws II*. Even if these movies were sufficiently bloody to appease the lusts of the most insatiably hungry vampire, even if the movies were sufficiently gory and sadistic to make a bulldozer throw up, American audiences must be addicted to blood flowing profusely, when it is not their blood. Hollywood's current propensity for bloodletting kindles Kipling's two knock-out lines about the old British empire:

> If blood be the price of Admirality,
> Lord God, we ha' paid in full.

There are several varieties of man-eating sharks: To mention a few there are the white, the blue, and the thresher. The basking shark, usually found in icy waters, often attains a length of thirty feet.

Without attempting to be grandiose, or "I told you so," this author had his say about sharks in a poem several years before the two *Jaws* movies:

Who's Zoo

The sharkiness of sharks
Beats the hoggishness of hogs all hollow,
And the Jacksonian mullishness of mules
Routs the elephantineness of pachyderms.
And, surely, the ebullient sass of jaybirds
Vanquishes all the canaries that graduated from Juliard.

To my nose, at least, the skunkiness of skunks,
Is infinitely preferable to the fishiness of fish.
The regal cattiness of cats is a diadem

When one considers the appalling chickenness of chickens.
Forsooth, the eeliness of eels is balm to the soul
When held parallel to the dark squidiness of squids.
(Anyone who prefers horsing around to monkeying around
Must like Bryan better than he likes Clarence Darrow.)

To deviate, which may be almost routine today,
Squirrels have luxuriant tails to stroke
But white whales with their shimmering tails
Are better than a wet version of *O! Calcutta.*

Anyway, as I said, I really dig sharks:
Whenever they bite your goddam head off
They never say it was done for a noble purpose.

Mostly About George Green and Jacob Fuller

Throughout the insular era, Goose Grease, a panacea for just about everything, was advertised by an aged Jehu and two geese that pulled a tiny wagon, part of which was cardboard, that extolled the merits of the grease. The episodic appearance of George Green and Jacob Fuller in small southern towns came as a sudden shower beats through the tranquil blue of a July sky.

There was never any prior notice. The elderly black and the two giant geese just showed up, usually around mid-morning; and before either of the geese could honk, the streets were quick with rapt human expectancy. On the dirt end of the town's main street, the black man would blow a trumpet. The sounds he always made were to "The Campbells Are Coming"; but, of course, small-town folks put it "Tra, la, tra, la, George Green and Jacob Fuller are coming."

As the giant geese pulled the miniature wagon, the old black man walked alongside the wagon, holding the toy reins and doffing his beaver hat to the throng. It was not long before the annual appearance of George Green and Jacob Fuller served as time, event, and bookmarks in local history. Many, many events were dated with "just before George Green and Jacob Fuller were here," or "right after" they were in town.

Most people decided the geese had found the spring for which Ponce de Leon searched with such indefatigable persistence. It never seemed to occur to anyone that the originals had died, that a new George Green and Jacob Fuller pulled the little dab of the Goose Grease wagon. Almost everyone in the community held the pair in the tenderest protective custody.

"As foolish as a goose" is a sacred, bucolic platitude; but it never applied to George Green and Jacob Fuller. They walked and acted as if they had just been awarded the Ph.D. at Harvard, and many of us expected the giant geese to stop and talk about current news.

220

"What is sauce for the goose is sauce for the gander," was penned by Tom Brown (1603-1703) in *New Maxims*, and it was Charles H. Poole in *Archaic Words*, who said, "The goose is a silly bird—too much for one to eat and not enough for two." (Today that same standard is ascribed to some local man who possesses an inordinate capacity for liquor. He is supposed to have said: "A pint is a terrible way to bottle whiskey. It is not enough for two drinks, but it is a little too much for one drink.")

Robert Burton (1577-1640) in his classic, *The Anatomy of Melancholy*, comes ringing down the halls of history with "All his geese are swans," meaning, of course, a supreme egotist who praises himself and everything he owns. John Lyly (1554-1606) is supposed to be the first man to wisecrack: "It is a blinde Goose that cometh to the Foxes sermon." Matthew Arnold, in his poem, "The Last Word," seems to tie a nice string around the entire package:

Let the long contention cease
Geese are swans and swans are geese,
Let them have as they will.
Thou art tired; best be still.

Natural Oddball

There must be as little public information about the zebra as there is about any living creature. Even if the zebra is not maligned, per se, as the poor mule is slandered, many jokes are told about the zebra, and most of the comparisons are with zippered clothing, convict's duds, and pajamas. Zebra is the generic name for several animals; and it is a native of Africa, belonging to the family of the ass, distinguished from Equs (the horse) because his body is banded, more or less, black upon brownish. He is also much smaller than the horse.

The typical mountain zebra (*Equs Zebrae*) inhabits south Africa but the breed is approaching extinction. A few of these are captured and afforded rigorous protection. About 1873 zebras abounded in herds on the plains. Today, we think of the zebra as being unfit for dray work, but sporadic experiments made since 1872 have shown that zebras can work in harness. However, any general advancement in being man-trained seems almost fatuous. Buxhell's Zebra (*Equs buchelli*) is the type usually seen at circuses and fairs, and in zoos.

The hard, warty patches seen on the inner side of the legs of horses, popularly known as "chestnuts," are thought to be survivals of scent or recognition glands and to be homologous to the similar glands on the limbs of other quadrupeds. Zebras and asses are distinguished by having these chestnuts on the forelegs only. (During the Middle Ages chestnuts, or callosites, were believed to be medicinally efficacious.)

From time to time the question is asked: Is the zebra a light animal with dark stripes or is it a dark animal with light stripes? The ground color of a zebra is a pale, yellowish brown and the stripes are black or dark brown. When the zebra and the ass are crossed, the light tan predominates as the basic body color in the offspring. The answer to the proverbial question is that it may be said that the zebra is a light brown animal with black or dark brown stripes.

For a long time convicts have been called zebras, and zebras have been called convicts. During World War II many non-commissioned officers were called zebras because of the corporal or sergeant's stripes on their arms.

In the 1970's *zebra* appeared to mean miscegnation, and in television shows about black families *zebra* meant the offspring of a white man and a black woman.

At the turn of the century *zebra* was applied to such hardcore Populists as Ignatius Donnelly, and "sons of the wild jackass." And there was a general political stigma. From the standpoint of the Democrat a zebra was a person who switched to the Republicans, Populists, or Fusionists. But this verbal apostasy depended upon the person who was criticizing. Hence zebra was virtually synonymous with mugwump, the man with his face on one side of the fence and his wump on the other side.

Brer Sparrow Found a Home

The late Dr. Thurmond Kitchin, President of Wake Forest University, once declared: "The Baptists are so numerous in North Carolina they are exceeded in numbers only by the English sparrow."

The gangster who would park his gat to write a birthday poem for his mother will gun down a yard full of sparrows just as if he were winning his moll a kewpie doll busting clay pigeons. We seem to have red days and special weeks for everything from the groundhog to "Miss Keg of Nails," but it is not likely that any official decree will ever contain a single word of kindness for the sparrow. It is about as hard to pry words of praise from American lips as it is to get Leo Durocher to dance at an umpire's wedding. Almost simultaneously, bucolic bards have stripped their lyrical gears canonizing almost every other bird, from the time of the Ark, to the birdie on Nellie's hat, to Alexander the Swoose, the uncanny hybrid turned into "half swan and half goose" by Tin Pan Alley.

For a fact, Robert Bridges, the late poet laureate of England, said he spent twenty-two years trying to think up a suitable poem, to dream up something new to say about the nightingale. As bad luck would have it, most of the nightingales Bridges started out rhapsodizing about were long dead when he finally finished his poem.

Actually, what Americans call a sparrow is usually called a weaver finch in Europe. The sparrow is not an American native, and the first sparrows were not brought here until 1850. Nicholas Pike, head of the Brooklyn Institute, brought eight pairs from England in 1850. It was believed that these sparrows would multiply and rid the nation's trees from foliage-eating caterpillars, particularly the span worm, which is the larva of the Geometrid moth. The first sparrows did not live long, and others, apparently a grand total of one hundred pairs, were

224

imported between 1850 and 1881. They did eat some of the worms that are foliage, but the sparrows wrecked vengeance upon gentler birds. They created infinitely more problems, in the long haul, than they arrested.

But the transparent, if elusive, truth is that the sparrow is something Americans can count upon when everything else is a mountain of Jello. They are as viable in our mores as brass door knobs and handkerchiefs in hay fever time. Yet we speak of sparrows the way we speak of our demented relatives whom we try to secrete in the basement when snazzy company comes.

The sparrow does have similarities to the Democrat in that neither belongs to an organized party.

Thus the ageless nomad is akin to falling leaves, when the autumnal wind blows without patience or memory. The sparrow is equated with charity drives, chiggers, summer complaint, leaky spigots, and the hucksters who ring the doorbell to sell light bulbs for good works while one is eating supper. Albeit, those few 19th century immigrants were made of true pioneer stock. They spread everywhere. An additional civic chore was added to protecting shade trees. They were sicked onto potato bugs; but if the potatoes were grateful, they spoke their gratitude underground.

As they taught rabbits lessons in the multiplication table, they were active, if unpaid, sanitation workers in the days of the horse. Then Henry Ford ended this line of work about the same way that the Wright boys put the kibosh on the stagecoach. Yet amid all of their vicissitudes, the sparrows have never played favorites. They take no more sass from a Volkswagen than they took from Old Dobbin. Never respecters of personages and never terrified by minor heroics, they had just as soon stake out squatters' rights on the banker's lawn as on the lawn of the village Oakies. But for this display of democracy, we return it with nothing but harsh words, works, and B-B rifles. Yet, our minor sadisms and stinging castigations turn up few Benedict Arnolds.

Other birds leave us for the downy opulence of Palm Beach, but the sparrow wouldn't give up one dusty lane or one automobile to splatter with his "doings" for Miami with Key West thrown in for good measure. Even when Old Man January sends rain in the form of marlin spikes, Brer Sparrow does not forsake his rustic abode. So, curse, and belt, and flay him, as though he is a winged Gunga Din; if he had big, sensitive ears, he would have deserted us long ago. And if we did not have him to curse, whom should we abuse when the legislature is not in session. Take three guesses and the first two do not count. Without the sparrow to berate, to have as a direct object for a hundred vexations and exasperations, there would not be enough couches extant to shrink us and rid us of the frustrations the sparrow helps us discharge, without fee, and in fee simple.

A Lotta Bull

The ox, a bovine animal, of the sub-family *bovinae*, goes back to prehistoric times. He seems to have been the original beast of burden, and the domestication of the ox began in the Bronze Age. An adult male is a bull; an adult female is called a cow; a young bull of either sex is a heifer; a young castrated bull is a steer, and an adult castrated bull is a stag.

Oxen were taken from Asia to Europe in ancient times, and scientists say they were tall and strong and this enabled some of them to survive the Glacier Period. Julius Caesar, much impressed by oxen, is probably the person who introduced the vastly improved, short-horned ox into Great Britain.

Cows sweat profusely because their sweat glands are distributed widely over the skin. The ox also has fewer sweat glands. The ox's sweat glands are developed completely on the muzzle. They do not drip sweat from the end of their nose, as is common with cows.

The once heralded black ox symbolizes death, old age, bad luck, or any trouble in general. "The black ox has not yet trod on his feet" is a proverb that was popular as early as 1546 when John Heywood mentions this in his book *Proverbs*. In Sappho and Phoa, written by John Lyly in 1591, this note appears, "Now cow's feet on her eye, and the black ox hath trod on her foot."

The allusion originally was to the black oxen sacrificed by the Romans to propiate the gods, and to Pluto especially, in his role as lord of the nether world. (White cattle were sacrificed to Jupiter.) In Rome the altar on which the black oxen were sacrificed was twenty feet below ground level, and the altar was never exposed to public view save when official sacrifices were being made.

In 1923 the late Gertrude Atherton published her extremely popular novel, *Black Oxen*, and she took the title from a line in

William Butler Yeats's poem, "Countess Cathleen": "The years, like great black oxen tread the world." (Among the Arabs the black camel is the symbol of violent death, of murder, specifically. The late Earl Derr Biggers used *Black Camel* as the title of a murder mystery.)

The ox has supplied the language with ox-bird, or ox-eye, or ox bot, a fly that attacks cattle, but is often applied to nagging humans, to several Ox Bow Rivers, ox pecker (the buffalo bird), ox gall (bile), the ox warbler (bird that hangs around cattle to sing there), and there is always Walter Clark's marvelous novel, *The Ox-Bow Incident*. "Big ox" and "dumb ox" are heard in daily conversations.

According to the late Glenn Tucker, once a White House correspondent, President Coolidge disliked Adolph Ochs, publisher of the *New York Times* and the noted reporter-editor Herbert Bayard Swope. Someone, looking for Swope, asked Coolidge if he had seen Swope. "Yup," the President replied glumly, "I just saw the Ochs and the ass going down that way."

The cow is the female of the ox family, and virtually everyone drinks milk and eats butter everyday. As Odgen Nash said:

> The cow is of the bovine ilk:
> One end moo, the other end milk.

(That is not a proper use of *ilk*. *Ilk* does not mean of the same kind. It is from the Anglo-Saxon *ilea*, and it signifies the same and identical. Knockwinnock (of that ilk) simply means that Knockwinnock was a man's name and also the name of his house and property. Albeit only an idiot would object to Nash's ringing rhyme.)

In his *Child's Garden Of Verse*, Robert Louis Stevenson has a poem that children used to say by heart:

> The friendly cow, all red and white,
> I love with all my heart;
> She gives me cream with all her might,
> To eat with apple tart.

> She wanders lowing here and there,
> And she can not stay,

All in the pleasant air
The pleasant light of day.

And blown by all the winds that pass
And wet with all the shadows,
She walks among the meadow grass
And eats the meadow flowers.

Oddly enough, in view of thousands of movies made and the millions of pages written about the cowboy, the word seems to have been used first, officially, in 1776, in the "neutral ground" of Westchester, Pa. During the American Revolution, the Westchester cowboys foregathered in an organization to plunder Tories and Whigs alike, and their specialty was stealing cattle. Thus, the cow rustler not only preceded the migration to the West, but was in vogue before Lewis and Clark explored the unknown vastness.

As a retaliatory agency, the British came up with a similar organization of ruffians known as the "Skinners," who plundered the Whigs and the Cowboys.

The animal that Stevenson said "children love," has given the language many side phrases. The cowpea, closely related to asparagus, grown chiefly in Asia, Central Africa, and the Malay Archipelago; cowpox, a variole, a disease among cows characterized by fever; cowslip, the stemless, perennial herb; cowberry, an aquatic plant; cow parsnip, the coarse, perennial herb that grows to a height of from three to six feet; cowbird, usually found in Bermuda; cow plant, of the milkweed family; cow wheat, common name for the *hemiparasite sciophisloriaceous*; and cowbird, which escapes the dangers of men and other animals much in the manner of the European cuckoo.

Finally, "cowpoke" had no relevance to a cowboy's purse. When cattle were loaded on freight trains to be shipped to the slaughter houses of Chicago, and other meat centers, the cowboy stood along the runway to the cattle car, poking the animals in the rump with a hard prod to keep them moving until the flat car with railings was filled to capacity.

"Watered stock," in the commercial connotation, actually arose from the fact of watering thin cows for the market. Daniel Drew, on the barons of the era of Commodore Vanderbilt, once bought a large herd of cows in upper New York, and he used drovers to get his cows to the New York City livestock market. In order to inflate the total poundage, Drew fed his cattle salt brick en route. As the herd approached New York City the animals were ravenously thirsty, and they drank an enormous amount of water. Drew drove his "watered stock" straight to the livestock market where he made a small fortune just on surplus water.

About the bull, William Carlos Williams wrote:

It is in captivity
ringed, haltered, chained
to a drag
the bull is godlike

unlike the cows
he lives alone, nozzles
the sweet grass gingerly
to pass the time away

he kneels, lies down
And stretching out
a foreleg lifts himself
about the hoof

then stays
with half-closed eyes,
Olympian commentary on
tye bright passage of days.

— The round sun
smooth his lacquer
with glossy pinetrees

his substance hard
as ivory or glass —
through which the wind
yet plays —
            milkless

he nods
the hair between his horns

and eyes mottled
with hyacinthine curls.

In provincial America the best known animal in the civilized world had to be the bull whose snorting prowess was plastered everywhere to advertise Bull Durham Smoking Tobacco, five cents a sack.

Bull Durham appears to be the first product to be advertised nationally and internationally. Thousands of dollars worth of premiums were rewarded each year for the return of empty Bull Durham sacks. The premiums ran a vast gamut from trinkets to real mantlepiece clocks.

For a number of years the company's art department was headed by Gilmer Koerner, for whom the North Carolina town Kernersville is named, despite the change in spelling. Koerner, who used the pseudonym "Rueben Rink" for many of his earthy, bucolic paintings, may have painted the original Bull.

There was hardly any series of American billboards that did not contain the roaring, uproarious Bull, and he seemed so alive and virile one expected him to ram a buggy or a Model T. His forelegs flailed the air, as the prodigious animal pitched on his hind legs. One series of these posters left nothing to the imagination relative to the Bull's sex. In this same series a heartsick cow stands a few feet from the Bull, and there is a wire fence between the two. The cow's insatiable, unrequited yearnings are within one of those balloons that commercial artists and drawers of comic strips used to employ. The breathless caption, emanating from the cow towards the Bull, is "Her Hero." It was Rosa Bonheur (whose painting "The Horse Fair" decorated so many parlors in insular America) who painted in the small board fence to conceal the sacrosanct portions of the Bull's anatomy, although everyone knew they were there, and Rosa Bonheur's screening fence amplified the Bull's anatomical dimensions. What was out of sight was not out of mind, not with these posters.

At one point, Julian Shakespeare Carr, wily Bull Durham executive and resourceful entrepreneur, seems to have told his advertising people to utilize all available space.

Thus it was that the Bull's egregious masculinity came to be plastered on the Egyptian Pyramids, and the removal of the Bull from the Pyramids cost the Durham firm a tidy sum. A bit later,

231

one of Carr's British representatives came to Durham with the startling news that Lord Tennyson, Lord Beaconsfield (Disraeli), Matthew Arnold, and Thomas Carlyle all smoked Bull Durham. While this news was obtained almost accidentally, Carr exploited it as an unpaid testimonial; and this may have been the first commercial for a product, in the truest sense of the word.

Another tremendous boost came when Owen Wister's novel, *The Virginian*, appeared in 1902. Wister was a friend of Teddy Roosevelt, and Wister had visited Roosevelt in Wyoming. Wister had the little yellow tags, the drawstrings of sacks of Bull Durham hanging down from every rancher and cowboy's shirt pocket. And when non-ranchers and cowboys around Medicine Bow rolled a smoke, it was almost always compounded from Bull Durham. When this news came back to Durham, it was exploited most successfully.

And it was the ferocious Bull that accelerated the manufacture and sale of ready rolled cigarettes. James B. Duke admitted candidly that his early company, W. Duke and Sons, could never hope to catch up with the Bull. Duke said, "There is no future for us in sack tobacco because of the Bull, and as for myself, I am going into the ready rolled cigarette business, and quickly."

The enormous whistle atop the Bull Durham factory was built to resemble a Bull, and its incredibly powerful bellowings could be heard ten miles away, in Chapel Hill, on a clear day. And when a rank stranger was assailed by these ear-splitting bellows, the Bull stampeded almost as many horses, pulling buggies, as were stampeded by mountain lions and snakes out west.

It is difficult to imagine any display of contemporary English poetry that is shorn of the late Ralph Hodgson's "The Bull":

> See an old unhappy bull
> Sick in soul and body both,
> Slouching in the undergrowth
> Of the forest beautiful,
> Banished from the herd he led,
> Bulls and cows a thousand head.
>
> Cranes and gaudy parrots go
> Up and down the burning sky,

Tree-top cats purr drowsily
In the dim-day gray below;
And troops of monkeys, nutting some,
All disputing, go and come.
All things abominable sit
Picking offal buck or sweine,
On the mess and over it
Burnished flies and beetles shine,
And spiders big as bladders lie
under the hemlocks, ten feet high. . .

Pity him that he must wake
Even now the swarms of flies
Blackening his bloodshot eyes
Bursts and blisters round the lake,
Scattered from the feast half-fed,
By great shadows overhead,
And the dreamer turns away
From his visionary herds
And his splendid yesterday,
Turns to meet the loathly birds
Flocking round him from the skies
Waiting for the flesh that dies.

"The Bull" is far, far too lengthy for complete reproduction here, and only the first, second, and last stanzas were just quoted.

In Ireland, of course, a "bull" is an incongruous statement, such as, "I'm an atheist, God help me," or "My mother had no children, God help her." It was in a book of 1802 called *Essay on Irish Bulls* in which Marie Edgeworth was off and running with "There is one distinguishing peculiarity of the Irish bull—its horns are tipped with brass."

Bull as in Irish bull, comes, of course, from *bulla*, and *bulla* is red ink imprint, a seal put on Papal papers to signify the importance of the document.

Bull enriches the language as a synonym for nonsense, usually extravagant bragging or statements that insult one's credulity. The "bull session" occurs everywhere, and every baseball park has a "bull pen." (This seems to date from the period when relief pitchers warmed up near a Bull Durham billboard inside the ball park.) To be poorly prepared but to go on and try to give the suggestion of rigid preparation is "to bull it through," and bull is often synonymous with policeman. "A yard bull" means a stupid person, and its chief use, certainly at times, seems to be a one-word reply or opinion. The "bull dike" is the lesbian who wears mannish clothing, and the "bull bitch" is any woman who uses masculine gestures or calls up the male countenance. A "bull cook" is the fellow who prepares the meals in logging camps and at similar enterprises.

Benjamin Franklin Was Right

Obviously America's winged symbol is the baldheaded eagle, the sea eagle. *Bald* is not ascribable to his want of feathers so much as it is suggested by the white feathers on this predatory bird's head. Although the bald eagle is as rapacious and as perverted to hideous vengeance as one of Al Capone's hoods, the eagle is applauded by many people who bless it for killing other birds which venture in growing crops. (Such an encomium reminds one of the old story of that revered St. Herod, of blessed memory, the greatest nuisance abater in all of history. In the same account, all Christians were admonished "to keep a vicious dog against the foot pads of charity and noble works.")

From the earliest time the eagle has been heralded for his might, his uncanny vision from tremendous heights in the sky, and for his amazingly fast lethal attacks. In the Bible the eagle is extolled for these same qualities. It is Isaiah who thunders, "They who wait upon the Lord shall mount up with wings as eagles." Albeit in some incidents the Biblical reference to vultures may have been translated as "eagle." Both are of the same family and are almost similar in appearance when airborne.

The Romans associated the eagle with Jupiter; and the eagle's features were emblazoned on the standards carried in battle by the Roman legions, from whence it has descended to the national ensigns of Germany, Russia, and the United States. The very ancient Assyrians and Egyptians utilized the eagle in many forms of art, and Xenophon says the eagle was on the old Persian standard.

But we agree heartily with Benjamin Franklin that the eagle makes a sorry national species, endangered or not. Franklin's suggestion of the turkey makes much more sense. This horrific bird seems more suitable in the Prussian Order of the Black Eagle, founded in 1701. As a popular name, *eagle* entails several raptorial birds, including the infamous lamb killer, found in the

235

Alps, the Pyrenees, and the Himalayas. Physically Lord Tennyson caught his physique accurately in his poem "The Eagle":

He claws the crag with crooked hands;
Close to the sun in lonely hands,
Ringed with the same world, he stands
The wrinkled sea beneath him crawls,
He watches from mountain walls
And like a thunderbolt he falls.

Until the coin was discontinued by the mint in 1913, a double eagle was worth ten bucks. There is (or was?) the Order of the Red Eagle of Bayreuth, (also called the Order of Sincerity). It was founded in 1705 by Margrave of Bayreuth, and the badge is an eight-pointed cross having in the center a medallion with a red eagle bearing the Hohenzollern Arms. There are several Eagle Groves listed in Rand-McNally; the famous Eagle Pass in Texas; the eagle ray is an order of fish; and the Fraternal Order of Eagles, operating in the United States and Canada, which, incidentally, has burial benefits and stipends for ailing members.

Benjamin Franklin's antipathy for the malicious bald eagle went unheeded, although Franklin voiced strenuous objections to an aloof predator as our national emblem. Then, as now, many Americans had never seen a live eagle, and Franklin's associates had scant interest in the bald eagle or knowledge of it. Conversely, almost everyone liked to eat turkey; and, of course, turkey was viable in the gifts brought to Plymouth Rock by Indians in the original Thanksgiving celebration. Again, the turkey in the backyard was a familiar sight, certainly from Franklin's time to the era when James Whitcomb Riley published "When the Frost Is On the Punkin." ("And you hear the kyouck and gobble of the struttin' turkey cock.") And insofar as we can ascertain no proscription against eating turkey exists among any ethnic or religious group.

Fortunately, Franklin didn't live to see the era when the rapacious eagle was the precise symbol for America's robber barons. He did not live to see the eagle as a representative of McKinley's blatant imperialism, when purblind national chest swelling traduced logic and compassion for smaller, poorer

236

nations. The invidious eagle ties to the maniacal obsession with chanting "We're number one," in numerous enterprises, in an endless array of childish pursuits.

Undoubtedly, the prodigious, unstoppable eagle was an apt emblem for the "big stick" tenure of Teddy Roosevelt, the dude cowboy and the slaughterer of many innocent animals. And, of course, the eagle is tailor-made for the strange mentality that adores raw power as this power was perverted by Messrs. Nixon, Agnew, Haldeman, et al.

According to the cherished story, Aeschylus (525-456 B.C.), the tragic poet and the "father of Greek drama," was killed when an eagle dropped a tortoise on his bald head. According to ancient stories, eagles caught tortoises and dropped them from great heights against rocks to crack their hard shells. Aeschylus is supposed to have been warned by that he would be killed when something fell on him; whereupon he sought safety by spending most of his time in open fields. The story of Aeschylus's bald head being cracked by a falling tortoise was told endlessly, and the tale appears in *Life of Aeschylus*, published in the 11th century. The *Life of Aeschylus* is appended to the Medicean manuscripts of Florence. Aeschylus is buried at Gela, and his adherents put this stanza on his tombstone, although there is no evidence that poet-dramatist was ever a soldier:

Beneath this stone lies Aeschylus, son of
    Euphoriion, the Athenean,
Who perished in the wheat bearing land of Gela;
Of his noble prowess the grove of Marathon can speak,
Or the long-haired Persian who knows it well.

Finally, there is nothing original about the selection of the eagle to symbolize the United States. Several orders of eagles were integral in the Junker military cult, and the Russians, long ago, paid lip and artistic tribute to the old baldhead.

When Titov, the Russian cosmonaut, yelled into his microphone, "I am an eagle," he was not indulging in rhapsodic grandeloquence, nor was he displaying Soviet arrogance. He was merely identifying himself. The name of his spacecraft was *Eagle* (in Russian this translates as "Oryol").

With his characteristic but not always wisely placed

237

ebullience, the late Vachel Lindsay canonized John P. Altgeld as "The Eagle That Is Forgotten." But Lindsay could turn himself on so quickly and so frenetically that he saw the country as "Every soul resident/In the earth's one circus tent." Since Altgeld spoiled his political future by pardoning some of the men unjustly convicted in Chicago's Hay Market bombings, Lindsay seems to have the eagle epitomizing the wrong side.

One can hear Lindsay's booming voice as he bullyragged a civic club meeting with:

Sleep softly. . .eagle forgotten. . .under the stone,
Time has its way with you there, and the clay has its own.
Sleep on, O brave-hearted, O wise man, that kindled the flame—
To live in mankind is far more than to live in a name,
To live in mankind, far, far more. . .than to live in a name."

(From what we know of foreign born Governor Altgeld, Lindsay would have served him and the nation better by invoking a bluebird or a cardinal.)

(This has no relevance to animals, save that every political convention is a better circus than Barnum ever assembled. When Bryan made his "Cross of Gold" speech in 1896, the Democratic delegates had righteous Protestant fits and fell in the middle of them. As Bryan spoke, Altgeld was seated by Clarence Darrow. When Bryan finished, Altgeld and Darrow reacted with the same spontaneous exuberance as the other delegates yelled. In the midst of the cheering, Altgeld said to Darrow: "What did Bryan say, and we are applauding so crazily?" Darrow scratched his head and replied, "I'll just be goddamed if I know.")

Elinor Wylie was fascinated by aloneness, even if she was never lonely. In "Let No Charitable Hope" she says,

Now let no charitable hope
Confuse my mind with images
Of eagle and of antelope;
I am in nature none of these.

It is the nation's juvenile, puerile addiction to physical prowess that suggests the mayhem of which the bald eagle is capable. It is this force that makes us turn our backs upon poetry and all such tender mercies and sustenances. What we are saying, in essence, is that the horse is man's superior because it can run faster, that the bull is man's superior because the bull has greater physical strength, and the mule is man's superior because it can absorb more punishment.

There used to be a fallacious jingle, a quatrain, about "Here's to the American eagle, that greasy bird of prey/Who flies all over the United States/And (censored) on Georgia." The response of a Georgia Congressman finishes the quatrain— formerly required memory work in America's pool rooms, livery stables, and around country stores—still bespeaks the adverse attitude to the eagle: "Here's to the state of Georgia/Its soil is fertile and rich./We don't give a turd for your eagle bird,/The bald-headed son-of-a-bitch."

Nonetheless this nation's compulsion for whatever is big and muscular is not likely to abate until a portion of the natural, accepted order is changed. We will applaud the eagle, and the "We're the number one" quack sloganry the eagle epitomizes until some ingenious rabbit catches a human in a human box or until some red bird sprinkles salt on a man's tail feathers.

The Snake, "Subtil" Or Otherwise

In "The Corsair," Lord Byron wrote:

Man spurns the worm, but pauses ere he wake,
The slumbering venom of the folded snake.

Genesis says: "Now the serpent was more subtil than any other beast of the field which the Lord God had made." ("Subtil" means artful or crafty.) In Chaucer's *Canterbury Tales*, the merchant repeats something ascribed to Aesop much earlier: "Lyk to the adder in bosom sly untrewe." This is supposed to be the classic case of gross ingratitude. Every story of a snake in the bosom goes back to Aesop's account of the peasant who found a snake half dead from cold and exposure. The peasant put the snake in his own bosom to restore life, and the peasant was killed when the snake bit him.

Scientists today count more than 2,500 species of snakes, of which around four-fifths are not poisonous. Venom is produced by modified salivary glands. The venom flows through a groove, or a hollow bore, on to the snake's fangs. Venom is removed from snakes for use in treating certain diseases, and to make antivenin for snakebites.

It was Virgil who gave us "a snake in the grass." "A snake lurks in the grass" appears in Virgil's *Ecologues*. "Snake" has meant an attractive girl, and it has meant a student who excells. A subway is called a snake, now and then, and snake eyes are the point of two in dice, with each die facing having one spot showing. A snake ranch is a filthy barroom or joint; and the snake's hips, popularized by James T. Farrell and by H. T. Webster, the old cartoonist, is any superior or remarkable person. In the southern states a snake doctor manifests cagy adroitness, for good or for foul purposes.

Actually "snake doctor" emerged from the era when snake

240

bites, and other poisonous animals were treated by madstones. Throughout most of the 19th century people believed that a madstone was profoundly efficacious for wounds made by rabid dogs or by snakes. Belief in the madstone's magical prowess was almost universal. Indeed Abraham Lincoln took his young son, Robert, all the way from Springfield, Illinois, to Terre Haute, Indiana, to have a dog bite treated by a madstone. Belief in the magical properties was likely stronger in the southern states than elsewhere.

The madstone was a round stone, about the size of an egg. It was placed upon the wound to suck out the poison. Many times the madstone was soaked in sweet milk; and when the madstone stuck to the wound, that meant that the poison was certain to be in process of extraction. In his remarkable *The Golden Bough*, Sir James Frazier says: "The Greeks believed in a stone; to test its efficiency, you had only to grind the stone to powder and sprinkle the powder on the wound." The American Indians believed steadfastly in madstones; and they said each white deer, an animal sacred to the Indians, was born with a madstone in its belly to obviate any poison the white deer might swallow while grazing. And a madstone, or something closely akin to it, figures prominently in Sir Walter Scott's *The Talisman*.

In addition to tempting Eve with the apple, the snake has left us with words and phrases such as: the Snake River; the snake bird (a darter), "snake-in-the-grass"; snake dance, originally done by the Hopi Indians; snake doctor (a dry-fly); the snake eel; the snake gourd or melon; snakeroot (antidote for snakebite); snake stone, an amulet; and snake wool, a plant or tree, depending upon geographical location.

There is a remote element of truth in the ancient bromide that snakes go blind during Dog Days (roughly July 16 to September 1). Before it sloughs off its skin, a snake assumes color of dull gray and this makes him appear to be blind. And just before the shedding process, the snake's eyes take on a milky look. This is ascribable to the separation of the outer coat of the eyeballs, but the eyes regain their clarity of vision after the shedding has been accomplished.

And it is another myth that a snake sheds its skin each year during Dog Days, or the hottest part of any local season. Sloughing may occur several times each year. They grow fastest in hot weather, and the more they grow, the more often they shed their skins. But this seems to be the only tenuous tie between Dog Days and the sloughing of skin.

Despite the general misconception, snakes do not dart out with their tongues to strike a human. The snake's tongue is completely innocuous. They do not sting at all. Conversely, they bite with their teeth and fangs. The continued motion of tongue is known to have some sensory significance, but scientists have not determined the precise nature of the movement. Since snakes do not have true ears, some scientists have assumed that the tongue acts as a substitute for the ears in registering auditory sensations.

Apparently the snake feels its way along the earth with the aid of his long, sensitive tongue. Several outstanding directors of zoos agree that the snake's tongue is a superbly delicate instrument, and that it serves to trace scents over the ground, by taste. But the myth about biting with the tongue used to be universally accepted. In *King Richard II*, Shakespeare has the monarch to say:

> And when they from thy bosom pluck a flower,
> Guard it, I pray thee, with a lurking adder
> Whose double tongue with a mortal touch
> Throw death upon thy sovereign's enemies.

Most of the snakes that go underground do not dig their own holes. Instead, they appropriate natural crevices and holes, and burrows made by other animals. At least four American species live underground: The "blind snakes" excavate their own burrows; the "ground snakes," the "coral snake," and the "shield tails" do not.

Scientists disagree about whether or not snakes are immune to their own poison. Many rattlesnakes have died from poison when they have bitten themselves, even if few shrinks know what prompts the death image among reptiles. There is always the chance that a snake will bite his own spinal nerve or some vital organ. Snakes are never likely to bite themselves save at the apogee of an injury or irritation. Since few leave suicide notes and wills for probate, the question of whether a snake is immune to its own poison will have to rest with a higher court.

Curiously enough, there are no native snakes in Ireland. The viviparous lizard is the only reptile found in Ireland, and it was there prior to the original Sinn Fein and the more recent hostilities in Ulster. A few years ago a small, harmless snake was found in Dublin; this lone snake, less than two feet long, caused such interest it was displayed in Ireland's Museum of Natural History. (Snakes are not found in Crete, Malta, New Zealand, the Hawaiian Islands and some other places.)

According to the cherished legend, St. Patrick banished all the snakes from Ireland. (He banished all the toads, too, but this gets very poor billing.) The St. Patrick legend is similar to the dragon stories from the Orient; and it symbolizes the conquest of evil by goodness, and in Ireland, the triumph of Christianity over paganism. In Christian art the patron saint is represented with a serpent at his feet.

There is the cherished belief that certain ornamental plants drive snakes away. The mountain ash is said to be especially obnoxious to snakes, both from the tree's odor and from the rank smell of its leaves rotting on the ground. For many generations American Indians and blacks planted snake calabash and the snake gourd. These were trained to grow over the dwelling. According to many colonial experts the offensive, fishy odors drove snakes away.

In his classic, *History of the Dividing Line*, William Byrd wrote (1729): "I found our Camp near Plants of the kind that rattlesnake root called Star-Glass. The leaves shoot out circularly and Grow Horizontally near the Ground. The root is the shape not unlike the Rattle Snake. The Rattle Snake has an utter antipathy for it, insomuch that if you Smear your hands with the Juices of it, you may handle the Viper Safely." Byrd adds that in the preceding July, "when these Snakes are in their greatest Vigour," he smeared a dog's nose with the powder of the aforementioned root, and although he trampled on huge rattlers many times, he was unharmed.

Thousands of farmers have sworn that a snake will suck milk from a cow's teat. Indeed this author has heard this assertion many, many times. No reputable jerpetologist believes this, and the U.S. Department of Agriculture stated: "Anyone who has ever milked a cow knows that the suction required to obtain a flow of milk is much greater to obtain a flow of milk than the pressure that could be exerted by any snake. Furthermore a snake has two rows of sharp, recurved teeth and the snake would find itself fully occupied, if a cow permitted such suction. The only way a snake could milk a cow would be to get the teat at least part of the way down the snake's throat." And, obviously, the snake's sharp teeth would have the cow writhing in agonies of pain from her ruptured teats.

The legend of the milk snake probably arose from the fact that snakes frequent milkhouses and dairy barns to prey on the mice that habitate both places.

Another cherished myth is that a snake's tail will wiggle until sunset. (This is in line with the turtle's biting down and holding tightly until a storm ensues.) In reptiles the spinal cord is more important than it is in most other animals, and the spinal cord influences the motions of the body more than the brain does. But in many animals the muscular system does not lose its powers of reacting to stimuli. (Any frog gigger knows that a frog's hind legs will show signs of life even after the legs have been separated from the frog's body.) The heart of a snake has been known to beat for twenty-four hours when the snake is dead, in the usual connotations of the word. The snake's reflex actions will make the tail wiggle a while after the serpent has been killed. And contrary to the popular misconception, snakes are not hard to kill. A sharp blow behind the head with a stout stick will gradually cause the death of even the largest of snakes.

A snake killed during the day may be imagined to wiggle until sundown, but this old wives' tale is predicated that amid the darkness no one can see the contractions of the snake.

Because it gives dingling notice before it strikes, the rattler has been called "the gentleman among snakes." Nonetheless the rattler, the most dreaded snake in North America, is not entirely the gentleman legend has created. The rattles of a rattlesnake's tail are merely rings of dried and hardened skin that do not come off when the snake sloughs its skin, because of the button on the end of the tail. When a snake is excited and poises to strike, it moves its tail nervously; and this causes the rings of old skin to rattle. Scientists think this rattling is a nervous protection over which the snake has no control.

The coach or coachwhip snake, slender, swift moving, brownish-black, is found in the American south and southwest. It has a long, tapering tail, and the scales are arranged so that it gives a braided or coachwhip appearance. The black whip snake, *Coluber flagellum*, is one of the few American snakes that can outrun a man on a smooth surface. The coachwhip has been the

244

subject of many myths among American Negroes and Indians. The Indians and blacks said this snake attacked humans and lashed them to death with their long tails. For a long time when a black was found dead on a highway, bereft of car or horse, it was roundly told, and believed, that he had been coachwhipped to death. Apparently, these stories about Negroes being killed by coach snakes were started by white masters as a deterrent to keep slaves from running away.

For a long time many southern Americans believed, or professed to believe, that killing and hanging up a snake was the only sure way to break a menacing drought. (One would have a hard job distinguishing which is more dangerous, a drought or catching a snake. At any event Dr. Samuel Fox Mordecai, longtime Dean of the Trinity-Duke Law School, perpetuated the myth with some lines he intended more as playful than as chauvinistic:

> If you come across a sarpant,
> As you travel in the north,
> Hang him, for God's sake,
> To try to break the drought.
> For if the hanging up of sarpants
> Be good to make it rain,
> The hanging up of Yankees
> Must be labor not in vain.

Hardly any animal manages to be so repellent and so fascinating, simultaneously, as the snake. (The fascination of many men for snakes is comparable to the cowboy who lost his pay at the faro wheel. His buddy asked, "Don't you know that machine is crooked?" "Yup, I know it's crooked, but it's the only one in town.")

Actually, Genesis says "serpent," not snake, and it was John Milton who said the snake "brought death into the world." Early in history virtually every venomous creature was called a snake. Indeed, the salamander and the crocodile were called snakes, betimes, until the 16th century. Even so, snakes do not swallow their young to protect their young, although this fantasy is hard to obviate. Just the same, big snakes eat little snakes when no other food is convenient. There are no known snakes with poison in the ends of their tails. Some, like the

245

red-bellied mud snake have sharp scales on their tails, and if handled, will strike with its tail. In almost every rural township someone points out a tree killed by a snake. (This is on a par with the story about the man who died of Dutch elm blight, although he was operated on by the best tree surgeon around.)

The hoop snake is not a man-made tale, but the hoop snake certainly does not roll itself into a ball, its tail in its mouth. And the glass snake, that can be busted up and put back together, must be found at a kiddie's novelty store. Although the puff, or puffing, adder is a true fact of nature, it is not venomous. It tries, and succeeds, in looking fearsome, although the African puff adder is a different bill of goods.

There is nothing but gas to the theory that snakes can charm or be charmed. The dumbest bird knows the snake is his enemy; and if the bird is killed, it is usually because it tried to lure the snake from its nest. The bird does not die because the snake charms him. He dies because he miscalculates the distance between him and the snake, and per force, flies within striking distance.

Cobras have never been charmed by flutes. Actually most snakes have tin ears. Music seems to have absolutely no appeal. And as is true of those imaginary fish that Kipling had flying along the road to Mandalay, no snake can fly. Yesterday, almost every community had a story about a man who stepped accidentally on a poisonous snake and died when the venom pierced shoe leather. The shoes were stored and forgotten. Some years later a grandson found the shoes, and since they fitted him, he put them on. He died because the stinger was still in the boot. (The fangs of a huge rattlesnake might pierce thin leather, but that would be the end of it.) Finally, snakes do not salvage their venom to poison their enemies. They keep the venom for the most pragmatic of all reasons: To kill their prey.

An Idler and a Nuisance

The ant, from the Middle English *ante, amet*, has benefited almost as much by PR men as the horse has profited from PR men. The ant, one of creation's most numerous and irritating insects, was off and running as a tireless worker when King Solomon spoke his familiar proverb: "Go to the ant, thou sullard: consider her ways and be wise." Again, in Proverbs, the ant in innumerated as one of the "four things which are little upon the earth, but they are exceedingly wise: the ants are a people not strong, yet they prepare their meat in the summer."

While the ancient Hebrews were tremendously impressed by skill and ingenuity with which ants developed a community of galleries and corridors underground, the Writ might have been more accurate and farsighted if it had said, "The ant bums its meat in the summertime."

This is, obviously, a minority report, but we think the ant is the playboy of the insect or animal world. If one had an Irish brogue he could star in Synge's *Playboy of the Western World.* Most ants are loafers and bums, and they hang around picnic grounds as if queing up to get welfare checks. Conversely, the squirrel, with an eye cocked to incipient falling weather, stores acorns. The robin, as parsimonious as Silas Marner, hoards bits of cardboard and discarded strings. The beaver uses its tail better than any can-can dancer as it builds in summer a comfortable haven for winter. The stork, always a feathered guardian *ad litem*, gathers food for himself and for his aged and infirm parents.

The ant divides his time between the picnic grounds and lakeside. He recalls the oldtime bum who could smell a free lunch at a saloon half a mile away. He calls to mind the shiftless, indigent relative who always shows up when a feast is on the table. Were it not for his microscopic size he would have been jailed for vagrancy long ago. And unlike the oldtime hobo, he will not eat his handout and then leave his benefactor alone. No. He hangs around to torment and pester the author of his largesse. He is a double first cousin to the village "radical" who hates everyone who has as much as four dollars because he, himself, is too good-for-nothing to get regular employment. That is why the ant goes about the lakeside haranguing the summertime balm with screeds about the exploitation of his breed.

While the crow went off to study elocution, the beaver engineering, and the snake legerdemain, the ant mortgaged his soul to the company store. He is, for all the world, like the man who ascribes his ignorance and tenuous finances to a massive lie, "I hadda drop outa school in the seventh grade to help out at home."

So, what else is new? The point, as the late George Ade might have fableized, is that if you can create the false impression that you are industrious, the soul of diligence, you will acquire the reputation of being diligent, and very few folks will muster the gall, run against tribal mores, to say, aloud: "Ant, you just aren't worth a dried apple dam." Hans Christian Andersen understood this when he wrote the tale about the naked king for whom the unscrupulous tailors pretended to fashion a glittering suit.

Happy Chimpanzee

According to "Abadaba Honeymoon," "Way down in the jungle land lived a happy chimpanzee/He loved a monkey, with a long tail,/Lordy, how he loved her." The chimp is a native of the equatorial area of Africa, ranging from the Atlantic to the Nile, within a belt about twenty degrees wide. The chimpanzee has many local and regional names in that area, and it is not clear if these names are all synonyms or if more than one species exists.

A chimp's presence in a community is ascertained quickly. For at regular intervals during the day they engage in a bout of far reaching, half human and half maniacal shouts and hoots. This ungodly noise rises to a crescendo that appears to be the laughter of a fiend. Then at daybreak that shouting becomes a concerted uproar that seems to rattle and shake the earth, for several minutes at a stretch.

At any sign of danger the male comes from his treetop with amazing agility, and he starts running, but not precisely on all fours as some viewers think. What he does is to use his great arms to aid his escape, to push away swinging branches and to knock creepers from his path. When on all fours his fingers are doubled on the palms, so that he walks on his knuckles.

At night each adult climbs a tree to construct a platform big enough for a bed. He bends branches and heaps twigs and leaves on his platform. The next night he constructs another such treehouse. And the female has her young on such a platform bed.

Chimpanzees have been seen in menageries and in zoological gardens of Europe since the middle of the 17th century. But for all of his amazing intelligence and ingenuity, the chimp is highly susceptible to disease, especially to diseases of the lungs, and a chimp does not live long in captivity.

Noiseless Patient Spiders

One hundred years ago, in 1863, Walt Whitman wrote his poem, "A Noiseless Patient Spider":

A noiseless patient spider,
I mark'd where on a little promotory it stood isolated,
Mark'd how to explain the vacant vast surrounding,
It launch'd forth filament, filament, filament, out of itself,
Ever unreeling them, ever tirelessly speeding them.
And you O my soul where you stand,
Surrounded, detached, in measureless oceans of space,
Carelessly, musing, venturing, throwing, seeking the
      spheres that connect them.
Till the bridge you will need be form'd, till the
      ductile anchor hold,
Till the gossamer thread you fling catch somewhere,
      O my soul."

I find little charm in spiders, Whitman to the contrary, although the webs are as inspiring and as gossamer as Whitman says, and, also, despite the important role spiders play in the economy of nature. Spiders are among nature's most numerous tenants.

If one looks closely on a dewy morning late in summer or early in autumn, one sees in the fields along the highways almost endless systems of spider webs. The tiny shreds of mist are caught by the spider's delicate webs, and the whole landscape seems to have turned into the most elaborate thin bridal veils. Quite literally, the webs cover all the low herbage. The entire landscape is overspread with the fragile tents and meshes of the arachnid hosts.

Obviously there is tremendous prejudice against the spider, against the bites of spiders. There are direct implications of

250

Mary Howitt's (1799-1888) "The Spider and the Fly":

Will you walk into my parlor?
Said a spider to a fly;
'Tis the prettiest little parlor
That ever did you spy.

"Little Miss Muffet" is of unknown origin, and it was printed first in 1805. Scholars and researchers believe that "Little Miss Muffet," as has occurred so often with other nursery rhymes, has departed completely from its original implications. Dr. Thomas Muffet (died in 1604) was a famous, early entomologist whose specialty was spiders. It is believed that Professor Muffet made a nuisance of himself by bringing every conversation around to spiders.

Albeit, some scholars see the nursery rhyme as a parallel to other ditties connected with the old cushion dance. At such a dance the young lady sat demurely and expectantly, lest something terrible occurred as she waited.

According to Proverbs, "The spider taketh hold with his web, and is in the kings' palaces." But Alexander Pope captured the magic of the filament one sees on dewy mornings in "Essay On Man":

The spiders touch, how exquisitely fine!
Feels at each thread and then lives along the line.

Many Americans swear that spider bites are dangerous, almost lethal, but naturalists say a spider's bite is no worse than a mosquito's bite, unless it is a black widow. And there is always the story about Scotland's being saved by a spider. In 1306 Robert Bruce, or Robert, the Bruce, was crowned king of Scotland, but soon afterwards his troops were routed by the British, and Robert, the Bruce, fled from Scotland, to take refuge on Rathlin Island, off Antrim in Ireland. One day as Robert lay on his pallet, in utter dejection, he saw a spider patiently trying to fix its web to a beam in the ceiling. The spider failed six different times. Bruce is said to have declared: "Now shall this spider teach me what to do, for I also have failed six times." In its seventh attempt the spider succeeded in fixing its web to the beam. Bruce emerged from his hiding place, and, after a series of successful battles, won the big fight at Bannockburn, in 1314. As a consequence of Bannockburn, the British recognized Scotland's independence. Because of the enduring story it is still regarded almost a crime for any Scotsman named Bruce to kill a spider.

Less well known is the story of Robert the Bruce's leprosy. Bruce had vowed to go on a crusade to the Holy Land, but this ambition was aborted by wars at home and his leprosy. The royal leper spent that last two years of his life at Cardrose Castle, on the northern shore of the Firth of Clyde. Bruce asked Sir James Douglas, (known as "James, the good") to take his heart to Jerusalem for burial. En route Sir James carried Bruce's heart in a small silver casket. Just before Douglas was killed by infidels, he threw Bruce's heart in the midst of his opponents, crying, "Go thou before as thou were wont to do, and Douglas will follow." However, one of the knights recovered the heart.

Bruce's recovered heart was taken back to Scotland, and it was buried with his body in Melrose Abbey. When Bruce's body was disinterred in 1819, the remains showed clearly that the heart had been removed.

(A royal leper is mentioned in the Bible. Second Kings says the Lord smote King Azariah (Uzziah) "so that he was a leper until the end of his days.")

The creatures we call daddy-longlegs are not bona fide spiders. They have the correct number of legs, eight, but these legs are much longer and thinner than the true spider's. And the daddy-longlegs is devoid of the apparatus which, in spiders, divides the body into two segments. However, these extremely long legs are a viable asset. As is true with certain automobiles which can jack up themselves by means of a central hydraulic system, the daddy-longlegs can, without benefit of hydraulics, raise his commonplace body high enough off the ground to avoid ants and other tiny pests.

In relationship to any insect, the humorous lines of Jonathan Swift are always analogous:

> For dogs have fleas upon their backs,
> Upon their backs to bite 'em;
> The fleas themselves have lesser fleas,
> And so ad infinitum.

So naturalists observe, a flea
Hath smaller fleas that on him prey,
And these have smaller still to bite 'em;
And so proceed ad infinitum.
Thus, every poet in his kind
Is hot by him that comes behind.

Poignant Gobble and Kyouck

Apparently that bird whose roasting is almost axiomatic at Thanksgiving and Christmas is called turkey because the Portuguese imported some of these birds from Africa, via Turkey. (The name of the country is derived from the Middle English *Turkye* and from the Old French *Turquie*.)

The domestic turkey (*Meleagris*) seems to be derived from the Mexican variety of turkey, and early in the 16th century some were taken to Europe. By the time of the early colonies in Massachusetts and Virginia, semi-wild turkeys were in great abundance in the forests around Plymouth Rock and Jamestown. And the bird eaten at Thanksgiving has enlarged American English in many "turkey phrases": Turkey-Trot, the popular dance; Young Turk, now a political liberal but originally a member of the young revolutionists in Turkey of 1920; turkey buzzard; Turkish bath; a turkey, to mean an athlete or a drama or musical that is a dud; Turkish Delight, candy; to have a turkey on one's back, turkey in the sense of easy money (a piece of cake in this hour's parlance); turkey, in the sense of a valise, popularized by those seeking silver and gold in the old west; turkey shoot, an easy task; and Turkish coffee, coffee pulverized in a thin sugar syrup.

The Indians and settlers found the turkey easy to capture, especially before the forests were cut, because it usually has the habit of running from its pursuer and not flying or landing atop a tree.

Turkey is available the year around now; but, somehow, it is not so mouth-wateringly succulent as it was prior to frozen foods and deep freezers in the home. Only a few years ago, turkey in the summertime would have been as incongruous as Pickett's Division charging at Gettysburg with Sherman tanks.

Yesterday many small-town families bought a turkey for Thanksgiving, but no one ever ate this specific bird. No, it died from old age, or from servile flattery; and, of course, it may have retired to St. Petersburg, to live on social security. The Thanksgiving turkey was put in a pen in the backyard, in the chicken lot, to be fattened for the Thanksgiving spread. Uglier than original sin the turkey bobbled around in the chicken lot. At first every member of the family talked about what a scrumptious dinner the turkey would provide. As it wobbled around with all of the grace of a fat, lady novice on roller skates, the children fed it table scraps.

As they fed this kyoucking monstrosity, they talked about which child would get which particular piece of it. Then, day by day, the incredible homeliness and clumsiness of the turkey fetched the children; and as Thanksgiving approached, the children began to feel cannabalistic. To stay the execution of the grotesque creature the kids hit upon the expedient of running the turkey around the wired-in chicken lot until it was as thin as a tall crow smitten with the gobbles.

Frequently, the father knew nothing about this ruse until he started to sharpen his ax. Then as he inspected the wreck of feathers and bones, some of the turkey's garbled and pathetic charm rubbed off on him. Henceforth, the road work ceased, and everyone agreed it was better to keep this specific turkey until Christmas. By then he should be fat enough to please a gourmet. Some mental hocus-pocus had to save the bird from the fiery furnace.

The father bought a second turkey at the meat market, already picked. In order to keep the neighbors from thinking they were curious or rich, the family told tiny lies about the first turkey. One son said they did not eat the turkey because it had to be wormed. Another said its liver was out of whack. After a week the old fowl had more ailments applied to him than were ever listed in the local veterinarian's books. It became a regular family pet, the same as the dog and cat. Nay more, it was not unusual to see such a turkey riding about town in one of those wicker basket carts that were pulled by a pony or a goat.

A story in Indian mythology has a direct bearing upon all of this. The turkey's owners probably did not know the story; but there is a tale in Indian mythology that at the beginning of a particularly rough winter, all of the fire in creation went out save for a few tiny sparks that spluttered in a hollow tree. An observant turkey went to the hollow tree to fan the sparks with his flailing wings. As the fire got hotter the flames crisped off the turkey's head feathers and left a long line of blisters along its neck and throat. And that, my gluttonous friends, is why the old turkey is baldheaded and pockmarked today.

Animal Memorials

As has been noted, the ancient Egyptians embalmed cats and buried them along with their masters. The Bluegrass Country of Kentucky contains many imposing life-size monuments to deceased thoroughbred racers. Other famous horses—Alexander the Great's Bucephalos, Robert E. Lee's Traveller, the Duke of Wellington's Copenhagen, Napoleon's Marengo, Stonewall Jackson's Little Sorrell, and many others—live in statuary bronze and paintings. It is doubtful if any small work of art equals the beautiful intensity of the marble model that Edward Valentine did of Lee's Traveller.

But the strangest and most anachronistic is the huge memorial that Roy Bean, "the law west of the Pecos," erected to his companion, Watch, the enormous bear. Bean, born in Kentucky in 1842, went west as a frontiersman, and during the Civil War he acted as a militant Confederate irregular in New Mexico and Texas.

Then when the Southern Pacific was being laid across Texas, Bean followed the working crews with a knockdown saloon. In 1882 he set up his saloon at Vineyard, Texas, permanently. He renamed the dusty village Langtry, for Lilly Langtry, the beautiful actress whom Bean had never seen save in photographs. He had himself appointed Justice of the Peace, and as "Judge" Roy Bean he dispensed "justice" more rapidly than anyone has done from Justinian to Warren Burger.

A frontiersman who ran up a bill of several dollars at Bean's saloon offered to leave his "son" as security; but when Ben drew his six-shooter to announce, "I don't want no goddam boy," the stranger returned with an enormous bear.

"Meet my son, jedge," the stranger said.

"Your son?" Bean asked flabbergasted.

"Yep, he's my son."

"Where's his Ma?"

257

"After spending two winters in my tent and getting pregnant with Son, here, she ran off to the Rockies with a grizzly, the damned huzzy did."

Bean kept the huge bear, and, as Bean explained, "He helps around the saloon and is the bailiff when court is in session, and all he wants is a little beer." The bear is said to have drunk thirty-two bottles of beer at one standing, never once leaving his place at the bar. The bear usually slept behind the bar, and there came the night he killed two gunmen who came to kill Bean.

From then on, Bean called the bear Watch. And Watch, aside from being Bean's constant bodyguard, acted as bailiff in court, after a fashion.

One day Bean, holding court in the saloon, fined a dead man $47.32, the total contents of his pockets, for carrying a concealed weapon. As soon as the fine was extracted from the corpse, Bean said: "Watch, stick him in the trash bin," and Watch dragged the dead man out.

Finally, though, Watch was wounded mortally by three gunfighters who came during the night to dispatch Judge Bean. Watch killed two of the marauders, and Bean hanged their dead bodies on a limb in front of the saloon, as "an object lesson to law breakers."

Bean sent to a neighboring town for a doctor, but Watch was beyond medical help. Bean buried him, with a simple headstone, and a bit later he had a huge marble statue erected in the center of Langtry to perpetuate "that noble friend, Watch."

The statue of Greyfriars Bobby, a small dog that lingered near the grave of its master, John Gray, in Greyfriars Churchyard in Edinburgh, Scotland, from 1858 until its death fourteen years later, is outside the gate of Greyfriars Kirk at Candlemaker's Row. (Bobby's collar—suitably engraved in 1867 when the Lord Provost presented it to the dog and undertook to pay the license—can be seen in Huntly House Museum in Edinburgh.)

The strangest cemetery this author has ever seen is one that was started many years ago by a black minister in Person County, North Carolina, who was enamored of chickens, tame and game chickens. He had a portion of his farm set aside as a cemetery for dead chickens. While I cannot remember any imposing marble, each grave had at its head a brief history and chronology written on one of those tags which undertakers stick at the front of a human grave while marble or granite is being chiseled.

And, as suggested, many Indians asked to be buried with their dogs so that the loving tie between the two would continue in the happy hunting ground. Horses were also buried with many Indians for use in the after life.

Fred, a famous fire horse of New Bern, North Carolina, is stuffed and remains on perpetual exhibition at the main fire station. This was done to express the community's gratitude to Fred for his many years of pulling the town's fire wagon. (Several other small American towns put fire horses on "pensions" when the day of motorized equipment displaced the horse. The reasoning went this way: Other civic employees were given pensions or monthly retirement by the city fathers when their working days ended. So it was asked why not do something similar for those other faithful town employees, the fire horses? In most places the "pension" consisted of a special meadow which no other animal used. This was the community's way of honoring its intrepid fire horses; and as this author can assert, it was considered an accolade for a boy when he was allowed to visit the retired horses on Sunday afternoon and feed them lump sugar at the fence.

The Berserker

To make a mockery of juxtaposition, there was the old cry, or question: "Is it an airplane, a bird, or is it Superman?" In Norse mythology, Berserk embodies many of the Superman gifts, and the pronoun "it" is certainly as applicable as "he" or "him." Today when someone exudes almost meaningless volatilities, we say the person "has gone berserk."

In the old Norse mythology Berserk was the nickname of the grandson of Starkadder, who had eighty mighty hands. Berserk, or Berserker, as he is called at times, always went into battle without any protective armour, and in every household he was hailed for the reckless fury with which he fought.

Actually, Ber-serk is an old Scandinavian word that means "bare-shirt," one who went into battle clad only in thin, conventional clothing. It was Berserk who killed King Swafurlam, and it was by King Swafurlam's daughter whom Berserk fathered twelve sons, each of whom possessed wild courage equal to Berserk's.

Berserk's mythological sons were called "berserkers," and later on the word berserk became synonymous with dozens of types of unmitigated fury.

Collective Animals

Insofar as one knows animals have not started any civic or patriotic organizations. Some may be anti-establishment, and it could be that they do not like green peas and creamed chicken enough to foregather once a week to eat and to salute the flag.

Most people know about a yoke of oxen and a bed of oysters. Several geese form a gaggle, and two horses make a team, just as eleven football players do.

Several gorillas are a wand; hawks are a cast; and more than one goldfish constitutes a charm. Clouds and chowders are groups of gnats and cats, although kittens are a litter. Ants form colonies, but coots are a covert, and swine are a drift. Basically birds fly in flocks, although quails big enough to be shot are a covey. Whales are a ham, elks a gang, and bees may be a swarm or a grist.

Those small cats that begin as kittens become a kindle when more than one mother's brood foregathers, and there are knots of toads, leaps of leopards, and leashes of greyhounds.

The mighty lion, the king of the jungle heads a pride, and crows are a murder, just as peacocks are a muster, and hounds a kennel or a mute. Some whales and all seals make up a pod; and if a fish is well known, it belongs to a school. We hear much less of cranes called a sedge or slege, or pilchards (known by the tradename of sardines) as a skeal.

Geese fly in skiens and bears ramble in sloughs, and a family of bears is a sleuth. Goats form a trip, just as kangaroos do; nightingales are a watch and plovers are a wing.

Young animals, like single women, often change their baptismal names. The tiny, isolated quail is a creeper, just as a lone swan is an eygnet. The small rooster will announce that he is a cockerel, studying for cock papers, if one listens to him. The eel is an elver and the baby kangaroo is a joey, although this is not what the late John O'Hara had in mind with *Pal*

261

Joey. Virtually everyone is familiar with the colt, the bunny, and the fawn; but fewer of us know that a small hare is a leveret, and that the young salmon is a parr here, and it is a smelt there. The turkey that just begins to learn the gobble-scale is a poult, and the mackerel is a pike or a blinker. The dog, in common with some other small animals, is a whelp before he qualifies as a hound or a bird dog.

However they are called, the ability of animals to survive in a world brimming with hunters, pesticides, and other pollutants must be the type of persistent courage and ingenuity which is grace amid adversity.

And it has taken many years of sedulous observation and considerable mental ability to fathom, all the way, D. H. Lawrence's admonition in *The White Peacock*: "Be a good animal true to your animal instinct." Lawrence expressed this same vital sentiment several times in his books, and on a slightly different level is the rough parallel between Lawrence's animal phrase and Shakespeare's "To thine ownself be true."

The Cat's Pajamas

All sorts of special days, such as Saluda, N.C.'s "Coon Dog Day," prove Cervantes's contention that "Every dog shall have his day. But if the faithful dog is celebrated in poetry, story, and song, no such national homage is accorded the housecat, or the alley cat, either. But the cat used to be sacred to the ancient Egyptians whose goddess, Iris, often took the form of a cat.

Dogs belong to men but cats are free spirits. Many people, who start out thinking they own a cat, live to learn that they belong to the cat. The dog pants and grovels for man's attention and affection. A loving rub is the ultimate accolade. Conversely, a cat is the original diva. She bestows the ultimate accolade when she lets a human rub her. And man is almost the same sycophants his dog is. Men fatten off friendly gestures and cheerful admiration.

In a world tending to monotonous sameness the eternally aloof and diffident cat endures as a supreme individualist. The cat is as imperious as the dog is subservient, and many cats would hold high political posts if they had anywhere to put their tails. Dogs like to think they are human, or certainly an extension of a man's personality. But it takes all of a cat's compassion even to admit, on rare occasions, that humans might qualify as cats if they stopped talking so much.

But once in every millennium, a cat gets her come uppsance, usually in a queer way, as this story demonstrates.

NOTE

I wrote "Mr. Pussy" before 007 or any of his swinging girlfriends came along. An English professor, who has a national reputation, told me: "Your story carries on, quite successfully, three satires, simultaneously." My smile was as buoyant as young Master Keats's soul was the day he first saw Chapman's *Homer* but I still wonder what these satires are?

For whatever it's worth, I didn't think of Robert Browning's "Pied Piper" until I was half-way through writing "Mr. Pussy." What I am trying to suggest is the fulsome storyteller, who, after infinite palaver, approaches a dramatic crescendo, and then, inexplicably, cuts, bolts, and runs. That's what I had in my mind, along with some fun.

Mr. Pussy

This is a tale I've heard told in Oxford, North Carolina, my hometown, a thousand times or more. Some of the people who told this tale were straight along and all right, from the ground up. Some others who swore by this tale swore, also, that the world was flat, or otherwise, eggs would fall out of the nest during the night. Several Sunday school teachers swore the tale was so, but so did many of the ones who voted three times for William Jennings Bryan, and I don't mean in three different presidential elections.

Mr. Pussy was a drummer, a traveling man. His card introduced him as a "Rodent Exterminator." Despite the grandiose language on the card, the word trickled around from county to county that Mr. Pussy was a cracker-jack rat killer.

The people who are alleged to have seen him in the flesh said he always wore the dark suits and string ties that used to be associated with undertakers. He wore an enormous black felt hat and a ruffled white shirt. He had a black moustache and long black sideburns, and his eyes were said to be so powerful that they could shine on still waters with the eerie clarity of two stars afflicted with a sullen squint.

Sometimes, when I heard the oldtimers describe Mr. Pussy, I thought of Edgar Allan Poe. Later on, as I remembered these descriptions, I thought of Paladin, the soft-talking gunslinger who used to shoot-up the parlor from television once a week. (Maybe this was because both men handed out such singular business cards.)

Mr. Pussy always came to town alone, whereas the other drummers usually traveled together. The other drummers rode the same train, and when they got to town they clipped in together for a hired hack to make their rounds of the rural stores, after they had called on the merchants in town.

Mr. Pussy carried a sample case, the same as the other drummers. His sample case was a big box, a sort of leather hat-box contraption, with several holes bored in the top. If an uncontrollable epidemic of rats raged in a community, Mr. Pussy might take his sample case and his business card to the town commissioners. The commissioners would hire Mr. Pussy the way health officers are hired today. But most of the time he called on merchants whose stores were overrun by rats or on large farmers whose crops were ravaged by rats. He would offer to do an exterminating job at so much per dead rat head, or he would guarantee to clean out a big store or a big corn crib at a flat rate.

Mr. Pussy always had a newspaper clipping down in his inside coat pocket that told how he had wiped out the rats in an entire country, in some little country down in Latin, or Central, or South America, somewhere down that way. He also had a gold medal which he wore from a velvet ribbon around his neck. The newspaper clipping said that some president or king, or whatever kind of ruler the country had, gave Mr. Pussy the gold medal for killing all the nation's rats. This medal had some kind of fancy inscription. Some of the local people said the inscription was in Latin and some said it was in French, and I think that one old man said it was in Greek. The local Sunday school teachers said it was in Latin, that it came, free, at the Philadelphia centennial of 1876. But the three-time losers, the Bryan folks, said, No, by God, it was in Spanish and that the ruler down yonder had it made up for Mr. Pussy especially. The straight along and all right folks said, "O foot," that you could have clippings or medals made up anywhere, but the flat-worlders denounced that as an infernal lie. They yelled: "O, yeah, Unca Sam would put your francis in the Federal pen for counterfeiting."

Because of the nature of his work Mr. Pussy didn't adhere to a regular schedule the way the other drummers did. No. You'd look up one day and he'd be standing there in front of the Confederate monument. He would roll a cigarette with one hand, against the breeze, and he must have had a startling resemblance to a black apparition, or to a gunfighter, as he stood there soundlessly in the shadow of the monument to the dead.

265

When he made his first step he twirled his big sample case the same paralyzing way a hired gun fingers his holster. And then, like a consecrated hawk to its prey, he'd swoop down on the place at which he had business. He'd put his sample case on the merchant's counter, and display his merchandise the same as the ones who sold snuff, or rubber boots, or lamp-chimneys. He had two samples, and both had collars and tiny chains.

Sample number one was Goliath, a huge yellow tom cat with whiskers as sharp and as sturdy as well-honed nails. When Goliath reared on his mighty hind legs, smote his broad chest with his front paws, and gave his lion's roar, all the customers and loafers broke for the sidewalk. Goliath was the lethal quintessence of King Kong. Instead of purring, Goliath rasped the way tremendous chains rattle, the way a hurricane rasps and snorts.

Lucretia, the other sample, was blacker than all the pits and all the starless nights combined. She was small, but according to all the oldtimers, the Bryans as well as the straight alongers, she could do three back flips without touching ground. It was even said that she had been trained for her profession on flying squirrels. Fast and deadly as evil, she could draw herself into a diabolically deceptive ball no bigger than a baby's mitten. Then, with terrible suddenness, she'd strike with the swift accuracy of an arrow.

There, you have the picture: Goliath, the broadsword, and Lucretia, the dagger up the sleeve. One was a brute and the other a winged serpent and each was as deadly as sin in England's grimmest first phases.

After the crowd around the store had quieted down, Mr. Pussy would take a rat from his outside coat pocket. If he was showing off Goliath he would throw the rat the way Mickey Cochrane used to throw to second base. Goliath would spring from the top of the counter, plowing ahead with the force of a Coast Guard cutter. A chair was less than a paper hurdle. Goliath hit it, knocked it to one side, and stormed on without even checking his prodigious stride.

If Mr. Pussy was sampling Lucretia, he would toss the rat as high as the ceiling, and often he would walk outside the store and toss the rat as high as a lamppost. Then Lucretia erupted angrily as a mean geyser. Usually she met the rat when it was half-way down to the earth. Some oldtimers say that Lucretia had the amazing grace of Hal Chase. Many compared her to Tris Speaker when the old Grey Eagle actually outran fly balls. Perhaps, Joe Dimaggio is the most suitable parallel in modern baseball.

After these brief exhibitions, Mr. Pussy always came straight to a contract, to the big hit. He worked it two ways: he would clean up a town better than Matt Dillon and move on. Or, merchants and farmers could order so many Goliaths or Lucretias, and Mr. Pussy's cat farm would fill the orders, by railway express.

The fee was larger, naturally, if Mr. Pussy took charge in person. That was fair, and all agreed that it was meet. The customer not only had the benefit of Mr. Pussy's personal supervision, but it was said, also, that his long experience in the business enabled him to smell a rat better than a temperance sister could smell out booze. They said, they all agreed, that Mr. Pussy's smelling genius worked even when he had a heavy head cold.

Now it so happened—sometime after Guiteau killed Garfield but before Czolgolz killed McKinley—Mr. Pussy was called to Oxford, North Carolina, my hometown, by telegram, mind you, to combat an emergency. The rats had taken over the largest store in town. The merchant tried bribery, cajolery, and cheese traps but nothing worked. Customers were afraid to walk on that side of the street. But as luck would have it, the store burned down to the ground the night before Mr. Pussy and Goliath and Lucretia arrived in Oxford, N.C. After the fire, most of the rats up and down the street took the hint and left town. (It was believed by some that the rats thought malicious arson had occurred, specifically for their own grim benefit. But this was not the case, as was· proven legally when the merchant had to go to court to collect from the insurance company.)

Well, Mr. Pussy was mad as if some smart aleck had sent him a rubber mouse on Christmas Day. He stomped around town for a day or two, vehemently cussing kerosene lamps and faulty flues, and hick towns that favor horse troughs and wells in lieu of hydrants. Just as Mr. Pussy was about to leave town, forever, he swore, an old man from the Shoo Fly section of our county, Mr. Tarapin-Eye Tulgin, sort of bumped into Mr. Pussy in the E Pluribus Unum Saloon, which was one of Oxford's best, if indeed, not the very best saloon.

They had a drink or two as they chewed the fat and talked about tricks in general. Then Mr. Tarapin-Eye said he had a sporting proposition to make to Mr. Pussy. Mr. Tarapin-Eye smiled foolishly and he rolled his eyes the way a sleepy fish does under a cloud of muddy water. From the way he talked you'd think all his brains were in his jawbone. Mr. Tarrapin-Eye said he reckoned Goliath and Lucretia could kill almost any kind of rat.

Sho, sho, he was sho of hit, but before he could go on Mr. Pussy almost slapped his gold medal in Mr. Tarapin-Eye's face. then Mr. Pussy vowed that in any reasonable time, Goliath and Lucretia could kill all the damned rats in the whole state.

Mr. Tarapin-Eye joshed along, agreeing, with all his "sho, sho's," and then he said he'd bet Mr. Pussy was a better gambler than he was because he had lost one plantation trying to fill an inside straight and he had lost another plantation when he finally filled an inside straight.

They had another drink or two, and as they stood there at the bar in the E. Pluribus Unum, Mr. Tarapin-Eye Tulgin made two or three half-witted bets for piddling amounts, for drinks and fifty cents and so on.

I imagine Mr. Pussy thought the old fellow was addlepated, but since the store had burned, I imagine he was glad for the chance at a little change and some free drinks.

By and by, Mr. Tarapin-Eye said how would Mr. Pussy take to this proposition: He had several corn cribs and a big stable that hadn't room for anything but the rats that were in them. Mr. Tarapin-Eye said he knew he was doing a fool stunt, a drunk trick, but he had a special rat, a pet, a sort of heirloom, he'd put up in catch-as-catch-can, fists-and-skull, no-holds barred, head-to-head fight with either one of Mr. Pussy's cats.

Quick as Lucretia going into orbit, Mr. Pussy whipped out some writing paper and wrote down the terms of the bet, in legal fashion, with all the "whereases." In fact, he wrote so fast he broke his pencil twice. The bartender and a goose grease salesman from Emporia, Virginia, were witnesses to the contract. The contract stipulated that if Mr. Tarapin-Eye's rat whipped one cat, then the other cat would exterminate all the rats free of charge. Conversely, if the first cat beat the rat, Mr. Tarapin-Eye would pay Mr. Pussy $100 flat rate, or a penny a head, whichever was the greater sum.

I imagine Mr. Pussy was afraid something might happen to his sucker. Anyway, he ran every step of the way to the depot and got his sample case. He and Mr. Tarapin-Eye got into the farmer's buggy and rode out to the Tulgin farm. The arena was a pit that was used for cock fights ordinarily.

As saturnine as Mr. Pussy was, he almost busted his ruffled shirt front trying to keep from laughing out loud when Mr. Tarapin-Eye brought out this rat about as big as a day-old biddy. It had a white beard all the way to the ground, a missing ear, one floppy ear, and large cataracts over both eyes. Its breathing was so tortured it was bound to have been born with acute and incurable emphysema.

Of course, Mr. Pussy wanted to know the joke. He said he had never heard of such a damned outrageous hotel bill. Who had ever heard of anything so insultingly preposterous? The very damned idea. Imagine, just imagine, putting one of his noble cats against a rat that was at Roanoke Island when the settlers arrived?

Old Man Tarapin-Eye laughed some, too. He pulled a jug down from a shelf in the stable. Both men drank a little, and Mr. Tarapin-Eye said that even if it was looney, why they'd come this far and they might as well have the fight. Mr. Pussy's retort was some sarcastic cuss words as he lifted Lucretia from the sample-box and snapped off the tiny chain.

When Lucretia saw the rat she might have thought Mr. Pussy was crazy or drunk. She shook, shrugged her shoulders, and emitted a deprecatory snarl, but she vaulted upon the aged bit of meat and beard and she toyed with it as if it were some sort of ridiculous hallucination. But when Mr. Pussy snapped his fingers, she snarled a real snarl and made a ferocious pass, albeit, it was executed with the grace of a ballerina.

Suddenly, the rat did a double back flip, bounced up behind Lucretia, did a sort of soft-shoe along her heaving back, and then ran around her belly, as if it were a clock, and whispered something in her ear.

Lucretia waddled over to a corner of the pit, sat down, crossed her legs demurely, and whimpered for milk. Mr. Tarapin-Eye, always the gracious host, picked up a milk bucket, but before he could reach the cow in the first stall, Mr. Pussy had killed Lucretia with a pitchfork.

Mr. Tarapin-Eye flung a red polka-dotted bandana to the rat,

269

and the rat dabbed at his cataracts. While the rat was dabbing his eyes with the bandana, Mr. Pussy yanked that tremendous Goliath from the hat box with such force the chain snapped. He kicked Goliath in the rear, and perhaps for the first time in his life, he raised his voice, and he screamed: "Kill that damn rat and be quick about it."

When Goliath went across that pit he sounded like old engine number 97 coming down that fatal grade. When the big yellow tom cat missed the rat and ran into the side of the pit the echo kicked up the dust back in Oxford, several miles away. But he was up in a lethal flash, up on his hind legs, and roaring as wildly as a lion with a splinter in his paw and a terrible toothache besides.

Just as Goliath was about to strike, the rat ran up Goliath's stomach and started doing a miniature buck-and-wing. Whereupon, old Goliath toppled over backwards and laughed himself to death. (There was some type of hemorrhage, no doubt, due to the paroxyms of laughter. Albeit, the death certificate, containing the precise cause of death, is not on record in the register of deeds office, if indeed, there ever was one.)

Although Mr. Tarapin-Eye hitched up the buggy as nicely as you please, Mr. Pussy walked back to Oxford, kicking at stones in the road, and throwing the sample case in the middle of Tar River. For months he walked around town blindly, perpetually in a palsied trance. He was a fruit jar of whiskey turned to talcum water, an anvil turned to jello. He spent his days, nights, and months stumbling around, always groping pathetically in shadows or inner darkness. During a storm, even a small one, he crawled under stores or porches. The only time he ever gritted his teeth and stopped his shaking was when some kind-hearted person would let him drown an ailing cat.

If he so much as saw a rat trap he shook so violently and foamed so wildly at the mouth he had to be given morphine. Finally, he lacked the wit and the will even to seek alms, but compassionate people left trays at their back doors for him. Eventually, he turned more and more to booze and he died one day in an agonizing delirium, screaming that rats were gnawing on his innards.

Well, I guess you want to know what that pursy old rat said to Lucretia?

Old man Tarapin-Eye always just grinned and said if you can't whip 'em join 'em, but kill 'em with flattery or tickle 'em to death. And all sides always agreed that he said that his rat was the very same one whose niece was courted by froggie. Remember the song:

> Froggie went a-courting and he did ride,
> Sword and pistol by his side, Um-huh.
> He rode up to Miss Mousy's house,
> And asked Miss Mousy for to be his spouse, Um-huh.
> 'Not without Uncle Rat's consent
> Would I marry the President,' Um-huh, Um-huh.

Everybody, flat worlders and straight alongers, knew that was a contemptible lie. Everybody denounced old man Tarapin-Eye as a blatherskite.

Can you imagine anyone with the unmitigated temerity to try to pass off as gospel the nutty story of a rat in a song being a real rat, and one that courted a frog? But that was the trouble with those oldtimey storytellers. They could stick to the truth for eight innings, but they'd louse it up in the ninth, just as surely as Mr. Pussy made a tragic mistake when he didn't get right back on the train when he learned the store had burned down the night before.

INDEX

274

275